Tarot Journeys

adventures in
self-transformation

Yasmine Galenorn

1999
Llewellyn Publications
St. Paul, Minnesota 55164-0383

FIRST EDITION
First Printing, 1999

Book editing and design by Astrid Sandell
Cover design by Lisa Novak
Cover illustration by Paul Mason

Library of Congress Cataloging-in-Publication Data
Galenorn, Yasmine, 1961–
    Tarot journeys : adventures in self-transformation / Yasmine Galenorn
      p. cm
    Includes bibliographical references and index.
    ISBN 1-56718-264-X
    1. Tarot. 2. Self-actualization (Psychology) — Miscellanea.
    I. Title.
    BF1879.T2G34   1999
    133.3'2424—dc21   99-33209
                                                          CIP

Llewellyn Publications
A Division of Llewellyn Worldwide, Ltd.
P.O. Box 64383, Dept. K264-X, St. Paul, MN 55164-0383
www.llewellyn.com

Printed in the United States of America

Also by Yasmine Galenorn

Trancing the Witch's Wheel: A Guide to Magickal Meditation
Embracing the Moon: A Witch's Guide to Ritual Spellcraft and Shadow Work
Dancing with the Sun: Celebrating the Seasons of Life

Dedication

As always, to Samwise, my dear husband who believes in me almost more than I believe in myself, and to our four feline children, Tara, Luna, Pakhit, and of course, little Meerclar.

To my loyal clients over the years who, through their trust in my talents, taught me more about the tarot than I thought possible.

To the cards themselves, I know you're alive and listening.

And again, to Mielikki and Tapio, my Lord and Lady. Thank you for sustaining my magick, my psychic gifts, as always, I surrender to Your call.

Blesséd Be!

Contents

Part Three: Surrender to Fate
The Search for Deconstruction

Part Four: Metamorphosis
The Search for Spirit

Preface

Writing is nothing more than a guided dream.
 —Jorge Luis Borges (1899–1986)
 Doctor Brodie's Report

In 1981, a year after I pledged myself into the service of the Gods, I received a deck of tarot cards as a gift. The man who bought them liked the pictures, but couldn't use the deck, so he gave them to me.

Little did I realize as I shuffled the cards and laid out my first spread, that my life would undergo dramatic changes from that action. Years would go by before I would manifest those changes, but the stage was set, the journey begun.

I had taken my first steps into magick, I had studied meditation for years, but the tarot opened an entirely new gateway. I found I had a real talent for the cards. From the beginning, my readings were surprisingly accurate.

It didn't take me long to memorize the meanings of the cards because I connected with the images. Excited about learning this new skill, somewhere within my heart I knew that my talent would help not only myself, but others. So I set about the task of becoming a reader. I knew there were other decks out there, but I decided to focus solely on the one I owned, at least in the beginning, so I wouldn't muddy my vision with differing viewpoints about the cards and what they represented.

I slept with my deck under my pillow, instinctively knowing that our energies would bond. I meditated on each card, examined the images, analyzed them, then let my subconscious mind guide me to new divinatory meanings. When I laid out a spread, I listened with my inner ear, waiting for the words that would add to what I already knew about the card.

After a year or so, I began to read for friends, tentatively at first. I admit to being nervous. Then, as now, I knew that some people who go to psychics take every word as gospel. Early on I recognized my responsibility as a reader and always cautioned my clients against blindly accepting my advice.

My confidence increased as the feedback began coming in. I could read with the cards, I was a good reader! I began reading for any friend who asked me and soon became very popular—too popular.

When you read the cards for free, without any expectation of an exchange, some people will take advantage of your goodwill—they won't leave you alone. Others ask the same questions over and over, wanting to hear a different answer because they refuse to work on their problems. After a while, I became cautious about offering my services.

Then, in 1988, a friend's mother asked me to read her cards. I did. After the reading was over, she looked at me and said, "How the hell did you know all that?" Before she left, she wrote out a ten-dollar check and handed it to me.

That was the first time anyone paid me for my time and it felt good. She respected the energy I expended on the reading. It broke me out of my fear of asking for money, although for the next couple years I still didn't do many readings for cash.

I had an 8-to-5 job at that time, I was trying to write on the side, and I was coping with a very unhappy relationship that I should have ended years before. I didn't have the time or energy to offer my services on a professional basis.

Everything began to change in 1990. I ended my relationship. Nineteen ninety-one saw me quit my job. I took my cats and moved into a converted school bus. I decided that never again would I pursue a job that stifled my true nature. To earn money for food and other supplies, I began to read cards for the public. It allowed me the freedom to write.

I soon developed a loyal clientele, some of whom still come to me today.

Over the past years, circumstances have changed dramatically. I live in a house now with my husband and our four cats. I have sold four books, and writing has become my career. But I still make time to read for my clients. I am touched by their loyalty.

I've also deepened my studies into the tarot. I own a number of decks now, collecting those I find attractive. I also use the tarot in magick far more than I used to.

Over the years, I've come to realize what an important tool in self-transformation it can be. One of the easiest ways to use the tarot for this purpose is through guided meditation.

There are many books of tarot meditations out there, but I have yet to find one that looks at the archetypical journey provided by the major arcana from a Pagan point of view. Most tarot meditations on the market seem to focus either Cabalistically or in a New Age fashion. I recognized the need for a book of meditations that explores the major arcana in ways and terms familiar to Pagans, Witches, and Wiccans.

As a tarot reader, I realize just how much knowledge can be derived from the deck—especially the major arcana—but it helps to have that guidance in familiar terms and imagery. I wrote *Tarot Journeys* to fill that void.

I hope that through use of the meditations within this book, through journeying through the major arcana, you will find guidance and inner direction to help you along your own personal path.

Introduction

*The beginnings and endings of all human undertakings
are untidy, the building of a house, the writing of a novel,
the demolition of a bridge, and eminently, the finish of a voyage.*
    —John Galsworthy (1867–1933)
      Markings

Writing *Tarot Journeys* has taken me into a new realm with regard to both the tarot and my own life. Like the Fool, I began with a simple concept—I wanted to explore the major arcana of the tarot through the use of guided meditation. I hoped, in the process, to help others reach a better understanding of this system of divination. When I write, no matter how analytical I may get, I always have the intuitive side of my psyche keyed in to what I'm working on. However, I believed, for the most part, that this book was going to be an intellectual project rather than a leap off the cliff into the depths of my subconscious. After all, I reasoned, I was working with universal archetypes. How could I open up my own interpretations to any degree without jeopardizing the integrity of the work?

What I did not realize when I began this book, but what became apparent during the writing, was that the writing of the book itself was a process, just like going through the meditations will be a process for you. I began to understand that if the work presented was to have any depth, any strength, it must necessarily reflect my own understanding of the tarot and the process that I underwent to produce it.

It occurred to me that my goal here was that the book be a useful guide—practical and hands-on, rather than just a curiosity or reference work. Once again, I understood as I delved into the writing of it that my own experience had to come through, for that is how I approach writing all of my nonfiction metaphysical work. So I present to you, my readers, my personal journeys with the hope that you might develop your own spiritual guide map through integrating some, all, or a few of the lessons I can offer into your life.

We in the Westernized cultures live in a highly analytical world, and while this most certainly has an important place in our lives—indeed we cannot function without reason and logic—we have neglected the intuitive side of life and assigned it a spot of importance somewhat above nighttime dreaming and somewhere below faerie tales. It's time to bring that facet of ourselves up to the mirror again, to look into the shadow of the subconscious, the realm of the inner self, and not flinch at what we see. For our shadow selves are as vital to our existence as our presented-to-the-world faces.

Guided meditation takes us into these shadow realms, into our subconscious. While I knew this—especially from writing my first book, *Trancing The Witch's Wheel*—when I approached *Tarot Journeys* the thought somehow eluded me. I believe this happened because the tarot seems such a vast topic—so much has been written on it, and so many interpretations exist. I wanted to take the common denominators and blend them together to attempt to form a more universal picture of the major arcana. Once I was into the writing of the meditations, I began to realize that I could do this while still putting my own spin on things.

But, as with all journeys, I did not realize at the beginning the full extent of energy and emotion that this particular quest turned out to involve.

Tarot Journeys has evolved from a simple book of meditations into what feels like a path for self-transformation. I'm not saying that everyone who reads this will come away feeling complete, whole and new. But I now believe that this book can lead you into an introverted, philosophical space where you can freely examine your desires, beliefs, fears, and wishes. The meditations are, yes, just meditations. But they involve very deep and pandemic symbols that speak to the "universal" consciousness residing within our conscious selves. These symbols, once triggered by our psyche, lead us into a greater understanding of our place in the nature of our race, our species, this planet.

During the writing, I would sometimes pace around my office, wishing fervently to be anywhere but in front of the computer. Like it or not, as I wrote the meditations, I had to experience them. And to work my way through all twenty-two meditations in a period of several months required intense shifts in mood and consciousness. I was on Inanna's journey, into my private underworld, and there was no turning back. Some of the chapters flowed freely, easy and quick. Others, I had to struggle with, to work through some of my own reluctance to tackle the particular card's meanings and how they relate to my own life. We all have our blocks, and this book can help you work through some of them, if you are ready and have the will to apply yourself.

My dreams, as well, felt the brunt of this book. They took on vivid and eerie twists until I woke as tired as when I went to sleep. I tend to have odd dreams anyway, but the months during the writing of this book could easily be grist for what my husband and I affectionately term "stoner films." At times they would echo the journey I was working on, the meditation I was writing. At other times they were filled with images that my writing brought into my conscious mind for me to address. Nightmares, yes there were some. Others were fantastical and beautiful. After a while I ceased to differentiate whether the dreams were sparking imagery for the meditations, or whether the meditations were sparking imagery for the dreams. I think, in retrospect, it involved a bit of both.

Reading the tarot for clients now has become much easier. The symbolism means more to me as I examine the cards of the major arcana. I consciously understand them on several levels now, and am able to articulate my interpretations with more confidence and surety. In fact, reading the tarot for myself has also become more of a journey and my usually accurate readings have taken on far more depth and meaning.

I've also experienced shifts in perception. I've began to understand each card and how the meanings relate to decisions I'm facing in my own life. I've resolved several issues that I've spent several years hedging about. For example, in writing the meditation for the Horned God (Devil) card, I had to face the fact that, being married for a few years now, I had let some of that wild passionate energy slip through my fingers. The meditation brought it up again and forced me to start learning how to integrate it into a married relationship.

Another card that gave me a lot of personal thought and resistance was the Tower card. I am not a person comfortable with life's events going on outside of my control, but through writing the meditation for this card, I was forced to face that sometimes you don't have much choice about what's happening around you. At times, disaster happens, things crash to the ground, your life seems to fall into a shambles. This also taught me that you do have control over how you react to these events. Through writing this book, I've grappled with my own inner demons and joys just as you, the reader, will.

Though I can't say I've fully won the battle, I feel more on track than I have in a long while. I have more self-confidence in my life-choices now, and have had the courage to explore and examine facets of myself that I had long ago shut away. Through doing so, I find that I am more comfortable with my evolving career and with my sense of being. I am Yasmine Galenorn as a whole, rather than seeing myself as a fragmented individual. I've come to integrate different facets of my personality that I didn't think were possible to integrate. Recently I was talking to a friend in Australia through e-mail. He looked at my web site and mentioned how wide and diverse my range of interests is. I wrote back and told him, "Yeah, I guess I'm tattoos and teacups." And that summed it up right there for me. I realized, with the writing of that sentence, that I could be complete, whole, and not feel like I was alienating different aspects of myself by allowing the others to exist.

I know this might not have happened, or at least the process would have taken far longer, had I not gone through the writing of this book, let myself slide into the meditations as I wrote them, and followed them through to the end.

Some people ask why I chose to focus on the tarot with this book. After all, there are so many different oracle and image-laden systems that might do just as well. The answer is both simple and complex. Simply put, I chose to examine the tarot because I wanted to, because I love the cards and have worked with them for so many years now. The more complex answer examines how I interact with the tarot and my underlying beliefs in the way it works.

When readers or clients or friends ask me how the tarot works, I have no concrete answer that I can condense into twenty words or less. There is no way of finding out for sure just what the process entails to produce an accurate reading, but I will do my best to articulate my personal beliefs. Remember, as always, they are just that—personal opinions.

I believe that the cards have a spirit all their own. The general imagery used has been standardized and used for so long, and by so many millions of people, that I believe a "spirit" of the tarot has evolved from all of this energy focused on it. So I believe that there is an entity, or energy, if you will, that embodies the essence of the tarot. We draw on that when we focus on the cards, when we lay out a reading.

I also believe that the cards act as a trigger for some people, to catalyze their intuition and psychic senses. Therefore we are not only drawing on the energy of the Tarot Spirit, we are utilizing our own psychic selves as well. Finally, the person asking the question is projecting, usually on a subconscious level, their inner knowledge about the issue into the cards as they shuffle them.

I have been in touch with this Tarot Spirit for many years, learning how to interact with it, how to utilize its powers, and meditating on it every time I laid out a reading. It seemed only natural that I incorporate it into my writing at some point.

I hope that you find something of value in this book. I hope that it helps your inner spiritual work as well as your ability to understand the major arcana.

Bright Blessings, and may the journey into the labyrinth always lead you to a deeper understanding of your own role on the vast stage that is our universe.

Practice is the best of all instructors.

   —Publilius Syrus (1st century B.C.E.)
   Maxim 439

Using *Tarot Journeys*

As my first book, *Trancing the Witch's Wheel*, offered you meditations for each of the Elements and Sabbats, so *Tarot Journeys* now offers you a meditation for each card of the major arcana. These meditations are for use either in a group setting or on a solitary basis by tape-recording the meditation and playing it back as you follow along.

For group use, I recommend that one person be designated as the guide. If your group plans to use the book on a regular basis, I suggest that a different person be chosen to read each meditation, so that everyone has a chance to participate.

In addition to the meditation, each chapter contains a brief examination of the major arcana card being explored and a "Guidelines for Use" section, which includes suggestions for items such as crystals, oils, and incense meant to enhance your experience. Also included in each chapter, you will find exercises intended to help you expand your understanding of the meditations. I encourage you to experiment with them.

Helpful Hints

Read the entire meditation thoroughly before using. If you are the designated guide, or if you are planning on tape-recording it, I recommend that you read the meditation aloud to familiarize yourself with the cadence of the words before using it.

In a group setting, schedule enough time after the meditation for group discussion. No one should feel pressured to share their thoughts, but through hearing other experiences, you may find yourself understanding different facets of the particular card and archetype being explored.

If you are guiding a meditation for a group, be aware that certain thoughts can trigger emotional responses. Watch the group carefully. If someone appears distressed or in trouble, gently inquire whether they need your assistance. More often than not, they can work through the problem without your help, but play it safe and be observant.

If you are taping these meditations, or if you are the one guiding the group, at the end of each paragraph pause for a silent count of ten (silently count out ten slow beats). Where I have indicated a *long pause* in the text, pause for about thirty beats. An *extended long pause* will be marked with the appropriate time. You want to give those meditating plenty of time to contemplate the ideas presented.

Please be aware that these meditations are essentially self-hypnosis. It is dangerous to drive right after you have finished. Always include the last paragraph of each meditation, which should bring you out of trance. I also recommend that after each session, you eat a light meal, preferably with protein in it, to ground yourself in the mundane world once again.

About the Tarot Meditations

Tarot Journeys is actually one long journey divided into twenty-two shorter ones. Each meditation can stand on its own, yet all are united. Working with the meditations in this book can better your understanding of your transformation through various lifecycles. The major arcana of the tarot follows a story, and this book is divided into four parts, each reflecting a leg of the Fool's journey. In the tarot, just as in life, the Fool starts out as a blank slate, knowing nothing. Then comes the search for the self, for personal identity, belief and wisdom. Part One: Coming to Wisdom comprises the first six meditations (the Fool through the Hierophant).

When a certain level of maturity is attained, then the Fool connects with the outer world. Just as the Fool built an inner foundation, s/he now begins to build an outer foundation. During this time, a career is chosen, love and family blossom, personal strength and power is attained. Part Two: The Growth of Will is comprised of meditations for the Chariot through the Wheel.

What many don't realize is that once we have built this foundation, there comes a time of disruption; a breaking down of the system. We find ourselves at the mercy of fate, having to sacrifice all but the most essential parts of our being. We are stripped to the bone, and through this tearing down we begin another transformation.

At this point in time, we find ourselves once again taking risks, burning those structures that have not worked. We winnow the chaff from the wheat. The difference of this process from that of the beginning (the Fool) is that we release and let go of only that which truly does not work. We destroy on a selective basis and what we are left with is strong, clear, and true to ourselves. Part Three: Surrender To Fate comprises the meditations for this process (Justice through the Tower).

The last part of our journey brings us to a higher understanding of ourselves, the world around us, and our relationship to that world. We hone our true natures, our intuition, and use that intuition to expand toward the future. We develop a sense of global consciousness. Part Four: Metamorphosis includes meditations for the Star through the World.

When we look at the major arcana in connection with the Pagan Wheel of the Year and the elements, we can assign each card a place in the scheme of the universe.

At the center, we have the World, the primordial energy; beginnings and endings, Alpha and Omega. Surrounding the World, we have the Priestess, the higher self who journeys into the labyrinth in search of the psyche so that she might better understand the world. We then divide the wheel into four parts, each correlating with the seasons. Within the seasons and sabbats, we place the cards according to their nature and energy.

Remember, new cycles (the Fool) can start at any point in your life, they can be very specific (career, love) or a general rumble throughout your day ("I'm dissatisfied and don't know why"). At the same time, this book will deepen your involvement with the tarot. Whichever way you choose to focus on this book is up to you.

Brightest journeys!

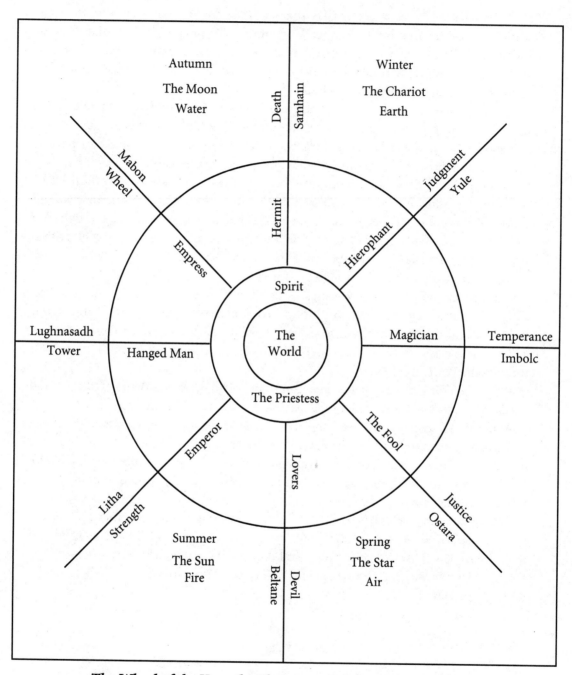

The Wheel of the Year, the Elements, and the Major Arcana

In the parched path
I have seen the good lizard
(one drop of crocodile)
meditating.

—Federico Garcia Lorca (1898–1936)
The Old Lizard (El Lagarto Viejo)

The Tarot
Using Meditation and Visualization

Where did the tarot originate? No one knows for sure. There are many theories on the subject, from the belief that its beginnings stemmed from the ancient Egyptians under the watchful eye of the god Thoth, to the theory that the tarot began with the Hungarian Gypsies. (Interestingly enough, the word *gypsy* is an abbreviated form of the word Egyptian.)

Others claim that forerunners of the tarot originated in India. Still others claim that the Chinese evolved the tarot. While it is widely accepted that the earliest playing cards come from China, the theory that they used these cards for divination has not been firmly established. So we come back to the fact that no one has concrete evidence to prove their case. But despite the lack of historical documentation, the tarot exists. It is one of the most widely used forms of divination (at least among Westerners) and can be uncannily accurate.

Modern tarot decks vary considerably from the standard playing cards commonly used in old movies. There are hundreds of decks on the market, ranging from simple black-and-white images to incredibly complex photo-montages.

In addition to tarot decks, we also find a wide variety of oracular decks—similar in design to the tarot, but with a varying number of cards. Usually an oracle deck will focus on one theme or one tradition, whereas the images on the tarot decks can span quite a range.

The standard tarot deck numbers seventy-eight cards. Of these, fifty-six of the cards comprise what is known as the minor arcana, while the remaining twenty-two cards make up the major arcana.

The Minor Arcana

The fifty-six cards of the minor arcana are divided into four suits—the most common terms for these suits are: Wands (vitality and spirituality); Cups (emotions); Swords (the intellect); and Disks or Pentacles (the physical world). Each suit consists of fourteen cards: Ace, 2, 3, 4, 5, 6, 7, 8, 9, 10, Page or Princess, Prince or Knight, Queen, Knight or King.

The minor arcana explores the events and people that make up our everyday world. These cards tell us whether or not it's time to go back to school, to move into a new house, to take a different job, to trust an uncertain love—they represent the backbone of our daily existence.

The Major Arcana

The twenty-two cards of the major arcana are different. Also called trump cards, they represent the higher forces that guide our lives. They tell the story of our evolution through life, or through phases of life.

As human beings, we tend to take three steps forward, one step back (sometimes more), then another three steps forward . . . and so on. We evolve at different rates. Some of us are very successful in our careers but unsuccessful in our personal relationships. Others seem to have more friends than they can keep up with, yet their health and finances suffer. Still others seem to have everything on track, everything going for them until a major catastrophe forces them to rethink their priorities and become centered and focused on those things that truly matter.

The major arcana typifies this struggle forward, this evolution of spirit toward a balanced and unified whole. It is the major arcana with which this book concerns itself.

The Fool's Journey

The first card of the major arcana is the Fool, and the Fool is the archetype of that part of our psyche that is just setting out on the journey of self-discovery.

The last card is the World. The Fool has, through evolution and maturation, come into his or her own power. Having been challenged to discover his or her priorities and, strengthened and tempered by difficult lessons, the Fool now meets the World with a global perspective, an ability to look beyond the self and to connect with a universal consciousness.

This journey represents a process of growth and understanding that allows us to advance beyond the sometimes shallow states in which we find ourselves. Challenged to examine our psyches, we evaluate our priorities, talents, and abilities while working through the fear and worry often connected to that evaluation process. By following the journey of the Fool, we journey into our own souls.

Guided Meditation

Simply put, guided meditation blends the discipline of focused contemplation with the art of guided imagery. Through guided meditation, we hone our powers of visualization, we develop a deepened ability to concentrate and, when pursued in a magickal way, we can use guided imagery to effect changes into our lives.

Guided meditation is intended to lead you on an inner journey, to stimulate imagination and creativity. By combining this process with the archetypical imagery of the major arcana, you should be able to clarify your intentions, motivations, and beliefs. Through using the meditations in this book, you should be able to reach your goals in a structured and enjoyable manner.

Because you go into trance during these sessions, the material directly addresses the Higher Self (the subconscious mind). Once in this self-hypnotic state, it is possible to discover hidden talents, motivations, and personal beliefs that you might not be aware of on a conscious level, beliefs and talents that affect your physical reality and day-to-day existence.

In coming to a clearer understanding of the self, it is possible to transform reality in positive and beneficial ways. You might find, during the times you are using these meditations, that your dreaming state reaches a new level. You may find yourself having magickal dreams, or perhaps lucid dreaming (in which you are aware that you are dreaming). Intuition and magickal awareness of other realms may heighten. You should also find an increased ability to concentrate and study.

Preparation for Guided Meditation

If you have never practiced the art of guided meditation, then you might want to explore some of the visualization exercises in my books *Trancing the Witch's Wheel* and *Embracing the Moon*. However, this is not a prerequisite for using the meditations in this book.

Think of visualization as a form of daydreaming. We all daydream, mentally picturing things we wish would happen; too often we picture things we're afraid will happen. To transform daydreaming into visualization, we must first begin with a focus, an intent. Decide, in advance, the subject of your visualization instead of just letting your mind wander. This gives you a solid foundation from which to work. Next, during your visualization exercises, always try to focus on the positive.

Now, I am not one of those people who believes that everything we think will come true. We must acknowledge our fears and negative feelings or we repress them and they grow stronger. During some of the meditations you will be exploring your inner fears and doubts, and within those meditations you will work through that fear to come to a place of detachment and release.

However, if we are deliberately attempting to visualize a change, we want to do it in the most positive manner possible. As humans, we tend to respond to the positive more willingly than we respond to the negative.

If visualization seems difficult for you, continue to practice. Through repetition, through training, our thoughts become disciplined to respond to our will. Any Witch, Pagan, or Wiccan will tell you that magick demands discipline. Chaotic thoughts breed chaotic lives.

Some Simple Suggestions for Practicing Visualization

First, relax in a chair or on your bed or a sofa. Make yourself comfortable. Take off your glasses and any restraining clothing you might be wearing.

Now, take three deep breaths. Let the air fill your lungs, then slowly exhale. As you exhale, feel the tension flowing out of your body.

You might want to set a timer to gently alert you when five minutes is up (a good amount of time for each particular visualization exercise).

When you are ready, begin to focus on one of the following scenarios. Play it through in your mind. Each time you find your thoughts wandering, gently bring them back to the subject at hand.

Listen to any messages you might receive during this time. It might be from one of the characters in the scenario (such as the dolphin) or it might just be an impression. Your mind is trying to tell you something when this happens.

Do not analyze while still in the exercise. Only after the time is up should you consciously think about what you heard. Then, ask yourself if it is fear talking, trying to force you away from making changes that, while beneficial, will force you to alter your perceptions or behavior. Or is it truly a ray of enlightenment rising from deep within your psyche?

You will have to sort through these messages carefully to discern the difference, but they can be very useful in analyzing your life and your patterns.

Practice these exercises at least once, preferably twice, a day. In a week or two, you should find both your discipline and focus sharpened, and you should then be ready for the meditations found within this book.

Visualization Exercises

· You are on a beach. See yourself swimming into the water and meeting a dolphin. Feel the waves lap gently around you. Smell the ocean air.

· You are in an orchard. Climb a tree, see every branch, feel every leaf brush your shoulder.

· You are eating a peach. Feel the texture of the skin. Smell the warm, dusky aroma. Taste the juice as it bursts into your mouth.

· You are making bread. Measure the ingredients with care. Hear the liquid as you pour it over the yeast. Stir harder as the dough begins to thicken. Feel the soft, warm dough in your hands as you knead it over and over again.

· You are walking through the woods to a small stream. Smell the different scents in the forest. Is it autumn or spring? Winter or summer? Hear the echo of birds as you wander along the path. Touch the cool moss that hangs off the trees near the edge of the water and taste the clear, cold liquid as it flows down your throat.

· You have just been told that you're getting the promotion you've wanted. Hear your supervisor telling you what a good worker you are. See the delight on your friends' and family's faces as you tell them the news. Touch the extra cash that goes along with the promotion.

· You are shopping for clothes. Thumb through the racks. Look at all the possibilities. Feel the material under your fingertips. Finally, you discover the perfect outfit, in your favorite color. Take the garment into the dressing room and try it on. It hangs gently from your body, fitting with absolute precision. Look at yourself in the mirror, smiling and confident.

- You are dancing to music you love. See yourself moving with easy, smooth motions. Feel the floor under your feet and your body swaying to the music. Hear the music and feel it pulse through your system. What are you wearing? Are you a belly dancer? Are you practicing the hula, or maybe you're freeform dancing to modern music? Experience being the dance itself.

- You are drumming around a big bonfire. Hear the crackle of flames and the pulsing of drums. Smell the smoke spiraling up into the air. See the shadows of other drummers. Feel the drum under your hands, the slight chill of the night air around you.

- You are looking at a picture that you've always loved. How many details can you make out? What are the images that stand out most in your mind? Touch the surface of the canvas—is it smooth watercolor or is it bumpy and textured from oil paint? If there are figures in the picture, do any of them seem more important than the others? Why is that? Could they symbolize something you need to think about?

Cleansing the Body

Before undertaking any in-depth magickal work, the practitioner should magickally cleanse themselves to remove any negative energies that might be hanging around, as well as to shake off the accumulated tensions and expectations from the day.

In *Trancing the Witch's Wheel*, I included an excellent cleansing meditation, but there are some simple actions you can take to get rid of most of the astral "garbage" that collects in your space, much like dusting away cobwebs.

You can smudge the area and the participants with cedar, sweetgrass, or sage. To smudge is to use the smoke from sacred or magickal trees and herbs to cleanse the aura and the space. A smudge stick is the easiest way to go about this. Smudge sticks are bundles of herbs (most often sage, cedar, lavender, and sweetgrass) which have been tightly bound together to form a thick "stick."

To use a smudge stick, first procure a heat-resistant bowl and fill it half-full with salt. Now light the smudge stick—they put out an incredible amount of smoke so you might want to disconnect your smoke alarm during this time. Just remember to reconnect the alarm when you are done. The flames will die, leaving the stick to smolder as waves of smoke billow out. Use your hand or a feather to gently direct this smoke around the room, or over your body.

When more than one person is participating, have Person A smudge person B; Person B smudges Person C; and so on. The last recipient smudges Person A.

If you have no asthma or allergy problems, breathing this smoke deep into the lungs and then exhaling slowly can do wonders in helping you release the tensions of the day.

Native Americans have long known about the sacred properties of these herbs and now we use that knowledge, too.

Use the salt-filled bowl to catch ashes and when you are finished, plunge the smudge stick into the bowl where the salt will smother the embers. Make sure the stick is completely free of embers and sparks before storing. I leave mine in the bowl of salt for quick access and to protect against wayward sparks.

If smudging is not an option, you can asperge your space and the participants. Soak a cedar branch in a bowl of spring water for an hour. If you don't have cedar, you can dissolve a small handful of salt in the water.

Now, using the branch or the tips of your fingers, gently flick water droplets around the room or over the body while visualizing the energy clearing and becoming lighter and calmer.

You can also use a magickal rattle and "rattle" the energy of the room, shaking loose the shadows and gunk that accumulates. Just hold the rattle toward each corner and shake vigorously while focusing on cleansing the room. You can rattle a person's aura, too. Just make sure you don't accidentally hit them with it.

After you have shaken up the energy, then use your magickal broom to sweep it out an open window. You can also use your broom to sweep the aura—again, taking care not to hit the person you're cleansing.

After you have cleansed your space and yourself, you can then move on to grounding, which is covered in the next chapter.

What once sprung from the earth sinks back into the earth.

—Titus Lucretius Carus (99–55 B.C.E.)
On The Nature Of Things
(De Rerum Natura)

Grounding the Self

Once you have cleansed yourself and the space where you will be meditating, you and/or your group should start the evening with a basic grounding of the body. This essentially means we connect ourselves to the Earth's energy. This keeps us from becoming too "spacy" or disconnected during the meditation.

Because self-hypnosis and guided meditations are such powerful tools, and because they can effect such a tremendous change in our psyches, it is important to remain grounded and centered within our lives.

Being grounded in no way indicates that you can't lift yourself out of the reality around you and create something new, nor does it mean remaining in a rut, or keeping yourself from fully experiencing the psychic work you are embarking on.

What being grounded *does* mean is that you will be able to come out of trance more easily when the meditation is over, you will be able to fully reconnect with the physical world around you, you will drive more safely after meditation and get more of the "mundane" tasks accomplished during your day-to-day life. Keeping grounded also ensures that your psychic work will be more effective, because when we ground our work, our magick can flow through our psyches and bodies easier.

Trancing the Witch's Wheel contains a very effective grounding meditation; and *Embracing the Moon* contains simpler, but just as effective, exercises for when you don't have enough time for a full meditation. Here, I present another meditation for grounding and centering. You should find it gives you good results.

Grounding the Body

You can perform this exercise alone or with a group of people. First, everyone should remove their shoes and any constrictive clothing. In a group situation, one person should lead the exercise, so they first should read and practice it several times. Allow plenty of time for the exercise.

- Take three deep breaths. Close your eyes and take another deep breath. This time, when you exhale, imagine that all the tension from the day is floating out of your body.

- Now, open your eyes as you reach over your head with your right hand. At the same time, point your right toe, resting your weight firmly on your left leg. Stretch the body. When you are stretching, do not strain, but fully stretch out your body.

- Now relax and lower your right arm.

- Reach up over your head with your left hand and point your left toe, resting your weight firmly on your right leg. Stretch the body.

- Now relax and lower your left arm.

- Stretch your arms out to the sides, holding them parallel to the floor. Flip your palms up, so that your fingers are pointing toward the ceiling. Now tighten, as if your hands are pressing against two walls, one on each side.

- Fully relax and then repeat once more.

- Bend over and gently shake your body as you hang limply, head aimed toward the floor.

- As you slowly stand, use your hands to stroke your aura with gentle, upward motions. Keep your hands about four or five inches from your body and quietly "fluff" up your energy, breathing deeply and rhythmically as you do so.

- When you feel centered, bring your palms together in front of you and close your eyes as you rest quietly for a moment.

Grounding and Centering: Guidelines for Use

Use this meditation before proceeding to the other meditations in this book. If you have don't have time for the meditation, at least do the physical stretching and breathing as directed above. You should attempt no guided meditation until you have grounded yourself. You can also use this meditation whenever you feel out of balance or before any major magickal working. Good for use on a regular basis, I recommend reviewing it on every full and new moon.

Flowers:	sage, cedar, sweetgrass, spruce, patchouli
Incense:	sage, cedar, sweetgrass
Oils:	earth, oakmoss, cypress, cedar, patchouli
Crystals:	hematite, tiger's eye, lodestone
Candles:	brown, green, yellow

Grounding Meditation

Relax and get comfortable. Close your eyes and take three deep breaths.

It is twilight and you are in the center of a large meadow. The sky reels above you, cloudless and pale, icy blue. Wiggle your bare toes and feel the soft blades of grass beneath your feet.

long pause

A light breeze touches your cheek.

As you stand on the mossy knoll, you hear a gentle sound. Look down. There is enough light for you to see that a vine has sprung from the ground near your feet and is growing rapidly. The leaves are glossy and dark, and some of them are striped with thin bands of white.

The meadow is quiet and peaceful. What a nice change from where you spend your days. Listen to the sounds of the birds as they echo through the twilight.

long pause

Take three deep breaths.

long pause

The ground seems so inviting that you decide to sit down. Take a moment to settle near the green ivy, which grows with surprising fecundity. It coils and twists and spirals and reminds you of the ancient labyrinths etched in stone on temple walls.

long pause

When you are settled on the ground, place your hands on the cool soil beneath you and feel the life that beats under your fingers. The Earth Mother sustains you, She is solid under your feet, a cradle in which you may rest when you are tired and weary. Listen to the drumbeat that is the pulsing of Her heart.

long pause

The evening is so peaceful that you lean back on your elbows so you can stare at the sky. Stretch your legs out in front of you as you watch the darkening expanse above. The silvery twilight is rapidly changing into the indigo of dusk and you think you can see one star shimmer and glisten.

A moth flies by, glowing an ethereal white. As you rest, a pale sliver of light shines over the horizon and you know it is the waning moon.

long pause

Now take another deep breath and let it out slowly.

long pause

A noise near your feet alerts you. It is the vine, twining closer and closer. You focus on the plant and to your surprise, you feel a wave of affection coming from the greenery. It is reaching out to you, offering you knowledge of itself and its realm.

long pause

You hear a whisper, perhaps it is only in your mind, but the ivy says, "My name is Jacinth, and I am here to help you ground into the energy of the Mother, of the planet. Will you trust me to help you?"

There is no sense of malice or danger and you know the ivy is telling you the truth. You feel safe in giving your assent. Take another deep breath and tell the plant you will accept its help.

long pause

The ivy rustles and you know you have made Jacinth happy by accepting the offer. You ask what you have to do, but Jacinth says, "Remain seated and do not fear me."

After a moment, the vine stretches out and coils around your feet. It gently begins twining up your legs. Jacinth's touch does not hurt, nor does the vine constrict you in any way.

long pause

As the vine continues coiling around your torso and onto your arms, you begin to feel very alive, very alert.

It is almost as if small root hairs are burrowing under your skin, taking hold so that you may become part of the ivy. The root hairs tickle, they feel firm and solid and grounded in the Earth and you begin to feel firm and solid and grounded in the Earth.

long pause

The vine now covers your entire body, and you can feel how very strong the plant is. Even though a simple twist could tear it away, this ivy has the tenacity and perseverance to cover the giant oak trees of the forest, it has the will to expand and cover the ground with sheets of itself.

long pause

The ivy's strength begins to flow into your body, and you realize that it is the essence of the very Earth, rooted and solid and secure. One life, made of many; a bloodstream flowing through all the world's entities; the Earth Mother under your feet is as much a part of you as you are of Her.

long pause

Feel Her strength flowing into your limbs.

long pause

Feel Her fertility flowing into your talents.

long pause

Feel Her vitality flowing into your heart.

long pause

Feel Her passion flowing into your loins.

long pause

Feel Her solidity flowing into your connection with the world around you and know that you are one of Her children, brother or sister to the ivy that encircles your body, to the stag that wanders through your forest, to the butterfly that lights on your sleeve.

extended long pause—2 minutes

Take three deep breaths and know that you are a child of this world. Feel your connection to your body and to the body of the Goddess under your feet.

long pause

Now, Jacinth begins to slowly pull back. It carefully uncoils itself, gently disengaging from your energy, but you still feel where the ivy's essence touched your own.

long pause

When you are free of the vine, stand and stretch. You are staring at the myriad stars overhead. Even as you connect with our world, your spirit can connect with the worlds beyond sight. All consciousness within the universe is intertwined, even as you were intertwined with the ivy.

long pause

Now, listen to my voice as I count from ten to one. You will become awake and alert, and the feeling of balance and groundedness will stay with you throughout the day.

Ten . . . nine . . . eight . . . you are becoming aware of the world around you . . . seven . . . six . . . five . . . you will awake clear and refreshed . . . four . . . three . . . two . . . you will be completely alert . . . one . . . take three deep breaths and when you are ready, you may open your eyes.

Suggested Exercises

1. When you feel out of balance, you should examine your life. Are you living your truths or have you been compromising your beliefs too much? This can make us feel off-center. Are there changes you can make that will alleviate this problem?

2. If you are not getting enough rest or good food, you will not be grounded or balanced. Take time to sleep when you need it and try to eat breakfast every morning. It may hurt the ego to say "I'm too tired to party," but in the long run it might help you to get an early night's sleep rather than getting blitzed.

3. Panic, fear, and worry can exacerbate that "spaced-out" feeling. But it is precisely when these feelings take over that we need the most grounding. In spite of your problems, try to take a few minutes out for grounding. It will help you cope on those days when nothing is going right.

4. A walk in the woods, pottering in the garden, even petting a cat or dog are all physical ways to ground ourselves and they're all good therapy.

5. Food, especially protein, can ground you quicker than just about anything. A thick slice of cheese, a few crackers, and an apple or banana should definitely help that "spaced-out" feeling.

Part One

Coming to Wisdom:
The Search for Self

One of the pleasantest things in the world is going on a journey; but I like to go by myself.

—William Hazlitt (1778–1830)
Table Talk

The Fool
The Journey Begins

The first card of the major arcana is known as the Fool. It is always assigned the number 0—ground zero, so to speak; the absolute beginning of a new cycle.

The Fool and His/Her Energy

Representing new beginnings, the Fool indicates that a new cycle in life is about to take place. This is the moment before change, the precipice from which we jump into new experience and new adventure, a turning point from which our lives will never again be the same.

The Fool is the inner adventurer, the part of our psyche that longs for change and growth. A potent reminder that we must grow, adapt, and evolve, the Fool prevents stagnation through inducing restlessness, a wanderlust that must be satisfied. When in the grip of the Fool, we become the seeker of knowledge, pulled by the allure of the Quest. We go charging off in search of our own personal Holy Grail.

In our daily lives, the Fool materializes as the college student who suddenly runs off to backpack across Europe. Another common embodiment of the Fool can often be found in the middle-aged man who, fearing age and the loss of his prime, packs up his wife and children and moves to the country to become a farmer, or moves to the city to become an artist. The Fool archetype appears in our lives when we realize that we aren't doing the work we are meant to, when we quit our long-standing jobs and change careers.

When a woman sees the last of her children out the door and suddenly decides to go back to school, when she leaves behind the traditional functions she has been taught to believe are her only or primary roles in life, she has discovered the Fool within herself.

The Fool can appear at any time, and will usually appear more than once, for we go through many major changes in our life-long journey. When we have the sense that many opportunities stand before us, that no matter which way we turn, we still have the ability to make things work out, we stand in the grasp of the Fool's energy.

At this time, if we feel we've made the wrong choice, we can still alter the outcome of the situation. Only later in the cycle, when we have made many twists and turns (decisions) along the path, do we find the ending of the cycle inevitable.

For now, at the beginning of a new phase, we can backtrack, we can slip from one path to another.

The Fool is truly foolish, for many of his/her choices seem almost insane, dangerous, or lunatic to those content and established in their lives. But the Fool also possesses a certain innocence that can protect; a Divine naïveté that inspires intuition and, like a stray cat or dog, often leads to people or places or events waiting to offer help.

The Spiritual Concept

Spiritually, the Fool becomes the Green Man, the Mad Hatter. He is King for a Day, ignoring the knowledge that he will later be sacrificed to the Gods. He is Dionysus, filled with joy and ecstasy and self-centered attention. He is the young Sun Lord, romping free and easy at Ostara.

The Fool is the Maiden aspect of the Goddess, running wild through the forests, unconcerned with family and career. She is the March Hare, the teasing nymph who does not realize her own power. She is Blodeuwedd, the Celtic goddess made of flowers; Eos, the goddess of dawn who teases the sun into the sky; and Eostre, the maiden of Spring who gives the Vernal Equinox its name: Ostara.

Within the Wheel of the Year, we place the Fool at Ostara, the season of beginnings.

The Card

Some common representations of the Fool include a youth approaching a precipice—uncaring and unseeing—too filled with life to notice the abyss looming below. The Fool is often dressed in bright, discordant colors, much like the jesters of the medieval ages; and usually carries a knapsack over his shoulder.

Guidelines for Use

This meditation is most appropriate for use during times when we are beginning a new phase of our lives. It can also be used during Ostara (the Spring Equinox), or as part of an ongoing journey through the major arcana, as the first meditation along that path.

Flowers:	daffodil, iris, tulip, daisy
Incense:	rosemary, rose, violet, frankincense
Oils:	frankincense, violet, rose, lemongrass
Crystals:	tiger's eye, a prism, lodestone, copper
Candles:	white, yellow

Meditation

Relax and get comfortable. Close your eyes and take three deep breaths.

long pause

You are standing in front of the door to a little shop off a side-street you happened to run across in your wanderings. Over the door hangs a sign that reads "Tarot Readings" in bright green and purple letters.

It seems fortuitous that you have come across this shop. For some time now, you have been curious about the tarot, wondering if you can learn more about yourself from the cards. Perhaps you already own a deck or two, perhaps you have used the cards for some time.

But today, you feel there is something new you can learn from the tarot, some knowledge about yourself that you have not yet encountered.

long pause

You examine your intuition and decide that the shop feels safe, protected, so you take a chance and open the door.

The room into which you step is small. The light is bright, but not glaring, and there are none of the dim shadows often associated with fortunetellers and psychic readers.

A table sits in the middle of the room, with a chair on either side. To your left, you see a small altar. You go over to look, but your intuition tells you that these are someone's sacred objects and so you keep your hands to yourself.

Atop the white linen tablecloth rests a vase filled with daffodils, bright yellow and fragrant with their spicy scent. A large wooden pentacle sits in front of the vase, and on the pentacle, a prism. It separates the rays of sunlight filtering in from the window into dazzling rainbows that dance around the room.

long pause

A stick of rose-scented incense gently smolders to the left of the pentacle, ash falling into a copper holder. To the right sits a bowl of water scented with rosemary and lemongrass.

There is another door against the back wall of the shop and you think that it might lead to the alley. As you turn back to the center table, a woman enters from the curtained door to your right.

The woman wears a gauze dress, lavender with a stippled pattern etched in gold. Gold hoops peek out from beneath her hair. A golden pentacle rests at her throat.

You notice a touch of silver intermingling with the ginger brown of her long curls and her eyes are ancient with knowledge and wisdom. She smiles to you and bids you welcome.

long pause

"You wish me to read your cards?" she asks.

Sit down at the table. The woman sits across from you.

"I am called Pythia," she says, "after the goddess of the oracle. What is your name?"

Tell her your name now.

long pause

Pythia takes out a deck of cards. She handles them easily, she must have shuffled them a thousand times before. She taps them on the table to straighten them and then hands the deck to you.

"Hold the cards while you think of this question: 'What do I need to know?' Then shuffle them seven times and return them to me."

Examine the cards in your hands. What pattern ornaments the back? Does it have any meaning for you, or is it random, a pattern chosen by fate? Now think of the question and shuffle them seven times, then give them back to Pythia.

extended long pause—1 minute

She spreads the cards face down on the table.

"Choose one," she says.

One? Surely you should pick more, you think. As if she is reading your thoughts, she shakes her head.

"Choose one card," she says again.

Look at the cards and pick one, but do not turn it over.

long pause

You give the card to Pythia. She turns it over and places it on the table in front of you.

"It is the Fool," she says.

When you examine the card, you see yourself in the picture. You are wearing a light robe over a simple dress or pair of trousers. The colors are jewel tones; yellow and green, blue and red. In your left hand, you carry a rose. In your right hand, a backpack.

A forest rises behind you and a few steps ahead lies a dark abyss, waiting.

long pause

Pythia smiles. "How exciting," she says. "You are beginning a long journey, a new adventure in your life. There are changes starting to happen, although I cannot predict where they will lead. For this is a journey that you must travel yourself. You must go alone and you must leave now if you are to seize the opportunities awaiting you."

long pause

The thought of such a journey is daunting. It seems a foolish thing to do, to run off without knowing where you are going, but still, a sense of anticipation shivers down your spine and you think that maybe it wouldn't be so frightening after all.

long pause

Pythia seems to sense your ambivalence. "There is no time for worry, nor for hesitation," she says, hustling you out of your chair. "The moment you entered this shop, you initiated change."

She presses a knapsack into your hands, it is similar to the one in the picture. Then she takes the card and tucks it into your pocket. "Keep this with you. It will aid you along your quest."

Somewhat bewildered, you find yourself aimed toward the door at the back wall of the shop.

"Remember, once the journey has begun, you can't come back to the exact place from which you started. Every journey, even the small ones, change us and we are never the same. Now go, knowing that I am with you even if it does not always seem so," Pythia whispers. Before you can stop her, she propels you through the door.

Much to your surprise, you find yourself standing in the middle of a wide, grassy meadow. A dark forest, cloaked in mist and shadow, rises between you and the distant mountains. A rainbow arcs over the sky as the sun slowly sets in the west.

long pause

You turn around. The shop, the alley, the city are all gone and you see nothing behind you but the wide expanse of open grassland. Take a moment to orient yourself.

extended long pause—2 minutes

When you have regained your composure, take another look around. A path runs through the grassland, down the knoll and into the forest. You follow it with your eyes until it disappears into the dark undergrowth. But when you look at the distant slopes, golden in the sunset, you notice that the path emerges from the other side of the copse to wind up through the nooks and crannies of the hilltop. It cuts through the mountain, up to the peak, and disappears over the top.

long pause

A wind gusts by, the cool breeze of the evening kissing your skin. Inhale deeply as the refreshing air fills your lungs. Feel it begin to dislodge any fears about change that you may have.

long pause

Now exhale, and as you blow the air out from your lungs, release these fears up to the sky, to be cleansed and carried away.

long pause

Inhale once more, this time the air brings with it a sense of anticipation, a stirring of wanderlust, and the desire for new adventures.

long pause

Exhale once again, and release doubts and insecurities that prevent you from trying new things, from taking risks when the time seems appropriate.

long pause

Now take a third deep breath. A sense of peace about the journey flows in with the cooling breeze.

long pause

Exhale slowly, and you will be ready to begin a new cycle in your life.

long pause

The sun is settling below the horizon. It is time to set out. Take a quick peek in your knapsack. What do you think you would need for such a journey?

Food, of course, and water. But what else? Look in the knapsack to see what you find. Perhaps there is a lantern there, or some rope. You might find simply a swirl of energy, ready to take the shape of whatever you need as you travel along.

Examine your knapsack now.

extended long pause—1 minute

A soft hooting from the forest below tells you that it is time to actually begin your journey. The sun is almost set, but the moon is beginning to rise and it will give you clear light under which you may travel.

Start walking along the path as you head toward the forest. For you know that somewhere deep in the glen lays the direction in which you must travel and while there may be many paths as you follow your quest, you have a sense of destiny about this journey.

The twilight shimmers around you. If you are not used to being out of doors, it may seem a little frightening. The knowledge that this afternoon you were sitting in a city shop and now you are traveling through an unknown land is enough to make anyone nervous. If you are a little scared, that's perfectly fine.

But remember what Pythia told you: once a journey is undertaken, you can never go back to the exact place from which you began. Every quest, even the small ones, change us and we are never the same.

long pause

You travel alone, accompanied only by the haunting call of birds as their cries echo through the approaching night. A shift in the grass here or there tells you that some small animal recently wandered by, but it is difficult to see at this time and you hurry down the slope, suddenly longing for the protection of the forest.

As you peer through the dusk, you see that the forest seems to be made up of maple and oak, cedar and fir, and the trees are thick with undergrowth. Huckleberries, fern, and vine maple wrap their way through the silent sentinels.

long pause

Just before you reach the opening of the wood, you see something in the middle of the path, blocking your way. It is a fountain, formed of agate and moonstone, and a ladle hangs from a nearby post.

long pause

You pause for a moment, then try to go around the foundation. A crackle in the air makes you slightly nervous, magick feels thick here and you aren't sure if you want to approach the shimmering water in the dusk.

But when you try to skirt the left, you find you can't get past. A field of energy blocks your way and seems to extend as far as you can see. You find the same thing to the right.

long pause

There is no help for it. You have to approach the fountain. Cautious, not sure what to expect, you make your way to the reservoir. The moonstone shines with a ghostly light under the rising moon.

Carefully, look over the edge and into the hollow of dark, glistening liquid.

long pause

The moon's reflection ripples as a gentle breeze moves across the water. A silvery face begins to take form in the water. It is the face of a woman.

long pause

"Who are you?" she says.

Tell her your name.

Her eyes glitter, they are the color of aquamarine and her lips open delicately as she says, "Before you can continue your journey, you must think about what you are ready to leave behind. Think about what behaviors you have outgrown, what beliefs no longer work for you. You must recognize that which has passed out of your life before you can search for new dreams, new goals, and new adventures."

Sit on the edge of the fountain and think now about what you are ready to release. What beliefs no longer matter to you? What habits are you ready to break? What lessons have you recently learned and integrated into yourself?

Think about all of these things for a moment.

extended long pause—2 minutes

When you have thought about her words, the spirit smiles and says, "Now you are truly ready for the journey. Now you are ready for new growth and new lessons. There will be many obstacles along your path, many parts of your psyche you have yet to explore. Your strongest ally is your own honesty and truth. Without honesty to yourself, you will never rid yourself of illusions and self-deception."

long pause

The water ripples as she says, "Take the ladle and scoop up a mouthful of water. Drink deep and you will be allowed to pass into the forest, to your next destination on this journey, where you will have to face yourself and your inner truths."

Take the ladle and drink.

long pause

As the water races down your throat, refreshing you, the fountain glows brighter and brighter and then, in the wink of an eye, it is gone, vanished into the night and the path into the forest is clear.

You know now that your next journey will take you into the wood. But for now, rest here, at the foot of the forest. All journeys take time, you cannot complete the cycle in a single evening.

long pause

Now listen as I count from ten to one. As I count, you will become awake and alert. Ten . . . nine . . . you are becoming alert and aware of your surroundings . . . eight . . . seven . . . six . . . hear the sounds around . . . five . . . four . . . you will be fully alert and refreshed . . . three . . . two . . . you are waking to full consciousness . . . one . . . take three deep breaths and when you are ready, you may open your eyes.

Suggested Exercises

1. Over the past year, what life lessons have you learned? How have you learned them? Examine how these lessons changed your life, your behavior, and your beliefs.

2. Paint a picture of yourself as the Fool. What does the precipice mean to you? What jump or leap in belief or action does it represent?

3. What are some things you've wanted to do, or to learn, but have been afraid to approach? Is there a way you can work beyond that fear? Sometimes the best attitude to take is: "Feel the fear, but do it anyway."

4. Think about all the major advances in your life. Look for the "Fool" moment that precipitated each one.

5. Create a ritual to welcome in change and new beginnings. Ceremonially burn slips of paper that represent your fears and the obstacles that hold you back. This is a good focus for group ritual. Just remember, it helps to have some idea of a direction you want to pursue before you open up a void.

I am true as truth's simplicity,
And simpler than the infancy of truth.

—William Shakespeare (1564–1616)
Troilus and Cressida

The Magician

Understanding the Truth

The second card of the major arcana is known as the Magician (in some decks, the Magus). It is always assigned the number 1.

The Magician and His Energy

The Magician represents our ability to communicate with the self and with others. After embarking on our journey (the Fool), we must take the next step which is to delve inward, to discover who and what we are meant to be. Only through the clarity of self-analysis, can we pursue our true paths in this life.

The Magician is the Alchemist, balancing the elements of earth, air, fire, and water, from which all life springs.

He reminds us to speak our truths, to act in accordance with our beliefs, to avoid hypocrisy. When we open up the Magician's magic box, we discover the truth behind the illusion, and while that can destroy some of the sparkle of life, it leaves us with a new sense of freedom.

The Fool is no longer quite so naive.

In our daily lives, the Magician appears as the teacher who forces us to really think about our reactions to what we study, read, and learn. The Magician also shows up in the guise of the person who accepts no excuses; who, instead, forces us to examine our apathy and lack of focus.

The Magician archetype can appear in our lives when we've strayed from our inner truth, when we discover that we've been lying to ourselves and to others in order to avoid uncomfortable situations. Representing the intellect, it is through this energy that our quest for meaning begins to take shape.

The Magician appears after the Fool because we must embark on the journey of self-discovery before we can expect results. Without the initial leap into darkness, without taking a risk on the unknown, we are too comfortable and too settled to journey within.

Only when we let go of the familiar and embrace that which seems alien do we discover the path home to our true natures.

The Spiritual Concept

In terms of spirituality, the Magician becomes Hermes, Mercury. He is the god of knowledge and communications. He brings us messages from other worlds. He is the Alchemist who successfully integrates and blends energies to produce a balanced whole. He is also the Coyote, the Trickster, who blinds us with illusion and challenges us to find the truth buried at the center. Coyote bites our heels until we pay attention and learn the lessons he presents.

The Magician is Brighid, in her aspect as goddess of sovereignty, who holds the chalice of truth, and Spider Woman, weaver of language and communications who encourages us to be as clear and concise as we possibly can.

In the Wheel of the Year, the Magician personifies Imbolc (Festival of Brighid), embodying the clarity of early Spring.

The Card

Some common representations of the Magician include a man (often an androgynous figure) holding a crystal sphere or a caduceus. We often find near him the symbols representing the four suits of the tarot. The Magician is sometimes portrayed as an aboriginal shaman, or as the Roman God Mercury.

Guidelines for Use

In our ongoing journey through the major arcana, this meditation should follow that of the Fool. Meditating on the Magician is also appropriate during Imbolc (February 2), or whenever we need to ascertain whether or not a certain attitude, belief, or opinion is actually our own.

Flowers:	lavender, fennel, caraway, dill, thyme
Incense:	lavender, peppermint, almond, sage
Oils:	lavender, almond, peppermint, lemongrass
Crystals:	clear quartz, sapphire, aquamarine
Candles:	white, blue

Meditation

Relax and get comfortable. Close your eyes and take three deep breaths.

long pause

You have been traveling on your journey for some time and now find yourself standing on a narrow, dusty path at the edge of a large wood. The sun has come and gone for the day and it is now early twilight. A chill in the air reminds you that winter is not yet over; the ground is still cloaked in a white shroud of snow.

long pause

The huge oaks and maples that litter the forest intertwine in a black silhouette of woven limbs. Here and there a dried leaf quivers, rattling as brisk currents of air gust along the edge of the wood.

You are dressed for winter, with your backpack hanging over one shoulder. If you like, you find a walking stick in your hands.

You have traveled far to meet the Magician who lives in the woods. It is said that he helps those who seek the path to inner knowledge and since you, too, are on such an odyssey, you have come to seek his aid. For several seasons you have cast about, carefree and adventurous, but now you feel the need to focus, to bring direction into your quest.

long pause

A screech startles you and you look up to see a crow perched in one of the bare-limbed trees. It looks at you with piercing black eyes and then swiftly wings its way down to land in front of you.

"This is the forest of Inner Sight. Only those who seek for truth in their hearts may enter," it squawks. Then, with a flap of wings, it asks, "Are you willing to face yourself honestly, to accept the truth of your being?"

Think for a moment before answering. If you are not ready to look at yourself honestly, then you are not ready to enter the forest.

When you know you are ready, then give the crow your answer.

long pause

The crow steps aside. The path is icy and littered with twigs and branches.

"The going is rough, there are dangerous parts that may attempt to trip you up, but if you persevere, you will reach the Magician," the crow says as it bids you enter the forest.

long pause

Your first steps onto the path confirm the crow's warning. Your footing is unsure, the worn path is covered with thick, glazed ice from which gleams a pale blue light.

When you set foot onto the slippery trail your boots go sliding out from under you and you find yourself falling to the ground. Though the ice is hard, your clothes are well-padded and the fall doesn't hurt much. It merely startles you and knocks the wind from your lungs.

long pause

You hear a slight cackle and look up to see the crow watching you.

"I warned you," it says. "Be cautious, your worst enemy in this forest is your own self." Then it flies away.

Stand up, if you have a walking stick you find it helps you balance. Otherwise, by leaning against one of the huge cedars interspersed with the oaks and maples, you can cautiously rise to your feet again.

long pause

The moon is high tonight, waning over the winter wood, and the sliver of light gleams like a crescent of ice. There is a rustle nearby and you think that you hear an animal cross the path ahead, but in the dusk you cannot be sure.

You continue and when you come to the brush where you thought you heard something, you see large paw tracks in the snow to the side of the path. Take a closer look—they are wolf tracks and your heart flutters for a moment. Wolves are usually benign, but it has been an exceptionally cold winter and there has been little game for them to hunt.

long pause

A snarl startles you. You look up to see a large gray wolf blocking the path. Its ears are back and its eyes gleam like sparkling yellow topaz.

long pause

"I am the guardian spirit of this forest," the wolf says, and his words roll like thunder. "Why are you trespassing in my woodland?"

Tell the wolf that you have come seeking the Magician.

long pause

The wolf's ears flicker. He gazes at you thoughtfully.

"So you seek the Magician's help? Then you must first pass my challenge," he says. "I am the Pack Master, the Wolf Father, and all who enter this forest must do so with my blessing. Will you accept my challenge, or will you turn and leave this wood?"

The wolf will not tell you what the challenge is, so you must make your decision based on your courage alone. When you are ready to accept the challenge, tell the wolf of your decision.

long pause

After you have given your assent, the wolf opens its mouth. Its teeth shine, they glisten, their razor-sharp edges trimmed with gold.

"Place your hand in my mouth as a symbol of courage, as a symbol that you are willing to accept all of your aspects, the fierce as well as the gentle. If you cannot master your aggression then you cannot use its strength, and the only way you can master it is to submit, to accept that every person has a wild and untamed creature residing within their hearts. It is your primal nature, and it rules over your courage as well as over your fear."

Think about what the wolf has said, and when you are ready, place your hand in its mouth.

long pause

The wolf gently closes his jaws so that his teeth are resting lightly on your flesh. Then he opens his mouth and allows you to remove your hand.

"You have passed the test of courage. You have my blessing to walk in this forest," he says and then turns and runs off into the brush.

Take a deep breath as you collect your thoughts.

long pause

The dusk is fading quickly but the wood is so laden with snow that the pale moon reflects against the blanket of white, making the night bright enough for you to see.

Cautiously pick your way along the path. Once in a while you trip over a branch or a twig, and now and then your feet feel like they are going to slide out from under you, but you manage to find a gait and pace that keeps you upright.

After a while, the path forks off into a "Y" and you must decide in which direction to go. As you stand thinking, a low hum emanates from the right-hand side of the path. Perhaps it is another wolf, you think, or maybe a different animal, but then a shimmer fills the air, green and yellow and orange lights all shifting and glittering, and out of the light steps a tall woman. She is lithe and ethereal, like no other woman you have ever seen.

She wears a dress of woven spider webs and her hair is crowned with a wreath of oak leaves and grapes.

"Halt, you who walk in this forest," she says. "I am the spirit of the vine, the spirit of wine and intoxication and forgetfulness. Drink of my delights and join me in ecstasy." You can smell the concord grapes that hang from her wreath. She holds out a jug of rich wine.

You are thirsty, but you hesitate to accept her offer. You sense there is something she has not yet disclosed, a price to pay should you accept the drink.

long pause

She senses your hesitation and laughs.

"Yes, there is a price, but an easy one. You abandon your search for yourself. What do you care? What fun is honesty and clarity and self-illumination? Better to drink of illusion and maintain your sense of balance through avoiding the pain that can attach itself to the truth. If you drink with me, if you walk my path, then you will enjoy your life and enjoy your days . . . my road offers an easy answer to difficult situations."

long pause

Her words spiral around your thoughts, they are persuasive and enticing, and you realize that she speaks the truth. If you accept her distractions, if you turn away from your search, you will live in a world of compromise and illusion.

The road to the self is not an easy one, but somehow you know that the rewards are worth the search. If you decide to accept the spirit's offer, you will have to leave the woods and abandon your quest.

When you are ready to tell her that you want to continue your search, then do so.

long pause

The spirit of the vine vanishes from your sight and you are alone in the hushed woodland once again.

long pause

Take three deep breaths as you compose yourself.

long pause

The path to the right has disappeared, so you must turn left. Now you enter a darker part of the wood, the trees are closer together and the snow on their blackened trunks and limbs creates an eerie sight in the moonlight.

Your footing becomes difficult, the ice a sheer glaze over the crusted snow. You fall and scrape your knee, then as soon as you get up, you fall again and bump your elbow.

long pause

An owl hoots from a nearby tree and its screech sends shivers racing down your back. There is a scrabbling sound, and you can barely see as the owl swoops down to pluck a rabbit from the snow. The rabbit squeals as the owl flies off, firmly grasping the hare in its talons.

long pause

Take a deep breath and continue along the path.

The trail begins to decline, sloping down toward a frozen steam. The stream is neither wide nor deep. You can see smooth river rocks under the frozen crust, and the skeletons of ferns that will flourish again when the spring finally comes.

long pause

As you begin to pick your way across the stream, you suddenly hear a crack and the ice fractures, splintering as you find yourself breaking through into the freezing water below. You lose your footing again and fall, this time into the chilly waters.

long pause

Exhausted and cold, you manage to crawl to the other side of the ravine and pull yourself out of the stream bed. Your clothes are wet and you are thoroughly chilled as you struggle to climb the other side of the path, slipping here and there in the snow.

Finally you make it to the top of the ravine. As you are wringing the water out of your robes, you hear someone approaching.

long pause

At first you think it might be the Magician, but when the figure enters a beam of moonlight, you find yourself staring into your own face.

Like you, and yet not alike, this being embodies all of your sadness, all of your mourning over the things you haven't done, the places you haven't seen, the experiences you may never have. Look into your own eyes and see the sadness that resides within your heart.

long pause

This replica of yourself stares back at you, unblinking. After a moment, you hear it say, "Turn and leave this wood. You don't want to know the truth of your failures, of all the lost chances, of all the opportunities you let go by. I carry these griefs within myself and protect you from knowing them too closely."

Know that what you hear is true. There is a part within each of us into which we thrust our fears of failure, our fears of success, our regrets over actions taken and actions left undone. When we do not examine these feelings, they grow in power and become our inner demons.

What are your inner demons? What hides in the heart of this double, this doppel-gänger who stands before you?

extended long pause—2 minutes

Once you have identified your inner demons, know that if you choose to leave them here, outside of yourself, thrust away from the light, they will only grow in power. You would have to turn and leave the wood, for self-confidence can only flourish where there is honesty.

If you take these fears into your conscious mind, accepting them for what they are— feelings and nothing more—then you will learn to experience them and let them go.

When you are ready, hold out your arms and invite your double to give you a hug.

As you embrace yourself, including all of your sorrows and regrets, you find that the negative emotions blend with your joys and your successes, and yet they don't over-whelm you. You can experience them without empowering them.

long pause

As you assimilate the emotions guarded by your double, the image slowly vanishes. You feel a sense of integration, of balance that may have been lacking.

Take a deep breath while you experience that sense of balance and integration.

long pause

As you look ahead, a faint light glows from around a curve in the path. Your footing seems a little more certain, a little easier here, and you quickly make your way to the light.

The wood opens into a small clearing. In the center of the clearing burns a bright bonfire. You can feel the heat from where you stand, it penetrates your wet clothing.

Near the bonfire stands a small tent, and in front of the tent, on a thick blanket, sits a man. He wears the skin and antlers of an elk, and around his neck hangs a necklace of quartz crystals. He sees you and motions for you to join him.

long pause

"You are cold and wet and tired from your journey," he says. He ladles out a hot bowl of soup from a kettle hanging over the fire. It is thick with vegetables and broth. He offers you a hunk of bread covered with melted cheese to go with the soup.

Eat quietly and relax as the food and the fire begin to draw the chill from your body.

long pause

When you have finished eating, he takes your plate and then returns with a small pouch made of fur. Something clinks from inside.

"You have passed my three challenges and so have won your way into my wood," the Magician says. "Do you seek the truth of yourself?"

You nod and he laughs.

"Then know this. I will help you on your quest, but what you learn tonight is only the beginning. You have shown courage, focus, and the willingness to embrace your fears and regrets, but there are many more steps to the path of self-realization."

He holds up the pouch. "I can help you by giving you a focus on your priorities."

A cascade of twinkling crystal runes pours out onto the blanket. He spreads them out so you can look at them.

"There are runes here to represent your home and family, your career, your schooling. There are runes to represent your values, your skills and talents. Still others embody the essence of the goals, hopes, and dreams that you can truly manifest into reality."

He leans closer. "No runes within this pouch represent an unattainable goal. Whatever you draw, you can achieve. You will choose three runes. Each one indicates one of your most important priorities at this moment. You and only you will recognize their symbols."

He pours the runes back into the pouch, shakes it, then hands it to you and says, "Draw the first."

Take the pouch, draw one rune and examine it.

What does the rune represent to you? Is it a priority that you are already aware of, or is it something you didn't expect? Whatever it is, know that your inner self is guiding you.

extended long pause—1 minute

The Magician sets the rune aside. He shakes the pouch again. "Draw your second," he says.

Draw your second rune and examine it.

extended long pause—1 minute

When you are done, the Magician sets the rune aside. He shakes the pouch and says, "Draw your third."

Draw your third rune and examine it.

extended long pause—1 minute

The Magician smiles.

"You must now think about these three priorities and decide how you will integrate them into your life. It is not a task you can complete in one evening. Achieving these goals will require consistent effort and focus."

He puts another log on the fire.

"You are tired and weary. I will bring you a blanket. You can curl up next to the fire. It will burn through the night and keep you warm."

As he speaks, you feel yourself drifting off. He wraps a thick comforter around your shoulders. Your clothing has dried and, as you curl up next to the blazing warmth, you can faintly hear the Magician say, "Your journey into my realm took courage and will. You focused on your goal and achieved it. Be proud of yourself."

long pause

When you wake in the morning, the tent is gone and you find yourself sitting next to the hissing embers of the fire. There is food for your breakfast, but the Magician has disappeared. Eat a light meal to prepare yourself for the journeys that lie ahead.

long pause

Now listen to my voice as I count from ten to one. You will awake refreshed and alert, remembering everything you learned about yourself on this journey. Ten . . . nine . . . you are becoming awake and aware of your surroundings . . . eight . . . seven . . . six . . . hear the sounds around you . . . five . . . four . . . you will be fully alert and refreshed . . . three . . . two . . . you are waking to full consciousness . . . one . . . take three deep breaths and when you are ready, you may open your eyes.

Suggested Exercises

1. Find a good book on goal setting and take stock of your current situation. Where do you want to be in five years? In two years? In six months? When you figure out your goals, then you can set priorities to help reach them.

2. When you faced the wolf, what did you fear most about the challenge? Did you fear he would betray you? Did you fear the actual pain of being bitten? Examine your reactions. Are your fears based more in emotions or in physical reality? When you examine and acknowledge your fears, then it becomes easier to release them.

3. Do you get distracted easily? Perhaps you are not working toward the appropriate goals. If your work does not challenge you, then you cannot expect to happily immerse yourself in it. Think about the goals you have. Are they appropriate for your nature, or do you think you might be happier pursuing something different? You must be true to yourself if you are going to create success you can be proud of.

4. Create a ritual in which you welcome the truths, both good and bad, about yourself. It is only through truth that we can change. Only through truth can we validate our personal strengths. False modesty is as damaging as false pride.

$\mathcal{I}$do not know whether I was then a man dreaming I was a butterfly, or whether I am now a butterfly dreaming I am a man.

—Chuang Tzu (369–286 B.C.E.)
On Leveling All Things

The High Priestess
Dreaming Your Path

$\mathcal{T}$he third card of the major arcana is known as the High Priestess (in some decks, simply the Priestess). It is assigned the number 2.

The High Priestess and Her Energy

The Priestess represents our ability to turn inward and seek enlightenment. The Magician seeks truth through analysis, the Priestess then uses intuition and magick to direct that truth. When we have come to a clear vision of who we are meant to be, we use the intuitive and creative powers of the Priestess to divine how to arrive at that state of being.

The Priestess is the center of the coven, she is the initiator into the hidden mysteries of the soul. She helps us use the elements—earth, air, fire, and water—which the Magician has taught us to balance.

She reminds us that we are the true originators of our own power. The Priestess also represents our link with the gods, she is the channel, the medium through which They speak. As the Fool moves into the realm of the Priestess, s/he begins to understand his/her relationship to the world of Spirit and the Divine.

In our daily lives, the Priestess appears as the catalyst who enters our presence, bringing with them a sense of wonderment and magick. Though they may pass through our lives, never staying for long, the catalyst has a profound philosophical or magickal effect on our existence.

We may meet an old lady on the pier who points out the connection between the ocean and ourselves, we might encounter the Priestess through reading a book on Witchcraft that touches our heart. We may even find the Priestess to be the little boy next door who looks at our artwork that we've done simply for fun, and asks why we don't sell them, because they're so good.

In other words, the Priestess can be of any age or gender, but she will always bring with her a flash of intuitive understanding that strikes like lightning and shakes up our world.

The Priestess archetype appears in our lives when we are ready for a leap in consciousness, when we've gotten clear on some of our truths and are ready for the next evolutionary step along our path. She represents the intuition, the hidden depths of the psyche, and it is through her energy that we grasp the spiritual nature of our quest.

Without the clarity of the Magician, we are not ready for everything the Priestess offers. Sometimes she may strike before we've achieved this clarity, and then it may take years to come to an understanding of what we learned through her powers.

When we have cast away false images of the self, the energy of the Priestess then leads us deep into our soul so that our path takes on a higher meaning in the personal perspective.

The Spiritual Concept

Spiritually, the Priestess becomes the Lady of the Lake, guiding Arthur to Avalon. She is also Morgana, goddess of magick and the sea, who challenges us to claim our own spiritual power. She is Isis, the Initiator; and Demeter, who takes us deep into the Eleusinian Mysteries. Through Hecate, the Priestess teaches us the balance of light and dark energies.

The Priestess also becomes the Priest, through Ptah, Opener of the Ways. He is Papa Legba, the god through whom one must pass to reach any of the others within His realm.

Within the Wheel of the Year, the Priestess personifies the element of Spirit, that which binds all Elements together.

The Card

Most representations of the Priestess include a veiled woman wearing the horns of Isis. She will often have a crystal ball or a bow near her, as well as the image of the Moon.

Guidelines for Use

In your journey through the major arcana, this meditation should follow the Magician. A meditation on the Priestess is also appropriate any time you feel you need to reinforce your intuition, or on the Full Moon.

Flowers:	lavender, gardenia, lilac, rose, mugwort
Incense:	frankincense, sandalwood, gum mastic
Oils:	honeysuckle, wormwood, lemon, camphor
Crystals:	clear quartz, aquamarine, moonstone, amethyst
Candles:	white, pale blue, lavender

Meditation

Relax and get comfortable. Close your eyes and take three deep breaths.

long pause

You are in the middle of the forest, once again on the dusty path that leads you through your journey. The snows and ice of winter have melted and the Wheel turns as another spring looms on the horizon.

The full moon rises overhead. It is tinged with silver, this luminous paper lantern that fills the sky. As you stand, watching the orb slowly wheel its way through the night, you think you hear the faintest of chimes on the wind, echoing under the moonlight.

long pause

A quickening in your blood tells you that its time to get moving. No longer the young, naive person who started this quest, your direction is still crystallized in thought—still a concept, and you know you have a long way to go. But you are more certain of yourself; you have some idea of who you are becoming.

You have heard rumors from passersby that a woman exists further within the wood. A Priestess, she is a seer of the soul, and can help you tap into your intuition and inner guidance. The Priestess only welcomes visitors on the nights of the Full Moon and so you must find her tonight.

long pause

Pick up your backpack and your walking stick, if you have one, and begin walking along the path. The woods are alive tonight, crickets are chirping, frogs are croaking. You even see a doe and her fawn slip into the brush as you pass by.

long pause

The forest begins to thin out a little and you notice that there are more hazel and willow trees here. The undergrowth is made up of ferns and nettle, and when you look up, you see more of the sky. The wind gusts past, leaving a cool, mossy scent lingering in its wake.

There appears to be a clearing ahead. As you step out of the forest, a lake stretches as wide and as far as you can see. The path ends at the lake but, under the powerful glow of the moonlight, you think you can see the distant shore.

long pause

Startled by your appearance, a flock of gulls circles the water, ethereal wisps of white against the black sky. They remind you of spirits as they fly past, screeching.

Bordered by reeds, the mossy bank is littered with trillium and crocus, and you know there must be a huge family of frogs living here because their croaking is so loud it seems to shake the earth.

The waters of the lake lap gently against the bank, the breeze stirs ripples into waves and carries the scent of fresh, cool water to calm your thoughts.

long pause

One frog, larger than the rest, hops out from the reeds and settles near you. He says, "Why have you come?"

You tell him that you are searching for the Priestess of this Forest, and the frog says, "You will never find her without first clearing yourself of the dust and grime from the road." It whistles and you hear a movement in the forest behind you.

A woman slips from between the trees. Her skin is a kaleidoscope of black and white swirls, which writhe and twist as you watch. Her long hair glistens with coppery high-lights, and her eyes mirror the brilliant green of tropical seas. She wears no clothes, but carries a towel in one hand and a basket in the other.

long pause

"If you seek the Priestess, then I must prepare you. She will never admit you to her land without the proper cleansing and purification."

Her voice is smooth, without deceit, and your inner guidance prompts you to accept her offer. The woman helps you disrobe. She folds your clothes and carefully places them in your backpack. Then she points to the water.

"Immerse yourself in the lake." She offers her hand, the mossy bank isn't steep but the ground is spongy and soft against your feet. As you step into the water, it tingles and you know this is no ordinary lake.

long pause

The woman smiles at your expression. "Close your eyes and inhale deeply," she says. Take three deep breaths.

long pause

As you slowly exhale, you feel the tension and cares of the journey slide away, water off duck's down, into the lake where it is cleansed and transformed into sparkling energy, returning to the world to be used again.

long pause

Now take another breath and dip under the water, fully immersing yourself in the lake. As the water closes over your head, you open your eyes.

There are sparkles all around you, sparkles of green and blue, of yellow and pink. They shimmer in the water and brush against your skin, renewing you, revitalizing your energy.

long pause

When you break the surface, the sparkling phosphorescence still surrounds you, it is floating in the water, and you see that some of it is shining on your skin. Make swirling patterns in the lake with your fingers, watch the whirlpool of stars flicker against your hand.

long pause

The woman laughs aloud and motions for you to join her on the shore. As you step out of the water, the drops of light slide away from your body. She hands you a towel.

"Dry yourself," she says.

When you are done, she takes a copper bowl from the basket. In the bowl, on a mound of salt, sits a burning ember. She drops a pinch of incense on the charcoal and huge clouds of smoke billow up. As soon as you smell the lavender and sage, your mind begins to relax and you find yourself at peace.

long pause

"Hold out your arms," she says.

Stand in front of her and hold out your arms.

The woman blows the smoke over your body, chanting a low incantation. The delicate white clouds gently touch your skin and lift off any remaining tensions or anxieties.

long pause

When she is finished, she calls out, "Wind, wind, blow this way, sweep the smoke and dust away." A huge gust of chill wind blasts past you, catching up the smoke to carry it away.

Your head feels clear, your body lighter, and your heart at peace.

Take three slow deep breaths as the woman silently helps you dress. She helps you into a robe, patterned with white and black swirls, and it reminds you of her skin. Then she stands back. "You are now ready to meet the Priestess," she says.

long pause

There is a noise in the water. A long, narrow boat is gliding toward the shore. On both bow and stern, rising like silent giants, are the heads of dragons. One is a dragon of ice, with sapphire eyes and talons of silver. The other is a dragon of fire, with ruby eyes and talons of gold.

The woman says, "Take your pack with you and step into the boat. It will guide you to the Lady's island."

Before you leave, you feel the sudden desire to ask her what the swirling patterns on her skin and the robe symbolize.

She smiles and says, "The white symbolizes light and clarity; the black, darkness and shadow. Both are necessary for balance, without the light there can be no shadow and without the shadow, the light would be meaningless. They intermingle at all times. Understand that no absolute exists when you are working with the magick and energy of creation. I am yin and yang; I am positive and negative; I am the struggle and balance of polarities."

extended long pause—1 minute

She helps you into the boat and you cautiously sit in the center with your pack at your feet. As soon as you have settled in, the boat glides away from the shore and heads out into the lake.

long pause

The water laps quietly as the boat slips through the gentle waves. When you have traveled perhaps half an hour, you see what looks to be an island up ahead.

You dock at a small landing, but there seems to be no one there to greet you. Climb out of the boat. Marble steps lead up the slope and you see, amongst a copse of elder and yew trees, what appears to be a small temple made out of the same marble. The steps and the temple glow in the moonlight.

long pause

You hear a meow and look down. Standing next to you, with a wide-eyed, innocent stare, is a huge black cat with a white belly and white paws. It stretches up to tap your knee, then turns and runs up the steps. You get the feeling you should follow the cat.

long pause

The steps lead to the temple, and when you get there, the cat races inside. As you stand at the entrance, debating whether or not to follow, a woman's voice echoes from down the hall.

"Enter under the full moon, you who seek the hidden mysteries of the soul."

A pale light glows from the end of the long corridor. Follow the light until you reach a large open-air room.

The walls gleam with alabaster, and Corinthian pillars rise from the four corners. Each pillar holds a shelf.

On the first shelf, a golden pentacle hangs behind a flowerpot containing a rose bush. Three roses adorn the bush, one is a white, slender bud, not yet opened. The middle rose has blossomed fully, crimson, its scent fills the room. The third rose has dried and become brittle and blackened, but still it grows from the branch.

long pause

On the second column, you see a billowing feather fan made of white and yellow and lavender plumes. It hovers about an inch above the shelf, quivering as if the wind might carry it away at any second.

long pause

Embedded in the shelf of the third pillar, you see a deep brass bowl. Within the bowl burns a bright fire. From where you stand, you can see no wood, no embers fueling the flames.

long pause

On the last shelf stands a gleaming silver goblet inlaid with amethyst and moonstone. It is filled with a dark wine stained with crimson.

long pause

In the center of the room, outlined by a beam of moonlight, sits a woman on a low footstool. She is cloaked in a robe the color of twilight and a sheer veil hides her face so you cannot see her eyes. She holds up her hand, motioning for you to stay where you are, right outside the door.

extended long pause—1 minute

"I am the Priestess. All those who search for me ask for answers to their problems. Know that I am no oracle and can offer you no solutions. My teaching provides a far greater gift. I offer you the knowledge of your intuition. If you would choose to open the door to your inner self, that you might seek the mysteries of your soul, tell me now."

The Priestess offers you the chance to be the initiator of change and of growth in your personal life, to make your own decisions. You can chart your course while knowing, intuitively, whether or not certain actions will be safe, profitable, or successful.

Think for a moment what this could mean for you on a personal level, and then give the Priestess your assent.

extended long pause—1 minute

When you have spoken, the Priestess holds up her hand. From her fingertips, a web of light shoots forth to cover the floor of the temple. Made up of hundreds of glowing strands, like spokes on a wheel, they leave a thin ledge of darkness surrounding the edge of the room.

She says, "One and only one of these strands belongs to you. You must find it before you can join me."

Examine the ends of the strands. You can walk along the dark band surrounding the web of light. Each strand sparkles with different colors, different patterns. Try to discover which strand belongs to you. If you touch one not aligned with your energy, you will feel a mild shock, not enough to hurt you, but strong enough to crackle at your touch.

Now circle the web, searching for the strand aligned to your personal life-path and energy. You know it is there, use your inner guidance to discover its whereabouts.

extended long pause—2 minutes

When you have found your strand of the web, the Priestess says, "Now, join me in the center of the temple."

Step onto the strand and follow it to the center.

long pause

The Priestess invites you to sit at her feet, where a soft rug and a thick pillow await. The glittering lights of the web disappear as you settle onto the floor. She motions for you to lie back; between the rug and the robe you are wearing, you are warm and comfortable.

As you lie on the floor, you can see the moon. Glowing directly overhead, it glares down so bright you have to shade your eyes.

The Priestess says, "Take three deep breaths." She gently lays one hand on your forehead. "Look at the moon. Stare at the moon and let yourself fall into the luminous orb that hovers above us."

The moon seems to grow larger, pulsating with energy. You think you can hear it breathe.

"Listen to my voice," the Priestess says. "I want you to go deep inside, down through the thoughts that clutter your mind, down through the fears that nag at you. Go down, down, deep within yourself."

long pause

"Still further, go further within yourself. Down, down to the center of your being, the core of your essence. Down past emotion and thought and analysis. Travel toward your core, toward your center."

long pause

"You see a light, a bright light deep within your core. It is as brilliant as the moon, and no one can touch this light but you. See the light within yourself, see the core of energy that makes up your essence."

long pause

"Take three deep breaths and let them out slowly. Now look at this light, deep within yourself. Behind the light, cloaked in the shadow, stands a mirror, dark and silent. Look for the mirror beyond the light."

long pause

"That mirror reflects everything you need to know about yourself and your life. It reflects the energy that is your core and your essence, your being, and your personality. Whatever you need to know about yourself or your actions, you can ask the mirror and it will show you the answer. Look into the mirror and see your true self reflected back at you."

extended long pause—2 minutes

"Take three deep breaths. Know that the voice of this mirror is not the voice of your heart, it is not the voice of your thoughts. It is the voice of inner knowledge. Whenever you have a question about you life, ask and it will tell you the truth.

"You have a choice. You may hear the voice as it is, or you may choose a form for it, a form which your inner guide can assume. You may want to choose a bear, or a salmon, or a bird, or a tree, or one of many myriad forms. Or perhaps you are happy with just hearing the voice. Spend a moment thinking about what form you would like your inner guide to take, if any."

extended long pause—1 minute

"If you have a question right now, go ahead and ask, and listen for the answer."

long pause

"Now come back to your conscious mind," the Priestess says. "Know that you can touch this guidance any time you choose to or need to."

You can feel her hand on your forehead again as you journey out of your inner core and back to the temple room. The Priestess smiles at you.

long pause

"This inner voice will always be with you," she says. "As long as you remain true to yourself, the voice will be easy to hear. The further you slip away from your path, the harder it is to listen."

She hands you your backpack. "Your clothes have been washed and dried. Change before you go back to the boat."

As you change clothes, you notice that the moon is almost gone from the sky and the first light of dawn is stirring in the east. The Priestess bids you farewell.

If you have anything to say to her, say it now.

long pause

When you step into the corridor, you hear a quick whooshing sound. You turn around, but find the temple room is empty and silent—the Priestess has vanished.

The black and white cat appears at your feet and leads you back out of the temple and down the marble steps. You climb into the boat and it starts to glide across the waters, to the far-distant shore of the lake.

The morning looks like it is going to be sunny and warm, and as you near the shore, you see a path, leading off into a wide field filled with late-summer flowers.

long pause

Now listen to my voice as I count from ten to one. You will awake refreshed and alert, remembering how to tap into the hidden realms of your psyche. Ten . . . nine . . . you are becoming awake and aware of your surroundings . . . eight . . . seven . . . six . . . hear the sounds around you . . . five . . . four . . . you will be fully alert and refreshed . . . three . . . two . . . you are waking to full consciousness . . . one . . . take three deep breaths and when you are ready, you may open your eyes.

Suggested Exercises

1. Practice quiet meditation every night before you go to bed, searching for your inner voice. Do this for a month and see how it affects your life.

2. When faced with a big problem, take a cleansing bath with lavender and lemon bath salts before making your decision. Lavender is a soothing herb and will calm your mind so you can hear yourself think.

3. Observe the moon every night for a month—simply note the changes as it goes from new to full to new again, and spend a few minutes tuning into its energy.

4. Remember: Intuition is not what you think and not what you feel. It's a little voice inside that says, "I know."

She said no more and as she turned away there was a bright glimpse of the rosy glow of her neck, and from her ambrosial head of hair a heavenly fragrance wafted; her dress flowed right down to her feet, and in her walk it showed, she was in truth a goddess.

> —Virgil (70–19 B.C.E.)
> *Aeneid*

The Empress
Touching Your Heart

The fourth card of the major arcana is known as the Empress. It is assigned the number 3.

The Empress and Her Energy

The Empress represents our ability to nurture ourselves and others. She is the caring, compassionate part of ourselves we often refer to as "heart." She is the mother who comforts, as well as the mother who disciplines—gently guiding her children.

While we do not need the intuition or analytical mind in order to be compassionate, when we have reached an understanding of both we find our connection to humankind deepens and in turn, we may be less judgmental of others who follow their own paths, even though their beliefs may not coincide with our truths.

The Empress is the caring mother, she may not have children of her own, but nonetheless she nurtures and guides others. She is the original Creatrix, Nature in both Her bounty and Her fallow periods. The Empress holds us when we cry, she listens to our problems, dries our tears, then sends us right back out again, encouraging us to rise to the challenge.

As the Fool enters the realm of the Empress, s/he becomes aware of how vast and large the Empress is, for the Empress embodies the cycle of life. The Fool begins to realize that everything s/he does affects others and begins to accept responsibility for her/his actions.

In our daily lives, the Empress may appear as our actual mother—or a substitute mother-figure. She consoles us, encourages us, rages with us, and then sends us back into battle because she knows we ultimately must stand alone.

We find the Empress in totem animals—the bear comes to mind—fiercely protective of her cubs; or the elephant, the matriarch of the tribe.

The Empress is the creative friend who writes or paints for a living, she is the horticulturist who tenderly nurtures her garden. The Empress is, above all, creative, and that must include destructive tendencies, for only by creating a void can we manifest new prosperity and abundance into our lives.

The Empress will never be a barren figure. She may be fallow, while new seeds (creative projects, babies, ideas) germinate, but she will never be one who actively pursues idleness. Relaxation and play, yes, but emptiness? Never.

The Empress archetype enters our lives when we are ready to create, when we have come to an inner knowledge of what we want to manifest. She represents the will to create, the moment of conception, and the attendant growth that follows. After she gives birth she then enters a period of compassion and guidance—creative projects, as well as children, need nurturing.

With the inner clarity of the Magician and the intuition of the Priestess, we have ascertained the direction of our personal life-paths. The Empress helps us nurture our vision and begin the process of creation.

The Spiritual Concept

The Empress is the Creatrix, she is Mother Earth, Nature Incarnate. Her names are many—Gaia, Spirit of the Earth. She is Ceres, goddess of the harvest and Sehu, the Cherokee corn goddess. She is great Isis, this time in her aspect as goddess of all mothers.

The Empress embodies the Full Moon. She is no longer the Maiden (waxing phase), nor is she yet the Crone (waning phase). She is full and ripe and sensual, ready for conception, ready to give birth.

She is consort of the Emperor (the Horned God); sexual and full bodied. She no longer reminds us of a blushing young girl.

On the Wheel of the Year, we can place the Empress at any corner. I choose to see her at Mabon, when the harvest is in full swing. She has conceived, given birth, and now we see the results of her bounty.

The Card

Most representations of the Empress include a woman in her early thirties. She is often seen as pregnant, holding a scepter or sheath of wheat or ear of corn. In some cards, animals graze in nearby fields, for the Empress is Queen of the Forest, Mistress of the Animals.

Guidelines for Use

Along our journey through the major arcana, this meditation follows that of the Priestess. It is also appropriate for Mabon (Autumnal Equinox), or anytime you need extra vision or energy for a creative project, or when you want to enhance your personal fertility or creativity.

Flowers:	rose, apple blossom, lilac, willow, magnolia
Incense:	frankincense, sandalwood, rose, jasmine
Oils:	honeysuckle, rose, tonka, vanilla, gardenia
Crystals:	rose quartz, amethyst, jade, ruby
Candles:	green, pink, mauve, purple, white

Meditation

Relax and get comfortable. Close your eyes and take three deep breaths.

long pause

You are standing at the edge of a lake, facing a field full of wild flowers, daisies and sunflowers, Indian Paint Brush and bachelor's buttons. A dirt path runs through the field, leading into a light copse of willow, oak, and maple.

The morning sun has climbed well into the sky and a golden glow of the light streams down to cloak you in its warmth. But a slight tang in the air tells you that it won't be long before autumn finds its way to the forest.

long pause

The lake ripples behind you, reeds and cattails border the water, and a mother duck paddles toward the shore, her ducklings desperately trying to keep up with her. Their quacking echoes through the lazy morning, along with the chattering of squirrels from high in the oaks where they are gathering acorns for the winter.

long pause

You have heard that these fields belong to the Empress, the Earth Mother incarnate. Perhaps, if you are lucky, you will get to meet her, for it is said that she gives all travelers comfort and rest in the shade of her willows.

As you wend your way through the fields, you notice a large patch of corn to your right. The ears are full and ripe, ready for picking, and you can smell the sweet sugar of the yellow kernels.

A sound in the distance catches your ear, the sound of laughter and jingling bells from the woods.

A large wagon, drawn by white horses, emerges from the glen. The driver is an older woman, cloaked in lavender robes. She is perhaps in her late fifties, and carefully steps to the ground.

long pause

In the back of the wagon, you see a tall woman surrounded by laughing children. She has hair the color of wheat, and her skin is the palest shade of green that you've ever seen. She wears a gown mirroring the peridot glow of sunlight throughout forest. Obviously pregnant, she allows the older woman to help her out of the wagon.

Immediately you recognize her as the Empress, for strength and power and beauty emanate from her aura. And when she walks, her feet glide through the grass, leaving no trace of her tracks.

Four children tumble out behind her.

The first, a boy, looks to be of Asian descent. The second boy is Black. The third child, a girl, is Native American, and the fourth, also a girl, has pale skin and bright red hair. You'd place her as Irish. They carry ribbons and balls and toys and begin to play near the wagon.

long pause

The Empress lays out a blanket in the middle of the field. Her assistant wanders off in search of fresh water. After a moment, Empress motions you near. As you approach her, she says, "I need your assistance. I need help to sit down. Will you lend me a hand?"

She holds out her hand. Take it and help her down to the blanket. When she is seated she offers you a space next to her. "Sit with me and rest for a while."

long pause

After you are seated on the blanket, the Empress proposes a bargain.

"When I planted the corn, I was able to do so alone. But now it is time to harvest the maize and I am in no shape to attempt it. If I wait any longer, its sweetness will ferment and the ears will rot. Pick it for me and I will give you food for your journey."

You realize there is no way she can harvest her corn. She needs your help. The morning is warm and you are in no hurry, so you can accept her offer.

The baskets are in the back of the wagon, along with a picnic hamper and a shawl, and you carry the baskets over to the field and begin stripping the ears off the stalks.

long pause

The work goes quickly and after a time, you find that the warmth of the sun and the droning of honeybees have lulled you into a drowsy trance.

There is a whisper in your ear, but you see nothing there and so at first, you ignore it. After a moment, it repeats itself, and you realize you are hearing the voice of the corn as the breeze ruffles through the drying stalks.

long pause

The voice crackles, paper-thin and rustling. It whispers to you, "I am the harvest, the rewards for work done. What do you seek to harvest, to create?"

Take a moment, as you are picking corn, to think about the question. What would you like to create, what seeds do you want to sow?

extended long pause—2 minutes

After you have carried the baskets to the wagon, the Empress gives you a large satchel of bread and cheese. She says, "Now I need help in turning the stalks over. If you help me, I will give you another gift for your journey."

Again you realize that you are the only one who can help her. The hoe and shovel are in the back of the wagon, so you retrieve them and begin to turn the stalks under the earth.

long pause

The scent of freshly turned soil lingers in your nose. Inviting and sour, tangy and dusty, it seems to rejoice as you bury the stalks and you understand that if there is to be another corn patch next year, the fields must be nourished. They are hungry for nutrients now that they've given up their yield.

Think about those seeds you want to sow, the projects you want to start. What do you need to prepare your fields for germination? What must you do to insure the growth of your seeds that they, too, might grow into the harvest?

extended long pause—2 minutes

By the time you are done it is almost noon and you rejoin the Empress on the blanket. As you sit there, a noise echoes from the forest. When you look over at the copse, you see animals beginning to emerge from the woodland. They are headed in your direction.

A mother bear leads her two cubs; a doe, her fawn. As you look closer, a fox and her kits come running out of the undergrowth, then a cat guiding her litter of kittens. A dog romps out of the forest behind the cat, her puppies tripping head over heels behind her. Lastly, with a loud screech, a blue jay and her fledglings wing down to sit nearby.

extended long pause—1 minute

At first you think there is going to be trouble, the diversity of animals begs for a fight.

But the Empress laughs and says, "Don't worry. They are watchful, but they know I will protect them for the moment. They are my own and I want you to meet them."

Look at the animals and watch their interaction. The mother bear cuffs one of her cubs, warning it to stay near. The doe nuzzles her fawn. The fox suckles her kits. The cat begins to groom her kittens. The dog rounds up her puppies. The jay shows her fledglings where a juicy worm is poking through the soil.

Take a moment to note the different methods of mothering and nurturing. Some are strict, others playful and caring. All are valid, all necessary. Watch the animals that surround the Empress and learn from them many different faces of love.

long pause

After a while, the Empress points to the children and says, "These are my children, too. All peoples of the Earth are mine," she says.

long pause

Just then, the two girls begin fighting. The Empress scowls for a moment and says, "It never stops. It is the nature of all creatures to squabble. Unfortunately, humans fight for all the wrong reasons."

As she is speaking, the Asian boy trips and begins to cry. The Empress looks at you with a heartfelt plea.

"Please help me. I will take care of the girls. Would you see to the boy?" She offers you her arm so that you can help her up.

long pause

The boy is holding his knee. Tears run down his face as he looks up at you, frightened. As you reach out for him, you suddenly find that you can see through his eyes. See yourself as a child might see you. See yourself from the outside.

Are you tall and intimidating, short and squat, do you have a smile on your face or are you frowning? How might you appear to a child? Take a few moments to explore how it feels to be staring at a giant, to be hurt and wanting comfort.

extended long pause—1 minute

Now you find yourself back in your body.

Look at the boy again. He is the face of the world. Every person alive was once a child, needing help at some time. Every child has known a moment of fear. Some children's lives are made up of pain. Some adults deliberately hurt their children. As the boy is crying, know that he cries for all the aching children on the planet.

What comfort can you offer? Take a few moments to hug him, tend to his knee. Know that even as you give help to him, you have helped the world.

long pause

The Empress succeeds in calming the girls. They are still teary-eyed from their fight, but they are holding hands now. She smiles wearily as she presses her hands against her lower back and arches gently.

"No job is more difficult than the raising of young and the tending of friends. Sometimes, no matter how good of a parent you are, no matter how much you care for a friend in need, they won't, or can't, respond. Nurturing exacts little gratitude, and far too many take on the responsibility without thinking about it. While animals breed out of biological urges, humans have options."

long pause

The wind has become brisk and the Empress asks you to bring her shawl and the hamper of food from the back of the wagon. When you return, she motions for you to sit again.

The children crowd around her as she adjusts the shawl around her shoulders and then opens the hamper.

She hands out sandwiches and fruit to the children and tells them to run off and eat. Just then, the older woman reappears with a large bucket of clear water. She gives the children their drinks, then leads them away, leaving you in peace.

long pause

The Empress offers you a sandwich. You notice she takes none for herself.

"My children always eat first," she says. "Some years the harvest is full and abundant and there is plenty for all. The winters are kinder then, for food warms the belly. But other years, scarcity rules and there is little to eat. Children die with their parents. It is the way of Nature, and since I embody Nature's principles, I must accept the inevitable. Death makes way for new life."

You realize that there is not enough food. Your sandwich is large enough for two, and she is expecting another child. Share some of your sandwich with her and notice how it makes you feel.

long pause

"Do you have children?" she asks, after you both have eaten. "Or have you chosen another path this life?"

Think about her question for a moment. If you have children, did you clearly think about it? Or did you engender them accidentally, without planning?

If you have chosen a child-free existence, do you parent cats or dogs? How do you express the nurturing sides of yourself? Think about these choices in life. Both paths are equally valid, if made from the truth of the heart and body.

extended long pause—1 minute

The Empress interrupts your thoughts. "May I hug you?" she asks. "You have been so kind to me today."

As you lean into her embrace, it is as if the entire world stretches out to hold you. Sink deep into her soft bosom as her warm arms encircle you with her love.

"Everyone needs nurturing," she whispers, rocking you gently.

long pause

After a moment, she lets you go and reaches into the basket. She takes out an object wrapped in linen and hands it to you.

"I promised you a gift for helping me," she says.

When you open the cloth, you find a crystal necklace fashioned from a translucent pink stone. Shaped like a heart, it dangles from a long chain of silver and gold.

"Wear this and it will remind you that my love is always with you. Even during the harshest times of your life, know that I am there, listening to your heart. Though I cannot save you from all mistakes, and would not even if I could, I can help guide you. My love, combined with your intuition and common sense, will keep you away from many dangers."

Fasten the necklace around your neck and take a moment to concentrate on the love that emanates from the crystal heart.

long pause

Now the older woman comes over and helps the Empress to her feet. "We must be going. The children are tired and the corn needs to be shucked and dried for the winter. Thank you for your help," the Empress says. "I would stay a while longer, but I have my responsibilities and I do not take them lightly."

Bid the Empress farewell as she climbs into the wagon, along with the children.

long pause

The older woman picks up the reins and they drive away. All of the animals have faded back into the glen of willow and maple. The sun is cooler, evening is not far away.

The next stage of the journey will take you out of the woods and into a village, and so you decide to rest here, in the field of wildflowers, for the night.

long pause

Now listen to my voice as I count from ten to one. You will awake refreshed alert, having slept in the bosom of the Goddess. Ten . . . nine . . . you are becoming awake and aware of your surroundings . . . eight . . . seven . . . six . . . hear the sounds around you . . . five . . . four . . . you will be fully alert and refreshed . . . three . . . two . . . one . . . take three deep breaths and when you are ready, you may open your eyes.

Suggested Exercises

1. Spend some time with your own or your friends' children. Pay attention to how they react to you as an adult. Try to play from their level—on the ground—so you can remember what it's like from a child's point of view.

2. Take time out to help someone who needs nurturing. It might be a pregnant friend, it could be your grandmother who can't get around too easily anymore, it can even be the friend next door who doesn't drive and really needs to go to the supermarket. You might find that giving to others isn't quite the hardship it appears to be when the gift comes from the heart.

3. Nurture yourself. Take long bubble baths, eat comfort food, go for a walk in the woods instead of cleaning house. Treat yourself the way you'd like others to treat you.

4. When you start a creative project, first think of what you'll need to nourish it to completion. Just like corn needs sunlight, good soil, and water, so an art project will need supplies, foresight, and an investment of time and energy.

5. You cannot help others or work on your own creative projects unless you have gotten enough sleep and good food and unless you value your time.

6. Remember, nurturing doesn't stop with humans. Do you have pets? They need a tremendous amount of love and attention to thrive. They are like children, just fuzzier and with four feet (birds have two feet, of course, and snakes none, but you get the idea). Allow plenty of time to interact with these feline and canine kids. The love you get back will repay you tenfold.

Life always gets harder towards the summit—the cold increases, responsibility increases.

—Friedrich W. Nietzsche (1844–1900)
The AntiChrist

The Emperor
Taking the Lead

The fifth card of the major arcana is known as the Emperor. It is assigned the number 4.

The Emperor and His Energy

The Emperor represents our ability to take control of our lives, to accept responsibility for our actions. He embodies the assertive, directed ability to act that we often refer to as "drive." He is the father, the leader, a person comfortable with authority.

We must have some control over our analytical minds in order to reason out what needs to be done (the Magician). Our intuition (the Priestess) allows us knowledge of whether or not we're headed in the right direction with a project or a task. We ascertain what is needed for growth in our lives, and our heart leads us to be compassionate (the Empress) to those under our command. Now, using our inner drive and ambition, we spur ourselves into action, initiating that which we have visualized and planned for.

The Emperor is the caring father, he may not have children of his own but nonetheless, he guides and directs others. He is an Originator, inseminating Nature that life might spring from her womb.

The Emperor advises us when we need counsel, he analyzes the situation and guides us to create order from chaos. He cares, but from a distanced vantage, forcing us to take responsibility for our own lives.

As the Fool enters this realm, s/he becomes aware of the strength wielded by the Emperor, for within his energy we discover our own powers of decision and self-confidence. Through the Emperor, the Fool comes to understand that s/he must make his/her own choices and decisions, and that those decisions will alter the course of the journey.

In our daily lives, the Emperor may appear as our actual father—or a substitute father-figure. He advises us, helps us plan our paths through life. He hears our worry and our self-doubt, then shores us up, strengthening our confidence and self-esteem before we charge ahead in the direction we have aimed ourselves.

We find the Emperor in the leader of the wolf pack, in the lion who rules the pride, or in the silverback gorilla.

The Emperor may be a friend who tells us the truth of what he sees, or a therapist who helps us analyze our lives honestly. He takes charge of the company and predicts trends and potential outcomes with uncanny accuracy. Above all, the Emperor leads, and at time, this forces him to be ruthless. His decisions affect many lives and he will decide in favor of the good for the many. Individuality can suffer at his hands because he takes his duty to those for whom he's responsible so seriously.

The Emperor archetype enters our lives when we are ready to put our creative dreams into action, when the time has come to manifest them into reality. We turn to the Emperor in order to actualize our goals. He represents the ability to manifest, the graduation from thought to action. He knows what he wants and is confident in his success.

With the Empress we have nurtured our vision and come to understand what we want; with the help of the Emperor, we begin to manifest that knowledge into reality.

The Spiritual Concept

The Emperor is the Originator, he is Father Sky, the spirit of the mind and thought. His names are many—Ukko, Ancient Father who rules the highest heavens. He is Odin, King of the Aesir and procurer of the Runes. He is great Osiris, whose word was law among the Egyptians. The Emperor embodies the element of Air, the intellect. He is the articulate, just, and wise counselor.

Consort of the Empress, he mirrors the sexuality of the mature man who no longer seeks the nymph, but instead slakes his thirst with a full-bodied mate of his own age and stature. He prefers a woman who will not shrink or blush in his presence.

In the zodiac, we find the Emperor connected with the sign of Aries, and on the Wheel of the Year, we can place the Emperor at Litha, when the sun is at full zenith and the Sun King rules the heavens. In the glare of the light, we see the Emperor's brilliance.

The Card

Most representations of the Emperor include a man in his late thirties or early forties. He is often seated on a throne, with banners and flags waving from a castle in the background. He is the King, wedded to the land through the goddess of sovereignty.

Guidelines for Use

In our ongoing journey through the major arcana, this meditation follows that of the Empress. We may also meditate on the Emperor during Litha (Summer Solstice) or whenever we need to empower our sense of self-assertion and self-confidence.

Flowers:	carnation, marigold, cayenne, ginseng
Incense:	carnation, tangerine, cedar, orange
Oils:	orange, carnation, ginger, parsley
Crystals:	carnelian, citrine, orange calcite, ruby
Candles:	orange, rust, brown

Meditation

Relax and get comfortable. Close your eyes and take three deep breaths.

long pause

You have come over the lake, through the fields and out of the wood, and now you are standing on a path that leads to a grassy knoll surrounded by a village. Atop the knoll sits a castle, purple and gold banners flying from high above the battlements in the blazing sunlight of noon.

The cacophony from the village drowns out your thoughts as you pass through the teeming streets. Townsfolk hurry by on their errands; here, a woman stops to look at fish in the open market; there, a man hawks leather goods and handcrafted clothing at another stall. The smells of cooking food and sweaty bodies mingles with the warmth of the day to overwhelm you and you find yourself quite dizzy.

long pause

Everywhere you turn, people are involved in the hustle and bustle of commerce, and they ignore you as you walk through their midst, so caught up in their business are they. There is a sense of strength here, a sense of purpose pervading the inhabitants of this area, and you feel slightly out of place. Everyone you see seems so secure with their role in the world that you begin to think about your place in this lifetime, what you need to achieve those goals and dreams that destiny has planted in your heart.

long pause

As you head out of the village, toward the castle, you come across a man sitting by the side of the road. He is wearing tattered robes and he motions for you to come closer. As you do, he bids you to sit down and speak with him for a moment.

long pause

"Rest by my side, stranger," he says. "For you are not from these parts, that much is obvious by your dress." He motions to the hurrying crowd. "Not one of them can spare a moment for me, they are far too busy with their lives to listen to a tired old man."

For a moment, you both rest in silence, then he turns to you and asks about your journey. As you tell him your experiences, his face lights up and he says, "I, too, journeyed far in my younger days. I understand the nature of the quest." After another pause, he asks, "So are you going to see the Emperor who lives in the castle?"

The thought of entering the castle hadn't really occurred to you until now, but the moment the words leave his lips, it seems like the most logical course of action.

long pause

He tells you that the Emperor sees all who journey through his town on a quest, that he has been known to inspire travelers and those who would take charge of their own lives. "But beware," the old man says, "the Emperor has little patience with laziness or self-doubt. If you go to see him, you must believe in yourself."

Even with this warning, you still want to visit the castle, to meet with the Emperor. Perhaps he can help motivate you on your journey. You have developed a vision for what goals you hope to nurture in your life; the Emperor might help you put those ideas into action. So far your journey has been very cerebral, now it is time to begin the actual work associated with your dreams and desires.

long pause

You smile at the old man and tell him that, yes, you would like to meet the Emperor.

He nods. "Then follow this path up to the castle. Keep a close watch, there are distractions along the way to keep out the ill-prepared or those who hold their goals too lightly." After he has spoken, he struggles to his feet and bids you good-day, then walks back toward the village.

With a last look at the throng of people, you turn and begin to wend your way up the knoll, through the long grass that reaches out from either side to brush against your legs.

long pause

As the village and its noise recedes behind you, you begin to notice a quickening in the air, a slight brush of anticipation. Back in the town, the energy was chaotic, hasty, and it set you on edge, but here, as you climb the hillside, the air currents flow past in a constant stream, a trail of flickering whispers that brush through your hair, past your ears.

long pause

Your knees begin to feel the ascent—while it looks slight and easy from the village, the knoll is actually a long slope, rising upward in a surprising gradation. Then, as you are forced to exert yourself more and more, your pace begins to slow and beads of sweat pop out on your forehead. You must take deep breaths as you push yourself up the hill. The effort is tiring and you begin to wonder if the trip is worth the reward.

long pause

A brief copse of trees stands between you and the castle, and you enter the glen with a sense of relief. The shade of the forest is a welcome respite from the sweltering heat and you think you can hear a trickling brook from within the glade.

long pause

Search through the trees, through the oak and maple and vine, until you find the stream. The water rushes along at a good pace, and although the stream is not wide, it is deep and clear, and the smell of cool water reminds you of how thirsty you are.

Rest by the water, dip your hand into the flowing brook and drink so that you might refresh your parched throat.

long pause

As you are resting, you hear a noise in the brush, the low trill of fluttering notes. Look to your left—out of the huckleberries emerges a short, dark figure—a satyr, no more than five feet tall. His legs are furry, ending in cloven hooves and he crooks one eyebrow while giving you a secretive smile.

long pause

"Where are you going?" he asks, his voice purring.

When you tell him that you are going to visit the Emperor, he shakes his head and laughs. "Why go to the castle above? All they do there is work, work, work. Stay here with me, with the nymphs who live in the wood, and play for awhile. Drink with us and dance the dance of ecstasy."

The offer is tempting. He raises his flute to his lips and the music that pours forth is the sweetest, most silver-tongued sound you have ever heard. After a moment, he lowers his pipes and again smiles.

long pause

"Stay here, go no further" he whispers, and out of the woods come three dancing nymphs to join him. Clad in sheer silk, they float on the air, twirling, with long hair trailing around their shoulders. The satyr begins to play again and his music coils around you, catching you up in a web of passion and desire.

The thought of remaining here in this wooded glade, of joining the satyr and nymphs in their dalliances, is so luxurious, so unbearably tempting, that you rise and reach out. But just as one of the nymphs takes your hand, you see another figure emerge from the bushes. An old woman hobbles out, and she limps between you and the wood spirit.

long pause

"Do not accept their offer," she tells you. "You will never be free if you indulge in their wine, if you stay for the dance. You will be caught here forever, as was I."

Her words startle you out of your reverie and she motions you to the side. The satyr and nymphs take little notice as you wander over to a willow tree where the old woman can talk freely.

"I too, came through the woods, long ago. I was young then, far younger than now, and was on my way to visit the Emperor," she says. "I hoped he might help me with my dream of opening a restaurant in the village. As I rested in the grove, the satyr and his nymphs came dancing out of the woods. Their offer of wine and play sounded so good, the climb had been so hot, that I accepted. The moment I gave my assent, I was lost. Their magick captured me . . . my dreams faded and while I still mused over how nice it would have been to own my own business, the work it required seemed overwhelming. I lost my confidence, I lost my belief that I could make it happen."

long pause

You begin to see through her rags now—once they were fine clothes. When you look into her eyes, you see the faded spark of dreams now long dead and hopes unfulfilled.

long pause

"My mind is clouded with wine," she says. "My life has been clouded with play . . . I lost my motivation. Don't let the same thing happen to you. Remember what it is that you have come for, remember why you are making this journey in the first place."

Think now about your journey, how you started in search of yourself. Think about the distance you've traveled, the goals you have set. Are you willing to give them up because at times they prove difficult? Will you quit when the work you must do requires effort and discipline? Think how you would feel if, in twenty years, you have achieved none of the goals you set out to accomplish? If you look back and think . . . *I could have been . . . I could have done . . .* knowing that only your lack of discipline and drive prevented you from capturing your fondest desires.

Take a few moments to think about the strength of your goals, about what you are willing to sacrifice in order to reach them. Reaffirm your stance, assure yourself that you will persevere.

extended long pause—2 minutes

While you are thinking, the satyr and nymphs have retreated into the bushes, they are gone, as is the old woman, and you are alone in the woods. You notice that the sunlight is now fading, you have been here too long.

As you pick up your pack and follow the path out of the glen, you find yourself back on the open trail leading up to the castle. A rock wall extends on either side of the path now, leading directly to the great doors ahead. Dusk is growing, the open sky above reveals the faintest pinpricks of white—distant stars shining overhead with their cool brilliance.

long pause

Lights burn in the windows of the castle and they provide some illumination as you stumble along. Now the grade is at its steepest and you find it helpful to use the rock wall for balance and leverage as you force your knees up the steep incline.

And then, as your breath grows ragged and panting, as your heart races with the exertion, you are there, at the gate, and a guard stops you.

"Have you come to see the Emperor?" she asks.

You nod your head, too winded to speak.

The guard examines your body and your pack to make certain that you carry no weapons. If you have any in your possession, you must now hand them to the soldier and she will give them to you before you leave this place.

long pause

She escorts you through the huge gate and into an antechamber where there are wash basins and mirrors. Take a moment to rest and wash the dust from your face.

When the guard returns, she bids you to follow her. You find yourself winding through a long passageway. The walls are granite, solid rock carved out of nearby hillsides, and they promise protection and security for all who venture within. You feel safe here, as if the very foundations of this castle are embedded deep within the earth. Stop for a moment and run your fingers along the walls, feel the solidity that resides within this structure.

long pause

The twisting hallway opens out into a large chamber. Illuminated by flickering torches, the audience hall is grand, with unicorn tapestries covering the walls. Scenes of vast forests filled with stags and rabbits have been painted across the ceiling. In the center of the room, on a tall throne carved of oak, sits a well-muscled, bearded man.

His hair is graying at the temples and wrinkles have begun to furrow his brow. He wears a long cloak of royal purple and a gilded crown sits atop his head. You understand that you are now in the presence of the Emperor. Take a moment to pay your respects.

long pause

The Emperor looks at you carefully, you feel he is studying you. He takes his time, and when he speaks, his voice thunders not the way you might expect it to, but is firm, and you sense that he is both fair and just. He says, "Welcome, stranger, to my lands. I understand you are seeking counsel. Be seated."

He points to an upholstered chair to his right and so you accept his offer and seat yourself.

"Look around you," he says. "This castle was a mere dream when I was a boy, and the village was squalid and people hungered but would not, or could not, work. I knew that if I was to achieve my dream, if I was to carve out a beautiful place to live, not only for myself but for others, that I would need to discipline myself, learn what needed to be done, and implement those plans."

long pause

"No one in the village understood the need for long-range planning, the people had little foresight and those in need were left to hunger and die. I changed that. I went away, found a teacher, and learned what needed to be done. When I returned, I taught what I had learned and accepted responsibility for seeing that our visions, hopes and dreams became grounded in reality.

"In return, the people made me their Emperor for they knew I would rule them justly and with wisdom. When I was a boy, many people died from hunger and disease. Because I was willing to discipline myself, to persevere, I learned how to motivate my people. The village now thrives, and my vision of a beautiful and comfortable life has come to pass."

He stops speaking and leaves you a moment to think on his words. Look around, see the order and peace that has been wrought here, feel the smooth flow of energy that pervades these granite walls.

long pause

"Now," he continues, "tell me of your plans. Tell me what you want to create, what visions you have for your own future." Spend a moment telling him about the goals and dreams that you have formulated on your journey thus far. Examine your priorities as you tell the Emperor what you want to accomplish.

extended long pause—1 minute

"Have you thought about your motivation?" he asks. "Why do you want to accomplish these goals? What do you need to drive you, to impel you to continue?"

Think about his question for a moment, then answer. You may find that the Emperor has suggestions that will help motivate you, or perhaps your drive is so high that he will just encourage you in your pursuits. Take a few moments to examine the strength of your drive.

extended long pause—2 minutes

"Now," he asks, "how will you implement your plans? Do you have all the skills you need to accomplish what you want? Or when you examine your talents, do you find, as we all do, that there are areas in which you might hone and refine your skills? Think for a moment about your resources? What do you need in order to accomplish your dreams?"

Examine all of your resources, don't overlook any help you might get, and then ask yourself what you still need before you are ready to begin working toward your goals.

extended long pause—1 minute

Now the Emperor steps off his throne. He kneels by your side, and when he looks into your eyes you sense that he has sat where you are now sitting, he has been on the same quest that you are now pursuing. His journey may have reached a different end, his goals may not be your goals, but he understands the energy needed to see a dream through to completion.

long pause

"Listen to me," he says. "You are unique in this world, no one can replace you. You use your talents and skills in a way that no one can copy. You must follow your dreams without caring what others say, yet you must also remember that you are part of the collective and your actions affect others.

"I chose to sacrifice my privacy that I might help others live a better life. Through doing so, my own life has joy and meaning. Perhaps this is not your path, but you must give thought to how your trek will affect others. Whatever our individual goals, we have a responsibility to those around us."

long pause

He reaches into his cloak and brings out a small book. "A gift for you," he says, "a remembrance of your visit."

Examine the cover of the book. The design will have meaning to you, look at the cover and see what it tells you.

As you open the book, you find one page inside. On that page are written five words: Vision, Motivation, Action, Flexibility, Responsibility.

Each word is written in illuminated typescript, beautiful and scrolling across the page. Examine the words.

Vision—you must have the vision to plan, the vision to look to the future and see yourself at a point in time when you have accomplished your dreams. Take a moment to think about your vision.

long pause

Motivation—without motivation, dreams stay within the mind and are never brought to fruition. What motivates you? What positive reinforcements work for you?

long pause

Action—the next step is to take action, to learn what you need to learn and then implement your plans so they might manifest and become reality.

long pause

Flexibility—we must always have a secondary plan, a back-up should our path be blocked. We must be willing to adapt and to re-envision our lives. There are always ways around obstacles, if we have the flexibility to look for them.

long pause

Responsibility—when we accomplish our goals, we must take responsibility not only for the end result, but for the means used to manifest that result. If our goal is to become a famous singer or artist, we accept the life that goes with being a public figure. We take responsibility for our actions and how they will be interpreted, we accept a certain loss of privacy. We must decide whether or not our goals are worth the effort. Will innocent people get hurt as we pursue our dream? Can we compete in a healthy manner without trampling others?

long pause

The Emperor says, "In your coming journeys you will find a teacher who will help you learn these skills, for truly, those five words represent training and discipline that, as human beings, we should all aspire to. Now, you may sleep here for the night and then continue on your way tomorrow morning. I would invite you to stay longer, but I do not wish to divert you from your journey. However safe my castle walls might be, you must have the discipline to continue back out into the world, to find your way."

If you want to ask him a question, you now may do so. Otherwise, pay your respects. Then listen for his reply.

extended long pause—1 minute

When you have said goodnight, the guard returns and shows you to a room where you may spend the night in comfort and safety.

Now listen to my voice as I count from ten to one. You will awake refreshed and alert, having slept in the safety of the Emperor's realm. Ten . . . nine . . . you are becoming awake and aware of your surroundings . . . eight . . . seven . . . six . . . hear the sounds around you . . . five . . . four . . . you will be fully alert and refreshed . . . three . . . two . . . one . . . take three deep breaths and when you are ready, you may open your eyes.

Suggested Exercises

1. Buy a planning guide or a daily organizer and begin to get your life in order. Allow yourself time to think about what you want to get done, and figure out your plan of action. THEN DO IT. Don't overwhelm yourself. If you try to do too much at once, you'll wear yourself out, give up, and then you'll feel worse than you did at the start.

2. If you have trouble finding time to pursue your dreams, then look to ways you can organize your life so you'll have the hours you need. Do you watch too much television that you aren't really interested in? Can you let some of the housework go? Can you combine chores, or delegate work to others? Can you break up your goal in small sections so it doesn't seem so unreachable? Often our lack of time can be attributed to poor usage of the hours we're given.

3. There are several good books you can read about organization and achieving your goals. Look in your local library or bookstore. (See bibliography for my suggestion.)

4. If self-discipline is a continuing problem, ask yourself if you really believe in your goals. Have you outgrown them? Do they need re-envisioning? Or do you just lack the belief that you can accomplish what you want to? If self-esteem is a problem,

then you need to begin building yourself up. Begin by setting very small goals that are easy to accomplish, and reward yourself for reaching these goals. It's all right to take baby steps at first.

5. Finally, you truly must believe that your goal is worth the time and effort it requires. Many people have been taught that they should neglect their dreams, that self-sacrifice at the expense of their goals is virtuous. But all too often, that kind of self-sacrifice leads to resentment and feeling cheated. To be responsible for your own happiness requires a certain amount of healthy selfishness. For when we are happy with our own lives, we tend to be more generous and caring toward others.

A fool sees not the same tree that a wise man sees.

—William Blake (1757–1827)
A Memorable Fancy

The Hierophant

Bowing to Wisdom

The sixth card of the major arcana is known as the Hierophant. It is assigned the number 5.

The Hierophant and His Energy

The Hierophant represents our ability to learn new skills, to understand the lessons coming into our lives, and eventually, to offer our knowledge to others. Through this card, we learn to value our goals and dreams, to prioritize and define the boundaries of what we choose to pursue. Understanding that one is simultaneously both teacher and student, the wise sage remains detached from the pupil while still being intricately linked to their development.

If we are unwilling to learn then we can never advance and grow in our chosen directions. We must

73

undertake hard work, persevere through difficult lessons, and fail and try again if we want to succeed in life. Once we have engendered the motivation to go after a goal, we must safely learn the methods that will allow us to pursue our dreams without tearing our world apart. As we learn new skills leading toward our goal, we also learn that we must combine those skills to create more than the sum of their parts.

The Hierophant is the teacher, the Challenger, who dares us to use our minds and our intuitions in a unified manner. He is a spiritual guide, demanding commitment to a cause, demanding sacrifice of time and freedom in order to learn. He is a disciplinarian who reminds us that any knowledge comes with a price. The Hierophant enlightens—he opens up new abilities that we never knew we had. The Hierophant advises and forces us to analyze our own path. If we do not accept his instruction, he will step aside and refuse to lead us further.

At times the Hierophant seems callous and uncaring. When we are tired, he insists we wake. When we fail, he gives us no quarter—only helps us examine our mistake and then orders us to try again . . . now . . . without rest.

He is the guru who appears when we are ready, the preserver of tradition and knowledge, the bard, the druid, the elder to whom all must listen.

When the Fool enters this realm, s/he accepts personal commitment, a commitment built through trial and error, through persistence, through repetition. The Fool learns or is cast out, the Hierophant has no room for sluggards and layabouts in his class. Here we hone our knowledge, here we strengthen our skills.

In our daily lives, the Hierophant may appear as an actual teacher—often the one we remember best from childhood. This teacher yelled at us, forced us to recopy our papers, threatened us with failing grades because he knew we could do better (and we knew it too). This teacher accepted no excuses; the dog never ate your homework!

But when we turned in an excellent report, that same teacher's smile said everything we needed to hear.

We find the Hierophant in our next-door neighbor, who shows us a new way to tend our roses, to fix our house.

The Hierophant becomes our mentor at work, or a friend who has accomplished what we someday hope to achieve. This person willingly shares their knowledge, yet they never give you the answers, only point you in the right direction as they insist you discover your own truths.

By remembering the past objectively, the Hierophant is record- and history-keeper for the clan. In times of bounty he reminds his people of famine; in times of famine, he encourages them to remember the bountiful years. The Hierophant encourages free-thinking. He may disagree with the Emperor, the leader of the tribe, but will never force his will on another, for the Hierophant knows that to learn, one must endure failure and testing.

The Hierophant archetype enters our lives when we are ready to learn new lessons, when we are actively pursuing a course and need to hone our existing skills or learn new ones. We refine our talent, which can only be done through self-discipline, practice, and perseverance.

We have used the energy of the Emperor to motivate us, we have taken the first steps on our journey toward a goal, now we accept the role of student and apply ourselves to our vision. No longer carefree, no longer footloose, we must buckle down and learn to work.

With the meditation of the Hierophant, we complete the first section of the Fool's journey. From here our choices narrow, from here we cut a channel through which to focus our energy and vision.

The Spiritual Concept

The Hierophant represents the gods of wisdom and knowledge. He blends thought and action. His names are many—Thoth, the Lord of time and knowledge. He is Buddha, the Bodhisattva. He is Kuei-Hsing—god of scholarship.

The Hierophant embodies thought and education. He is the teacher, the counselor, the guru.

She is Athena, goddess of wisdom; Minerva, goddess of education; and Sefkhet-Seshat, Egyptian goddess of record-keeping, scribes, and language.

The Hierophant is connected to the zodiacal sign of Taurus. On the Wheel of the Year I choose to place the Hierophant at Yule, when the days are short and thoughts turn to learning, books, and indoor pursuits. In the chill glaze of ice, we learn the discipline of a keen mind.

The Card

Most representations of the Hierophant include a man in clergy's robes. Often seated on a dais, he stares through those who come to him for advice, observing their inner selves and judging their ability to discipline their thoughts and actions.

Guidelines for Use

In our ongoing journey through the major arcana, this meditation follows that of the Emperor. The meditation for the Hierophant is also appropriate during Yule (Winter Solstice), or whenever we need to reinforce our self-discipline and our desire to learn, even though we might make mistakes in the process.

For this meditation, you might want to review your discussion with the Emperor in the last meditation, paying special attention to the book he gave you as a gift.

Flowers:	sage, rosemary, basil, vetiver, pepper
Incense:	sage, lavender, cedar, myrrh
Oils:	sage, lavender, myrrh, frankincense
Crystals:	clear quartz, aquamarine, sapphire
Candles:	blue, indigo, violet, white

Meditation

Relax and get comfortable. Close your eyes and take three deep breaths.

long pause

You are standing on a dusty path that leads into a wide meadow covered with snow. The air is chilly and you feel an ache in your bones that tells you you've been traveling for too long without a rest. The last light of afternoon is flickering and you know it will soon be dark.

In the center of the meadow stands an oak, taller than any oak you've ever seen. A door at its base leads into the tree trunk, and you can see a house built in the limbs and branches at the crotch of the tree.

long pause

You have come to this place to meet the Hierophant, the teacher the Emperor predicted you would find. Along your journey you have heard rumors of how wise this man is, how much his pupils learn from him. Now you have found his home and you are ready to ask him if he will teach you that which you need to know in order to manifest your dreams.

long pause

The clouds are blowing in on the chill wind, and thick flakes of snow begin to fall. A golden light is glowing from the window of the tree house and your feet propel you down the path, into the meadow and over to the door.

The tree is far wider than you first imagined, at least fifteen people could hold hands and still not circle the base. Knock and wait for an answer.

After a few moments the door opens and a young girl, holding a candle, peers out at you. She wears a robe that matches the silvery sky and her eyes reveal an age far older than her years. She stands back and bids you enter.

"The night is cold. Be welcome, stranger."

She leads you to the center of the trunk where a staircase circles high into the upper reaches of the tree. Without a word, she begins to ascend the steps, indicating that you should follow her.

As you pass through the tree you get the feeling of immense age and strength surrounding you. While the tree is hollow, you sense it is still very much alive and that the very cells of this oak are saturated with years of magickal workings and energy. You cannot help but reach out to touch the hard, polished wood and when you do, a surge of power races through your body.

long pause

The staircase opens up into a large parlor. The girl stands back, allowing you to pass in front of her. She says, "Please be seated. My father will be with you shortly," and then disappears through a door to your left.

Two rocking chairs and a small divan encircle a glowing fire—but when you come close to warm yourself, you discover that no wood fuels this flame, and no smoke rises from the hearth. Warmth soaks into your body, though, and regardless of the source, the heat is welcome after the bitter cold of the outdoors.

Sit in one of the chairs and look around. The room has a golden quality to it—a warm, homey environment. A long plank table with matching benches sits in one corner, and books line the walls. You begin looking through the titles and discover some that you've already read, still others that you've never heard of.

Several doors lead out of the parlor. Before long the girl reappears, with her enters a man wearing a brown tunic and trousers. He is bald, bearded, and carries a long staff bedecked with feathers, fur, and crystals.

long pause

He holds out his hand to you. "Welcome to my home," he says. "You must be hungry and cold from your journey. Come, dine with us."

You feel a need to explain your presence, a desire to assure yourself that he is, indeed, the Hierophant. But when you start to speak, he raises one hand.

"Patience. There is time enough for discussion. Now to eat." His daughter has set the table with plates and mugs, and the Hierophant brings a steaming tureen of soup to the table, along with a crusty loaf and a golden wheel of cheese. He fills your mug with milk and bids you sit and eat in silence and peace.

long pause

After you have eaten, you find the food has warmed more than your belly. The chill from the snow is gone and you are quite comfortable.

The man escorts you back to the fire; he sits in one of the rocking chairs while his daughter curls up on the divan. "So, you seek a teacher?" he asks.

As you nod, he continues. "My students learn five lessons. Since you have seen the Emperor, you know what those five lessons will be. Tell me what they are."

You remember the book the Emperor gifted you with, and the five lessons inscribed within. Now tell the Hierophant what those five lessons are.

long pause

He smiles when you have finished. "Very good . . . vision, motivation, action, flexibility, and responsibility. You must understand, I have no answers for you. I merely help you discover this knowledge within yourself. Now then, my daughter Morgan will take you to your room. Sleep well this night, you will need your energy."

The little girl takes up a candle and leads you through one of the other doors. You find yourself in a small room with a porthole-sized window. A thick feather mattress lays waiting for you on the floor and a patchwork quilt will keep you warm through the night. Morgan leaves, shutting the door behind her, and as you blow out the candle, you can see the snow falling through the window. The meadow gleams icy and distant from your perch in the trees. Lay down under the quilt and sleep.

Take three slow, deep breaths.

long pause

As dawn creeps through the window, Morgan shakes you until you open your eyes and whispers, "Get up, get up now. My father awaits you in the parlor."

Still tired, you stumble out to find the Hierophant standing by the bookshelves. He points to the table where a slice of bread and butter and a glass of milk waits for you.

"Eat," he says. When you have finished your breakfast, he motions for you to take your place on the divan. He sits beside you and says, "Close your eyes. I am going to take you on a journey. Take three deep breaths and let them out slowly."

long pause

His voice is soft and low as he continues. Follow his words and let them lead you within yourself with the Hierophant as your guide.

See your goal, your dream. Examine it carefully. What makes it so special for you? What do you expect from the outcome? Where do you want it to lead you in your life? Is it a major turning point, or just another means to an end? Is it a career move, an emotional transformation, a physical manifestation? Examine your vision thoroughly. Walk inside of it, get to know it, understand just what you are asking of the universe.

extended long pause—1 minute

Now hold that vision as you see someone walk up to you. This may be an actual person from your life, or a composite of people you have known. Whoever it is, they do not support your dream. They say your goals are unrealistic and taunt you for trusting in your talents. Listen to their derision for a moment and examine their comments. Do they make any valid remarks, or are they just envious? Remember, just because they may have a valid point, you should not negate your vision. However, they may expose issues you need to address as you pursue your goal.

extended long pause—1 minute

You must stand your ground when people like this come into your life. Speak to them. Do not defend yourself—defense merely encourages them. Instead, be firm and secure in your own beliefs. Counter their remarks, address their concerns, and silence the doubts and fears that exist within your own mind.

long pause

Visualize your goal. How much do you want it? How important to you is this dream? Would you give it up for a two-week holiday? Would you give it up for a year's free salary and benefits? If you won the lottery, would you drop your preoccupation and let your dream go? Suppose your goal takes five years to accomplish? Will you still pursue it? How about ten years? Is it worth ten years of your life? What are the boundaries you'll draw to getting it? If you were offered your goal free and clear, but at the expense of a friend's well-being, are you so obsessed that you'd take up the offer?

extended long pause—1 minute

You must define healthy boundaries for yourself. While your goal should maintain an important priority, you need to value your ethics, even when it comes to pursuing a dream. Take three deep breaths and relax.

long pause

You can still hear the Hierophant's voice, though it seems to be coming from a long way away.

See yourself pursuing your dream. What makes you continue? When the odds seem overwhelming, what drives you on? Motivation is an absolute necessity, so you must discover that which encourages you. See first one door close, then another. What will keep you motivated in the face of rejection? Do you need a support network? Should you keep a journal of your successes to encourage you when the going gets bleak? Do little rewards at the end of a hard day help? With what will you replenish your energy? Music? Dinner out? A long walk in the park? Playing with the cat? A new book . . . sweater . . . briefcase . . . ?

long pause

Sometimes we believe that work should be its own reward, but humans need encouragement, support, and praise. Examine your motivations, your reward system, and see if you might need to update or upgrade those special treats you give to yourself.

extended long pause—1 minute

Take three deep breaths and relax.

long pause

The Hierophant sits beside you. You hear him speaking.

"I know these questions are not easily answered," he says. "They can make your head spin, but you will return to them time and again during the rest of your journey. Right now, we seek to stimulate the subconscious so that it begins the process for you."

Take another deep breath and let your tension out as you exhale.

Once again see your goal, and this time see yourself actively pursuing it. What are you doing to manifest the dream? What activities must you perform? Follow through with some of the steps you need in order to accomplish your goal. Be in the moment. What are doing? How are you doing it? See, feel, hear, touch . . . taste . . . give yourself over to the pursuit of your goal for a moment and experience how it feels.

extended long pause—1 minute

You must also learn flexibility. Suppose that your goal isn't working out the way you want it to? Suppose you aren't getting the response you hoped for? Maybe you don't enjoy this as much as you thought you would. Attempt to re-envision your dream; think of alternate plans should your first attempts fail. Remember, most inventors and artists have many failures behind them before they succeed. If you give up because of one failure, you will never reach your goal and you will sit there when you are old thinking:

"I could have been . . ."

"I could have done . . ."

Examine your alternatives and if there are none, begin to create them now.

extended long pause—1 minute

"I realize this is tiring work," the Hierophant says. "But anything worth having requires perseverance and energy. We have but one more lesson and then you may rest. So take one more slow breath and listen to my voice."

See yourself accomplishing your goal. You have it in hand, you've done it, you're at the pinnacle of this cycle. Now look to how this accomplishment affects your life.

Perhaps it won't change you as much as you thought. If you never believed you were a worthy person, accomplishing a goal isn't going to change that. Or perhaps you thought you could achieve something wonderful without having to be responsible for the results. Remember, every major breakthrough will engender some kind of fallout and you must accept responsibility for what you create. Think through what might happen when you have reached the end of this particular quest.

extended long pause—1 minute

Lastly, remember that at the end of a quest lies the beginnings of another. Life is a cycle and even though you may accomplish something wonderful, there are always new paths lying beyond the one on which you presently walk.

The Hierophant wakes you from your trance. He bids you to sit at the table and refresh yourself with food and drink.

"You see," he says. "I do not give you wisdom, but only help you discover it within yourself. Now you have come to the end of the first part of your journey. You have all the tools you need with which to accomplish your goals. Your path now leads you into the growth of your will, a time when you build dreams and connect with other souls and hearts. You must claim your personal power and see your fortunes rise. Events and other people will rule your life during the second phase of your quest."

If you have anything you want to say to the Hierophant, do so now and listen for his reply.

long pause

He stands and gestures to his daughter. "Morgan will see you to your room for the night, then tomorrow she will replenish your pack before you head off on your quest again. Good fortune and remember your lessons." And with that, the Hierophant quietly exits the room. Morgan escorts you to your room where you may rest and sleep until morning.

Now listen to my voice as I count from ten to one. You will awake refreshed and alert. Ten . . . nine . . . you are becoming aware of your surroundings . . . eight . . . seven . . . six . . . hear the sounds around you . . . five . . . four . . . you will be fully alert and refreshed . . . three . . . two . . . one . . . take three deep breaths and when you are ready, you may open your eyes.

Suggested Exercises

1. What skills would you like to learn? Take a class on a subject that interests you or pertains to a goal you have set for yourself. Remember, a teacher does not necessarily have to be a person—your teacher can also be a book, an audio or video cassette, or a class through the computer or the television.

2. Make a list of your worst distractions and plan out a time to pursue them. If you try to negate them entirely it will be worse than if you indulge them in moderate amounts.

3. If it has been a while since you have tried to learn a new skill or concept, remember that the mind takes time to adjust. Be gentle, yet persistent, with yourself.

4. Study with a partner. You'll be more apt to apply yourself if someone else is there; and studying with someone else provides a dose of healthy competition, not to mention the encouragement you can give one another.

Part Two

The Growth of Will:
The Search for Foundation

Bid me discourse, I will enchant thine ear,
Or, like a fairy, trip upon the green,
Or, like a nymph, with long dishevell'd hair,
Dance on the sands, and yet no footing seen
Love is a spirit all compact of fire,
Not gross to sink, but light and will aspire.

—William Shakespeare (1564–1616)
Venus and Adonis

The Lovers
Binding Ties

The seventh card of the major arcana is known as the Lovers. It is assigned the number 6.

The Lovers and Their Energy

The Lovers represent a dual, yet connected, set of energies within our lives. On an inner level, the Lovers archetype represents an ability to integrate differing aspects of ourselves, to blend and merge opposing facets of our personalities so that we might arrive at a sense of peace and wholeness with all aspects of ourselves. On an outer level, the Lovers represent the interconnecting relationships that we evolve with others—most often of a romantic nature, but it can also indicate the bond between close friends.

The Lovers are enmeshed with one another; they reach out, touch others' lives, and interact on a social level. They remind us that no one can act with independence all of the time, that whatever we do will affect others. When we give ourselves over to the Lovers' embrace we become vulnerable. We open ourselves up to the possibility of being hurt, as well as the potential for incredible bonding.

The Fool no longer travels the road alone when s/he encounters the energy of the Lovers. If integration and connection occur within the self rather than with another, then we tend to find a sense of unity and contentment in our lives that precludes bitter loneliness.

In our daily routines, the Lovers can manifest as potential lifemates, partners on a romantic level. They appear as the desire to begin a family, to bond and wed (with or without the formal ceremony). The Lovers bring with them sexuality, passion, and desire for companionship.

The Lovers archetype can appear in our lives when we're ready for a relationship, when we have outgrown dalliances and want something longer-lived. This energy shows up when we are tired of going the route alone, when we want to enlarge our social circle.

On an inward level, the Lovers archetype can appear when we're ready to resolve two or more issues that have been tormenting us, disparate energies that we have, until this time, been unable to mesh together. (An example: an inability to choose between two differing, yet equally appealing, sides of ourselves—such as being drawn toward both Native American spirituality and Western European Paganism. The Lovers energy would help to find a comfortable blend between the two paths).

While the Lovers can appear at any time during our lives, they most often show up when we are ready for a break from constant focus on career, on education. They can make life difficult—sometimes they pop into our lives when we don't have a lot of time to pay them the attention their energy demands.

The Spiritual Concept

In terms of spirituality, we look to devoted pairings of the gods and goddesses. The Lovers become Isis and Osiris, Ishtar and Tammuz, Inanna and Dumuzi—divine pairings in which love included personal sacrifice.

Perhaps we can best see differing aspects of the Lovers by examining the cycles of the Earth Goddess and Horned God:

- love is found with parents and family: the God transforms (quickens in the womb) during Samhain. During Yule, He is reborn to the Goddess who, recovered from mourning Her lost love, is ready now to give birth to Her new family;

- we leave our parents and begin our own family: the weaning of young Lord from the Goddess during Imbolc leads to the new cycle of fertility by the magick wrought during Ostara;

- we enter our prime years of sexuality and romantic love: the Goddess and the Horned God discover Their passion during Beltane and reach the zenith of Their pairing at Litha; and

- we learn the sacrifice and loss that, in one form or another, always accompanies love: the God voluntary sacrifices His life during Lughnasadh as the Goddess assumes her cloak of widowhood, then as He begins His cyclic descent into the Underworld, She mourns the end of the Harvest Cycle/Pagan year.

In terms of the zodiac, the Lovers represents the sign of Gemini. On the Wheel of the Year, we can place the Lovers card at the festival of Beltane, best personifying the passionate romantic and sexual union between partners.

The Card

Some common representations of the Lovers include a woman and man entwined in a passionate embrace. Often the images will be merging or blending into one another. In some cards, we find a priest or the Hermit presiding over their union.

Guidelines for Use

In our journey through the major arcana, the Lovers meditation should follow the meditation of the Hierophant. Meditating on the Lovers can also be an appropriate part of a Beltane ritual, or whenever we feel a need to explore our interest in love relationships, friendships, or the integration of opposing facets of ourselves.

Flowers:	rose, carnation, basil, cinnamon
Incense:	rose, jasmine, musk, vanilla, tangerine
Oils:	rose, jasmine, ylang ylang, orange, musk
Crystals:	rose quartz, garnet, ruby, diamond
Candles:	red, pink, mauve, white, magenta

Meditation

Relax and get comfortable. Close your eyes and take three deep breaths.

long pause

You wake early in the morning on your journey. You met the Hierophant some months ago and since then, you have been following your path, honing your skills, until you think you are ready to settle and go about the business of life. But you still feel a restlessness, a certain anticipation, and you know that you have not quite found the place which you will call home.

The path, still dusty, is now a familiar companion. You have been through valley and glade, forest and prairie, and still the path winds up toward the mountains in the distance. The peaks are closer now, but seem veiled in mist and shadow and you do not know how long it will be before you ever climb their slopes.

long pause

The morning is fine—spring is merging into summer—and as you wander along the path, you find your mind trailing off first one way and then another. A large hill stands to your right and the path curves around the hill, you cannot see what lies on the other side.

As you round the bend, a gladed wood lays ahead. Oaks and maples are burgeoning out in their growth, their leaves dappling the ground with shade as the sunlight glimmers down to splash across the fern-shrouded floor. With a light heart, you enter the forest.

long pause

The trees are filled with bird song as you meander down the path. Huckleberries show their blossoms, the wild rose will soon be in full bloom, and the sun is hitting you just right, so that you feel lazy and sleepy and energized all at the same time.

The scent of water lures you down a short side road and you find yourself standing in a grotto, next to a pond that shimmers under the sunlight. Fed by a stream that trickles in one side and out the other, gentle ripples glide across the water, the breeze encouraging them onward and you feel the need to rest here, to let yourself relax and drift.

Sit down, take three deep breaths, and then lay back against the mossy bank and listen to the droning of bumblebees. They buzz past your ears, on their way to the lilacs growing next to where the stream gurgles its way into the grotto.

long pause

As you lay there, drifting on the scent of lilacs and roses, you hear a noise. You open your eyes and see a woman crossing the grass. She is beautiful as the sunrise, honest of face and opulent in body. She wears a long white dress of filmy gauze and when she silently lowers herself to sit next to you, you find that her eyes mirror every color in the rainbow, shifting from one hue to another in a kaleidoscope of swirling colors.

long pause

She holds a mirror in her hands and offers it to you. "Look," she says, "look into the mirror and see yourself as you were when you were a child. If you had difficulties when you were young, if your life was unhappy, now you have the chance to nurture yourself as you wish you would have been nurtured. If your childhood was happy, remember those times in which you felt protected and loved."

Look into the mirror, see the child you once were, and either remember the love you received, or if your childhood was scarred, then honor and love the child within as you wish had been done.

extended long pause—1 minute

Now the image is changing.

"Look into the mirror," the woman says. "See yourself as you are today. See both your strengths and your weaknesses. Embrace both, for together, they make up your life, your existence. Perhaps their nature will change as you continue in your journeys, but right now, accept yourself for who you are and love yourself as best as you can."

Look into the mirror, see yourself in an objective and detached manner, and simply accept what you see. Do not judge, do not fault, simply accept and love the person that you've become.

extended long pause—1 minute

When you have finished, she takes the mirror from you. "To love others, you must love yourself. You must accept yourself. That is the first lesson of love."

She holds out her hand. On it rests a beautiful butterfly. The insect sits lightly in her palm and is so beautiful, so exquisite, that you find yourself envying her. She laughs gently and says, "I offer the butterfly to you. Take it from my hand."

With little thought, you snatch at the insect. With it tight in hand, you know that you possess one of the most beautiful things in the world. But when you open your palm to peek in, the butterfly has been crushed, broken and now it lies dead in your grasp.

long pause

The woman reaches down and blows gently on the butterfly and, before your eyes, wings and body mend. It rises to its feet once more and crawls back on her palm.

"You see," the woman says, "if you hold the object of your love too tightly and do not allow it to follow its nature, you will destroy what you have attempted to protect. Now gently, slowly, take the butterfly and carefully allow it space on your palm. Let it take the time it needs to grow accustomed to you.

Reach out once again and gently coax the butterfly onto your fingers, hold it lightly and watch as it tests your skin, tests the air, and then willingly climbs onto your palm and rests there.

extended long pause—1 minute

You feel a sense of devotion and care emanate from the butterfly to your heart, then it flies off to seek its dinner.

"Do not fear," the woman says to you. "Your friend will return. All creatures need to nourish themselves, and love needs nourishment too. Sometimes we find that one person cannot supply all of our needs—they cannot always be our friend, lover, parent, child, mentor, and servant. So we make friends to support our differing interests, we seek out teachers to guide us, we turn to our family for emotional support. Just because your loved one chooses to spend time talking with others doesn't mean that they don't love you. They simply know that it's unreasonable to expect one person to fulfill all of their differing needs.

"A balanced and well-rounded individual will have many facets to their personalities, and they will have more than one person to address the differing needs each facet requires."

long pause

Now, think of yourself. Think about all the different aspects to your personality. If you are in a relationship, does your mate have exactly the same interests as you? Or do you find some dissimilarities within the connections you have made together?

Perhaps you enjoy hiking and your partner prefers shopping. Or you like reading adventure stories while your partner prefers to work on the computer.

Or you might not be in a relationship, but you have several friends with widely diverging interests, and you talk about cooking with one friend, work with another, and movies with yet a third.

Think about the differences in personality among the people who are your companions, and then try to understand how impossible it is for one person to fit our every need.

extended long pause—1 minute

The woman stands up, indicating you should follow her. She leads you through the glen, alongside the brook, until you have reached a clearing. Within the center of the clearing stands a large palm tree. Under the palm tree, you see a love seat. The woman points to the love seat and says, "If you will sit there, please."

When you sit under the palm, you can hear the gentle strains of music, coming from far away it seems, and you see a sparkle of energy rising before you.

From the middle of the glowing energy, you sense a series of questions.

What emotional aspects do you hope your potential mate will possess? If you have a partner, think about their emotions, their sensitive side. Do you want your partner to be caring of others? Do you want them to be empathetic, or do you hope that they will be able to control their emotional side? Are you more comfortable around reserved people? What is your partner like? What makes you comfortable?

long pause

What can you offer in the way of an emotional commitment? Are you ready for a long-term relationship? Do you shy away when you think of marriage? Do you want children or are you happiest when you think of just the two of you together?

long pause

Now think about the intellect of your potential spouse, or your current partner. Are they witty? Charming? Keen-eyed and observant? Are they more intelligent than you are and does this make you uncomfortable or secure? Think about what conversations you would like to have, or that you do have, and what you find interests you most during these debates.

long pause

And what about your own intellectual pursuits? What do you find interesting? Are you rabid about politics or would you rather discuss the latest novel topping the bestseller list? Does your mouth water when you see a piano and sheet music, or would you rather sit in on a discussion about car repair? Think about what you have to offer in this department and don't sell yourself short—everyone has interests, you just have to discover what makes your eyes light up and your mind start to whir.

long pause

Next, what would make you happiest to come home to after a long day at work? If you are in a relationship, what makes your heart flutter when you see your partner? What actions or words makes you want to take them in your arms and never let them go? You are trying to discover the keys that unlock your heart, that resonate in your soul.

long pause

Next, ask you what you can do to encourage a happy and congenial home-life? Will you remember to bring home flowers without it being a special occasion? Can you find the best in your partner when they're feeling down about themselves? If the cat walks all over your new sweater and leaves a trail of fur, do you get angry or will you laugh and pet the kitty before reaching for a lint brush? What can you do, while still being honest with yourself and your partner, to make the days happier?

long pause

What are you willing to compromise on and accept in your current or potential part-ner, should the love and other connections be there? Can you accept a sloppy house or is cleanliness and order too important to you? Will you be happiest with a bookworm or do you prefer to be outdoors most of the time?

Do you need a person who will be happy dressing up for evenings out, or are you the blue jeans and t-shirt type? Even then, if they prefer dress clothes, never putting on a pair of overalls in their life, but don't insist on the same for you, can you live with that com-promise? Think about what you can adapt and adjust to versus what are absolutes in your life.

long pause

Examine the sexuality of this person. Will they be the opposite gender than you? The same? Are you conservative in the bedroom or experimental? Do you need someone with a high sexual appetite, or are you content with a little less? If they are willing to forego the handcuffs and riding crop, will you wear lace and leather?

Remember, when it comes to sexuality each person is an individual and you will each have to discover your own needs and then talk together about how best to meet both sets of desires.

extended long pause—1 minute

Next, turn your mind to the appearance of your current or potential partner. Do you have a preference about looks? Most people do, but supposing you met someone who met all of your needs but they looked quite different than what you usually are attracted to. Can you allow a friendship to grow and out of that, a potential relationship? Can you tolerate differences?

Beauty has as many faces as there are people and you must keep in mind that what is beautiful to you may not be desirable to another. Before judging someone unattractive, make sure that it isn't society talking, but truly your inner self that finds no spark, no interest there.

Think about all the different people you've met, and how many you found attractive, whether or not you were in a relationship with them. If you are in a relationship now, think of your current partner—what drew you to them in the beginning may not be what holds you together now. Think of their assets, of what you find attractive now.

long pause

Appearances can be deceiving, you should not expect more out of your potential mate than you are willing to uphold yourself. Fifty years from now, your partner will have aged and so will you. Relationships must be built on more than physical appearance to last the test of time.

Now look at the ball of glowing energy and see it begin to sparkle and take form. Out of the glowing energy steps a figure—if you are in a happy relationship, it is your current partner. If you are unattached, or if you are in a relationship that fulfills few or none of your needs, then you find the figure represents a potential mate—a person who would meet the most important of your needs.

long pause

Offer your hand, then stand and walk away from the palm tree, onto the path that leads out of the clearing. The journey feels different when you aren't alone, when you are with someone else. You stumble a little and your partner catches you before you fall. A little while later, your partner trips and you are there to stop them from tumbling to the ground. Think about that responsibility, about the connection that allows you to interact so closely with another human being.

long pause

Now look down at the ground, you see that your partner walks a different path than you follow. Their path runs parallel to your own, yet it is a separate and unique. No one ever will pursue the exact quest, the exact journey, you now follow. You will forever be an individual, even when you find a partner with which to share your life. How does that make you feel? Does it frighten you? Is the thought a relief?

long pause

The forest gives way and you enter a town. The streets are well-kept, the houses clean and homey. As you walk along, you see families and couples out for their evening strolls. Now and then you see an older couple wandering by, arm in arm, and you can tell that their love has matured, deepened into a connection that transcends appearance and health.

long pause

Simultaneously, you and your partner look into each other's eyes. Without speaking, you both know that this is the town where you wish to make your home, to establish your career and to raise your family, be it just the two of you, or a house full of children.

long pause

As you turn the corner you see the house of your dreams. There is a for sale sign in the front yard, and you know that you have found your home.

Now, listen to my voice as I count from ten to one. You will awake refreshed and alert. Ten . . . nine . . . you are becoming awake and aware of your surroundings . . . eight . . . seven . . . six . . . hear the sounds around you . . . five . . . four . . . you will be fully alert and refreshed . . . three . . . two . . . one . . . take three deep breaths and when you are ready, you may open your eyes.

Suggested Exercises

1. If you are looking for a relationship, make three lists for yourself—one of attributes you want in a partner that you aren't willing to compromise on. The second lists the attributes that you have to offer a partner. The third should be of qualities that you want in a relationship. Refer to your lists weekly, think about them, and change them as need be. Then, whenever you meet someone, you will be able to see if they fit your needs, and perhaps avoid potential disasters.

2. Remember—to find love with another, you must discover it within yourself. People will treat you the way you treat yourself. If you see yourself as unworthy or unlovable, then you will most likely incur that response from others.

3. If you are having trouble integrating differing sides of yourself, see if they can coexist without changing either of them. You can be both spontaneous and conservative, you can drink both herbal tea and vodka martinis—no one is mono-dimensional by nature. Realize that there are days when one side of your personality is going to dominate and accept that balance doesn't necessarily mean equal proportions all the time.

4. If you are having difficulty resolving internal conflict, perhaps you are trying to fit into a mold you think you should fit into. Sometimes we attempt to force ourselves into behaviors or beliefs that aren't right for us and this causes severe distress. If the conflict becomes too difficult, then you might want to consider seeing a professional therapist for help—therapy can work wonders and it doesn't always take a long time to resolve some issues.

5. All the compromise and therapy in the world won't save a relationship that isn't meant to be. If your partner simply doesn't want to be with you, there's nothing you can do. You're better off letting go so that you can recover your sense of self and start new again. Never compromise your ethics for the sake of anyone—no relationship is worth denigrating yourself for.

*I go among the fields and catch a glimpse of a stoat or
a fieldmouse peeping out of the withered grass—The
creature hath a purpose and its eyes are bright with it . . .*

—John Keats (1795–1821)
to George & Georgiana Keats

The Chariot

Boundaries and Directed Focus

The eighth card of the major arcana is known as
the Chariot. It is assigned the number 7.

The Chariot and Its Energy

The Chariot represents our ability to set boundaries,
to push through our commitments to victory. We
firmly establish ourselves within our career and family,
building upon the foundations we laid with our work
through the prior cards of the tarot.

The Chariot represents the driven, focused part of
ourselves. It contains our actions, our deeds, all directed
toward specific ends.

Using this energy, we make connections within our
community, we become recognized for who we are
and what we do. The Chariot has a limited supply of

fuel, however, so one must selectively discriminate where one's energy is to be used. We throw ourselves into the present with an eye on the future; we accept our ambition as a natural emotion; we use our aggression to compete in a healthy manner.

The Fool's carefree days are over, s/he has accepted responsibility and now lives up to it. Instead of innocent naïveté, s/he now has mastered his/her skills and actively uses them with an aim toward personal victory and success.

In our daily lives, the Chariot appears less as a person or persons, and more as events occurring to us or being initiated by us. The Chariot is our first job in the career of our choice, it embodies our wedding and subsequent first years of marriage. The Chariot can represent our first house and the home we make out of that house.

The Chariot archetype can appear in our lives when we've completed our education and are ready to take on the business world, it represents the birth of our first child, the writer's first book contract, the artist's first gallery show. The Chariot, in essence, is the beginning of our foray into the professional side of our chosen lifestyle, the successes that give us confidence.

Only after we have honed our skills, only after we have met the person we want to marry, only when we've decided to become parents, can the Chariot come roaring into our lives. We use the drive that propels us forward (the Emperor), and the skills we have honed (the Hierophant) or partner we meet (the Lovers) to pursue our goals.

The Chariot also represents, as said above, setting boundaries and limits on what we will accept from others. We decide what is most important, what we can compromise on, and then stick to our decisions. Through the Chariot, we find ourselves maturing. We are no longer young and idealistic—we have learned some necessary truths and are ready to go about the business of compromise to complete the work we want to do.

The Spiritual Concept

In terms of spirituality, the Chariot becomes the element of Will—the Spirit that pervades the Universe, the Spirit that resides within each person. The Chariot represents our personal soul and the connection of that soul to the material world.

The Chariot represents victory and therefore we liken it to the goddess Nike, the Grecian personification of that energy. We also find the Chariot in the Roman goddess Victoria, who began as a goddess of military success and through time, gradually shifted to symbolize the spirit of victory as a whole.

We also find the Chariot in Ptah, Egyptian god of artifice and building.

We find the Chariot connected to the zodiacal sign of Cancer, and we can place the Chariot, within the Wheel of the Year, as the element of Earth—found in the northern quarter, for the Chariot represents manifestation, building, foundations, and the solidity of results gained from actions taken.

The Card

Some common representations of the Chariot include: a knight or charioteer holding the reins of a chariot, which is often winged (to represent Nike, the winged goddess of victory). In some decks, the Charioteer will be holding a chalice, which represents the Grail; in others—a scepter or flaming torch. You may find banners waving in the background, or other symbols of victory.

Guidelines for Use

In our ongoing journey through the major arcana, this should follow the meditation on the Lovers. Meditating on the Chariot is also appropriate for any time when you need to infuse a project with extra energy for manifestation, or when you are working with the element of Earth.

Flowers:	allspice, basil, mandrake, ginseng, fern
Incense:	tangerine, lime, cinnamon, carnation
Oils:	bergamot, carnation, lime, tangerine
Crystals:	tiger's eye, malachite, citrine, carnelian
Candles:	brown, burgundy, pumpkin, rust

Meditation

Relax and get comfortable. Close your eyes and take three deep breaths.

long pause

You and your mate have found the house that will be your new home. You have settled into your family unit. You may have children—perhaps you or your mate had children before you met. Perhaps you have no children, but cats or dogs instead. But whatever the mix, you indeed feel very much part of a family.

You are standing in the empty living room of your ideal home. You have just bought this house and now you must decorate, you must make it your own.

Look around carefully, what do you see? The room should reflect your personality and that of your mate's, as well. Think for a few minutes, about what sort of home you would like. It must meet the needs of your family, reflect the lifestyle that you are now pursuing and yet remain comfortable, a safe haven in which to retreat.

Take a moment to furnish the room, make sure everything truly fits your style, and that of your family's. When you are satisfied, stand back and admire your work.

extended long pause—1 minute

It feels like a red-letter day to you. You are happy with your family, you found a home you love, and you recently started working in a position that suits your needs. You aren't where you want to be yet, but you are getting there.

Your days are full now, busy and complicated. There seems to be very little time to think anymore. Look back to the beginning of your journey—when you started off as the carefree wanderer. So much has changed since then. You can feel yourself maturing, you can sense yourself growing.

Think now about the responsibilities in your personal life—in your home life. Have you reached a point where they consume much of your free time? Do you have children? If so, what part in their upbringing and care do you play? If you are child-free, then what other responsibilities do you have? Even pets can exact a lot of energy from us . . . they need our care and our love.

Our relationship with our partner demands attention, too. Sometimes we must look after aging parents, or other family members. Think about your life and examine how much energy you give to these demands. They may be tiring, but look for the good that you get out of them, the good you do others. What can you learn from the care and nurturing of your family members? If you do not have these sort of responsibilities yet, think of what they might feel like and how you might respond to them when they do enter your life.

extended long pause—2 minutes

Now, you have furnished your house, and it is time for you to go to work. You have found a job very close to what you were hoping for. While you are still in the lower echelon of workers, you know you will be able to advance within this position to the success you have often imagined. For now, you are content to work your way up the rungs, to pay your dues, so to speak.

Now, think of what that position is, or what it might be when you find it, and dress yourself in the proper attire for the job. Take a moment to examine yourself in the mirror. What do your clothes say about you? What about your posture? You are happy with yourself right now, you feel on the road to success. How does this feeling affect your stance?

long pause

When you have finished examining your image, then pick up your keys and wallet, or keys and purse, and leave the house, taking care to lock the door behind you. You now have something to lose, possessions and family members whose welfare and upkeep matter to you, so you take no risks when it comes to protecting them.

long pause

To get to work, do you take the bus? Do you drive a car? A motorcycle? How do you commute to your place of business? Perhaps you have opened your own shop out of the garage and you work right next to your home. Perhaps you work in a large office building downtown. Or you work in a small boutique, or a restaurant. Think of the career you are pursuing, or will be pursuing, and envision the work environment. As you commute to work, think about what you like about your work place, and what you don't. If you have complaints, think of ways you could resolve them.

extended long pause—1 minute

You arrive at work. Do you work behind a desk? In front of a stove? Behind a counter? Are you working toward an executive position? Are you actively creating something? Do you supervise others? Think about your career, or potential career, and postulate what might be waiting for you when you get to work on a Monday morning.

long pause

Prioritize your duties, see yourself going about them in a confident, efficient manner. Envision yourself finishing tasks on time, and receiving praise for your efforts and attitude. How does that make you feel? Can you build your self-esteem, knowing you deserve those compliments? Take a moment to examine your feelings of self-confidence and personal esteem.

extended long pause—1 minute

Now your supervisor comes over to you, or a new client enters your door, who wants you to do something that you know you either don't have the time or abilities for. Are you comfortable saying no? Are you able to establish a set of boundaries beyond which you won't go? Can you ask for help when you need it, or do you feel obligated to take on the entire task yourself?

long pause

Sometimes when we are presented with a task beyond our abilities we feel embarrassed or ashamed of admitting our need for help, but remember, if you attempt something that you know you're not ready for, you're probably setting yourself up for failure. It might be better to ask for the help, to ask for an extension in time, in order to successfully accomplish your goal or task.

Now your supervisor or client asks you to take on a task beyond your means. Envision yourself asking for help or extra time. Be firm and clear about your position, don't be apologetic. You might find that if you are open about your needs, you will get a more positive response than you expected.

long pause

Later in the day, you hear about a new position opening up. It promises raises in salary, responsibility, and job satisfaction. One other person, a stranger, wants to apply. How do you feel about competing for the job?

long pause

Next, imagine how would you feel about competing if your rival was a person you disliked?

long pause

Now, imagine that this person is your friend. How would you feel about competing for a job with a friend? How do your feelings differ than if you don't like the person or if they are a stranger?

long pause

Competition can be a healthy impetus to improve our lives, it can spur us on and give us the motivation to make necessary changes in ourselves and in our situations.

As human beings, we need to compete, but we also need to establish a set of ethics about how far we are willing to go in order to procure something we want. Take a moment to think about your personal ethics. What actions do they preclude? What will you do in order to get a promotion or win a contract that you want? Are you comfortable with your ethics or do they leave you feeling a little queasy?

Perhaps you need to redefine your sense of right and wrong. Are you espousing one set of values and living by another? Examine your value system and whether or not you are living by what you believe.

extended long pause—1 minute

The workday is over and you are on your way home. You have a few errands to run, and then chores to finish before and after dinner. But you know that your family is waiting for you, they are tired from their days too, and yet you are happy. There may be minor complaints, occasionally an argument, but for the most part you have entered a hectic, contented part of your life on this cycle of the journey.

When you arrive home, see your mate, or your potential mate, as they greet you. Their day has been a little rough, so the two of you curl up on the sofa before tackling the evening chores and spend some quiet time.

As you look out of your living room window, you sense the peace that underlies the seeming chaos of your days. Through the busyness, through the hustle and bustle, you have found joy. The strength of your home—whether it be with a partner or in comfortable solitude, whether it be with children or pets—gives you a solid foundation upon which you are building your life.

Take a few moments to savor that sense of foundation, of security. Breathe in the peace and love and stillness, breathe out the chaos and errands and jumble from the day. Take two more deep breaths, letting the tension slide from your body.

long pause

This day has been like the majority of others that now slide through your life. Sometimes you look back on that carefree state and nostalgia hits you, for it seemed so free and easy, but you also know that you were searching and that part of what you were searching for is the life you are now leading. You aren't sure what the future will bring, but for now you feel solid and secure within the life you are building. This part of your journey feels stable, a foundation built in stone.

Now, listen to my voice as I count from ten to one. You will awake refreshed and alert. Ten . . . nine . . . you are becoming awake and aware of your surroundings . . . eight . . . seven . . . six . . . hear the sounds around you . . . five . . . four . . . you will be fully alert and refreshed . . . three . . . two . . . one . . . take three deep breaths and when you are ready, you may open your eyes.

Suggested Exercises

1. This meditation is meant to immerse you in the day to day existence that encompasses our lives as we pursue a goal and as we grow in maturity. Think back to different cycles in your life, to when you felt like everything was set and solid. Recognize that you needed that sense of solidity to continue on, to learn what you needed to. But realize that sometimes what we thought was so solid can change drastically, quickly, and be aware that this is simply a part of the journey.

2. Now that you have undergone this phase of the Fool's journey, can you identify where you want to be in your life? Are you actively pursuing those goals? You can't sit back and expect things to happen without making an effort—the Gods help those who help themselves and, for most of us, we achieve according to how much effort we make.

3. Do you fit the image of what you want your life to be? Or is your image a little off? I used to have a picture of what I was supposed to look like once I became a successful author. I finally realized that I can only look like me, I can only dress according to what my tastes are, and that my images were based on a false sense of reality about my personal situation. I have also had friends tell me that I don't dress witchy enough. I have to ask them, what does the average Witch look like? Wearing a long

gypsy skirt with ankle bells and a wreath of flowers around my head only fits a small part of my personality, definitely not my entire lifestyle.

4. Can you say no and mean it? If not, do you have a hard time disappointing friends? Or are you secretly afraid that people won't like you if you tell them no? Perhaps, you were never allowed to say no when you were a child and now it's hard to give yourself permission. Practice saying no, perhaps with a friend who understands your predicament. Set up scenarios with your friend in which you are asked to do something you either don't want to do or don't have time for, and establish setting your boundaries until you are comfortable. You can also use visualization to practice boundary-setting.

His mind his kingdom, and his will his law.

—William Cowper (1731–1800)
*Verses Supposed to be Written
by Alexander Selkirk*

Strength
Claiming Your Power

The ninth card of the major arcana is known as Strength. It is most often assigned the number 8.

Strength and Its Energy

Strength represents our inner strength, our powers of self-confidence and self-esteem. Within this archetype, our growth blossoms and we feel we have reached a pinnacle in our lives. With the inner conviction of our beliefs, our lives run more smoothly. We master the majority of our problems and forge a satisfying existence.

With Strength we heal what is possible, so that we might attain a sense of wholeness, of completeness. We head toward what appears to be the zenith of our careers, we know we have talent, creativity and find ourselves willing to tackle anything. It seems that all we need is one last push to put us on top of the world.

The archetype presented in the Strength card leads us into a period of rejuvenation, regeneration of self-esteem and ability. We look in the mirror and love what we see, we have a sense of eternity—surely nothing can topple our position.

When we look back on ourselves as the Fool, we no longer harbor much nostalgia, but instead see how very young we were. We now understand that all our searching, all our struggle, was worth the effort.

In our daily lives, the archetype of Strength appears less as a person or persons, and more as inner feelings toward ourselves and our accomplishments. The energy of Strength appears through promotions at work—but more in our satisfaction with our careers. We reach new heights in our family life—the newness is over and we settle into a happy and comfortable routine. We *think* we mirror the Empress or Emperor at this stage in our lives.

This sense of Strength appears in our lives when we've worked our way up our career ladder, when we've overcome the 2 A.M. feedings and the terrible twos and our children are somewhat well-behaved and manageable. We find our Strength in our continued success as writers, artists, in the recognition we begin to receive from others for our work. We are by no means beginners at this game of life, now we are among those that we once looked up to.

The Strength card also represents our sense of generosity, for when we are in a good place with our lives and ourselves, it becomes much easier to give to others. We find Strength in our sense of power, but we have developed a control over that power. We are the wise father, the guiding mother, the fair and just employer. We know how to achieve a balance between teamwork and individual accomplishment, and at this point, we cannot see ourselves altering our course.

The Spiritual Concept

In terms of spirituality, Strength becomes the element of success. Strength blends spiritual and material progress and represents the accompanying peace that can result from that blend.

We can liken the archetype of Strength to the goddess Amaterasu, the Japanese Sun-goddess. We also find Strength in the Greek Eos, goddess of the dawn, and in Freya, leader of the Valkyries and goddess of Fire.

We also find Strength with the Norse god Tyr and the Greek hero, Hercules.

Leo is the astrological sign associated with this card, and we can place the Strength, within the Wheel of the Year, at Litha, alongside the Emperor, for Strength represents the expansion of light, the growth manifest during summer, the glory found in the sun.

The Card

Some common representations of the Strength include a woman riding a lion or tiger. She has bested her beast, tamed her power, and now uses it without shame or guilt. In some decks, a serpent, often with its tail coiled in the figure eight (for infinity) will be resting near the woman. You might also find symbols such as the Egyptian ankh present, symbolizing the life-force inherent within the nature of Strength.

Guidelines for Use

In our ongoing journey through the major arcana, this should follow the meditation on the Chariot. Meditating on Strength is also appropriate for Litha, or any time when you need to infuse a project with extra energy for healing or success. You may also use this meditation when you are working with the element of fire.

Flowers:	cinquefoil, sunflower, walnut, saffron
Incense:	frankincense, tangerine, carnation
Oils:	orange, tangerine, carnation, lime
Crystals:	carnelian, citrine, garnet, ruby
Candles:	red, orange, yellow, gold, white

Meditation

Relax and get comfortable. Close your eyes and take three deep breaths.

long pause

Early morning promises to be warm and you have the entire weekend to yourself. You have accomplished much in the past months, and your peers have been very good about acknowledging your successes. Now, though, you simply want to be off to enjoy your own company and your good fortune.

You have decided to climb a hillside that lies near your town. It is a short drive or bike-ride there, and with several days at your disposal and the weather promising to be perfect, the moment seems right for exploring the lightly forested slope.

Gather what you think you'll need for your journey—you will want water and food, and perhaps a walking stick.

long pause

Now set out, either in your car or on a bike. As you head out of town, you remember when you first approached this city and your life here. The road you are following today leads away from that life, and yet you know that you won't be going far, not at this time.

Sometimes you wonder to where the road leads, you know that eventually the path journeys to the mountains in the distance, but you aren't prepared to find out. Not today. You have your wonderful life and your family here, and those roots tunnel deep in your heart. But still, now and then, you find your eyes turning toward the trail and you muse on what might have been.

long pause

A junction ahead divides the main byway from a narrow dirt path. Pull off of the road and leave your car or bike here. The trail winds up the hillside, through a thick patch of ivy and ferns. Trees dot the slope, huge oaks and maples shading the way. Their leaves are grown wide and sway gently in the light breeze.

The sun lights up the sky, filling the robin's egg blue with a golden glow. As you take to the path, sweat begins to bead against your brow but you don't mind. You have plenty of water and your body is in good shape. In fact, the workout feels exhilarating. At first you stride along at a quick pace, so accustomed have you become to hurrying through your daily routine, but as you ascend further up the hillside, your pace begins to slow, you no longer feel the need to rush.

You have the time to notice the birds chirping in the bushes, the water burbling along in the creek that shines through the trees. Stop and take a deep breath. Breathe in the peace and stillness surrounding you, breathe out the hustle of your life. Let a sense of solitude fill your body and soul. Surrender to the peace.

long pause

When your mind and body are still, then slowly continue your climb. The trail winds in and out of the light glade, a gentle path along which you begin to see benches and tables at which travelers may rest. At times you see a person here at one table, a family there at another, all enjoying the beautiful view.

After a while, you come to a giant old maple overhanging a picnic table. The shade obscures the brightest rays of the sun, but beneath the tree the air is warm and lazy, and you decide to rest here for a time. Sit down at the table and drink some of your water, then pull out your lunch and eat. Take your time, savor whatever foods you brought. Today is your day to enjoy yourself and the lunch you packed should reflect that.

long pause

After you have eaten, rest your pack on the table and examine the tree. A giant of a maple, its leaves are so big they cover both of your palms and more. Examine the leaves, the veins that run through the green expanse. Think of the energy required for a tree to grow thousands of these each year. Place your hands against the trunk of the tree and feel the strength that resides within the maple—the age and wisdom and power collected over the years, over the decades.

long pause

Now think of your own life. Of the power and wisdom you have collected. Think of goals you've accomplished. Think of all your successes over the years, of everything you've done right.

extended long pause—1 minute

Each success has brought with it a certain amount of inner strength, of confidence. Sometimes we overlook our successes and focus only on our failures. By doing so, we disservice ourselves. Most inventors will tell you that for every success they had a hundred . . . a thousand . . . failures. Failure is simply part of the process and should we not achieve our desired results, we simply dust ourselves off and try again. We must keep striving, keep moving forward.

Now lay down and rest with your back against the tree. Close your eyes and take three deep breaths.

long pause

As you rest, a snuffling catches your attention. Open your eyes. A large tiger stands over you, with a wild, fearful look. You sense that the cat has a secret wound, that it is hurting. The tiger looks at you with suspicion, and you begin to worry, for it far out-weighs you.

"I will eat you up," the tiger says. As you warily sit up, you think you recognize a spark, a look in the creature's eyes.

"I will destroy you," it says, and the voice sounds oddly familiar.

Once again the tiger speaks. "I will never allow you to succeed because you risk the chance of failure." With that statement, you begin to understand.

The spark in the tiger's eyes is the spark that you sense from your own inner demons, from the low self-esteem and self-doubts that can plague each and every one of us.

The tiger's voice is your own internal censor, berating you, ignoring your successes and rubbing your nose in your failures.

The tiger's words are those of your fears and worries—the plague of guilt and shame that we carry around in our secret hearts. Terrified that we cannot control or rise above these emotions, we repress and bury them, but they come back to stalk us.

The tiger's wounds are your own, wrought from years of self-doubt, from years of focusing on failure rather than success; from secret embarrassments and shames brought about by our guilt-producing culture. Rather than heal the source of the problem, you have covered these wounds with a veil of gauze, thinking that if you pretend they aren't there, perhaps the pain will go away. But underneath those makeshift bandages, the wounds have festered. Now, when your life is on an upswing, they interfere with your abilities to fully enjoy and trust your results.

long pause

Brute force will not win out here. To tame your inner demons, you must use your will, self-confidence, and the esteem that comes from knowing you have succeeded many times and that you will continue to succeed.

Look at the tiger now, see the fear and doubt and worry that inhabits its heart—your heart. Have empathy for the beautiful cat, for the tiger threatens you out of fear, not malice. What can you say to ease its fear? To heal its pain? What can you say to help it understand that these emotions are simply feelings and nothing more? That you are willing to rise beyond those fears? That you have succeeded before and can do so again?

Think about what you want to say to the tiger, and then, with the generosity that comes from a happy, productive lifestyle, explain why the tiger need not fear your efforts to succeed, why you should be friends rather than enemies. Believe in what you say, for in your heart you hear your own truth.

extended long pause—2 minutes

The tiger pauses to consider your words. As you watch, you realize that we are seldom kind to these frightened aspects of ourselves.

We often berate them, ignore them when we can. We repress our fears and try to whip them into submission. The tiger within needs nurturing to be able to grow beyond fear and shine with true strength.

As the creature thinks over your words, reach out and gently stroke the soft, supple fur. Tell it that you care, that you will try to gently help it over the fears that rise with new situations. Offer your comfort and watch how quickly the tiger turns into a playful kitten, begging for attention, lapping up the care and self-love you offer. Each stroke heals a portion of the pain.

extended long pause—1 minute

The tiger seems happy now and you can fully sense the connection between yourself and the cat. You know that you still have your fears and reservations, but your inner beast no longer tries to control you, to stop you from enjoying your successes. When you revel in your accomplishments, without becoming arrogant about them, then the fearful part of your heart will take a step toward the sun, a step toward joy and peace.

long pause

Rather than stalking you, the tiger asks if it may walk by your side. No longer a threat to your sense of well-being, you can see what a strong ally this creature can be. The tiger will warn you if a true danger does arise, it can protect you from being too vulnerable to others who may not have your best interests at heart.

Far from just carrying your fears for you, once you have cleared out the inner demons and healed the wild beast within, the tiger offers you the ability to discriminate between right and wrong, between safe and dangerous. It represents your sense of self-preservation and healing.

long pause

You gather up your things and, together with the tiger, once more begin the ascent up the slope.

You meet fewer people along this part of the trail—not all have the strength and perseverance to hike this high. The ground is rougher, the trees fewer, but you find the going a challenge rather than a problem. You have the endurance to complete the climb, the will to push ahead.

The tiger keeps pace with you, occasionally warning you of an unstable rock or hole in which you might trip. You begin to discuss your fears together and the answers to some of your worries are easier than you might have thought. Think about a problem you've been avoiding and ask the tiger what it might suggest. Listen for the answer, for your inner self often knows what you need to do to overcome difficulties.

extended long pause—1 minute

By noon, you have reached the end of the path. Both you and the tiger are panting, but the exertion sparks off a sense of inner strength that makes you feel like you could conquer the world.

The view from this point overlooks the town. In fact, from this plateau, you can see the faint outline of the roof of your house. You are tied to your roots, but you are also becoming aware that your journey is not yet finished. There is more to come.

As you stand here, you begin to realize that you have spent so much of your recent time in pursuit of goals for yourself and your family that you have lost sight of a certain sense of individuality—a sense of solitude that you need in order to balance out your energy.

long pause

Perhaps you have need of a retreat, of a time in which you can balance your inner and outer lives—your spirit and your body—your thoughts and your actions. As you are pondering this possibility, you notice that yet another twenty feet up the slope, shadowed against the mountain, lies the opening to a cave.

Cautiously picking your way around the loose rock, you climb up the face of the peak. The tiger follows behind, encouraging you on while still maintaining a certain amount of reservation about the whole idea. After all, you are off the path, no one knows you are here and if you slip, you could easily fall and hurt yourself.

A shower of pebbles from beneath your feet sends you sliding about five feet down the granite face. With scraped knees, and fingers bloody from grabbing hold of the rocks protruding from the slope, you grit your teeth, determined to reach the cave.

long pause

The tiger clears its throat and starts to say, "Are you sure you want to do this? You might get hurt—"

Once again, you feel the fear creeping. You have the opportunity to thank the tiger for the warning, but also to reassure it that you want to continue toward your goal and that you would appreciate support. Speak to your inner self. You know you have the ability to complete the climb, so calm your doubts and fears.

long pause

The tiger relents and surprises you when it even goes so far as to help push from behind. With a surge of energy, you both go tumbling up to the ledge next to the cave. Congratulate yourself, you have succeeded once again—you have climbed the mountain peak. From here, the view is so panoramic that you feel you can see forever.

After a few moments, turn to the cavern and peer inside. No light enters the shaft and you can see no further than the threshold.

long pause

Through the darkness, a silent call beckons you. You know that you must enter the cavern, must search out the hidden secrets that lay in wait for you.

The tiger says, "I cannot join you. This act needs to be done without fear, without doubt. Your path leads next to a vision quest and within that quest lies no room for hesitation. Give yourself over to whatever waits within. But I will guard the entrance and I will be here when you return."

long pause

As you stand by the cavern, you know that the next step in your journey will lead you over the threshold, into the unknown. It is too late in the day to continue your quest, and so you cuddle on the ledge with the tiger, warm against the thick fur, until the morning.

Now, listen to my voice as I count from ten to one. You will awake refreshed and alert. Ten . . . nine . . . you are becoming awake and aware of your surroundings . . . eight . . . seven . . . six . . . hear the sounds around you . . . five . . . four . . . you will be fully alert and refreshed . . . three . . . two . . . one . . . take three deep breaths and when you are ready, you may open your eyes.

Suggested Exercises

1. Make a list of all your successes. Each time you are tempted to qualify them, or to list a failure, stop yourself. You are to focus solely on what you have done right in your life. Keep this list where you can see it and whenever you have accomplished another goal, add it to the list.

2. Make a second list of all the things you've wanted to do but were afraid you couldn't, or were afraid that you would fail. Examine the list carefully while asking yourself these questions: Are my fears justified? Do I not have the necessary skills to attempt my goals, or is my fear based on insubstantial evidence? Sometimes we may not have the physical capability to perform some deed or act—if you can't swim then it would be foolhardy to attempt a scuba dive. But more often than not, our fears are based on looking stupid—I can't dance because I'm too fat; I can't paint because I've never had training.

3. If, after honestly examining your list, you want to try something but your fear still holds you back, ask yourself if you can try in private, with no one else there to see whether or not you succeed. And remember—failure is a relative term. Anytime you attempt a new activity, you've already achieved a form of success. True failure occurs when you quit trying.

4. Note the successes of your friends and congratulate them. We build our own sense of worth when we truly revel in others' success, for we have made the world a brighter place in which to live.

5. If you have trouble seeing anything you do as a success, turn to close, loyal friends for help. Tell them that you can't seem to see what you are doing right and ask them to help you write your list. More often than not, you'll be surprised to find how much other people notice your talents. In our culture, we aren't encouraged to focus on our strengths, we're taught to be humble, to wear a false sense of modesty. As a result, we often have a hard time pinpointing our talents.

6. Remember, the world tends to see you as you see yourself. The energy you project to others will be reflected back on you. If you see yourself as worthless, as a no-talent failure, then you will project that image to others and they will treat you with disdain. If you see yourself as self-confident, as someone with talent who is equally happy to recognize the skills and talents of others, you will be treated the same in return.

7. Envy often masks inadequacy. If you are envious of a friend's success, then perhaps you need to take a long look at yourself and see where your self-esteem needs shoring up. Sometimes we may also feel that others reach success with far less effort than we are putting out. Luck does play in a hand in our lives and by accepting that as part of life, we go a long ways toward easing our sense of bitterness and envy.

He went back through the Wet Wild Woods, waving his wild tail, and walking by his wild lone. But he never told anybody.

—Rudyard Kipling (1865–1936)
The Cat That Walked By Himself

The Hermit
The Lonely Road

The tenth card of the major arcana is known as the Hermit. It is most often assigned the number 9.

The Hermit and His Energy

The Hermit represents our inner solitude, our retreat into ourselves to balance spirituality with daily life. We go alone, into our private worlds, and if any should desire to go with us, they keep up as best they can. Often, at this point, we do not realize that we bear a lantern that attracts others—we have come to a point of wisdom that other people are still seeking.

Without realizing, we have become the trailblazer, the path-forger. The difference between our position and that of the Hierophant lies in the fact we do not seek to teach others. We are on an internal quest, a retreat for meditation and contemplation.

We've come to this space hoping for solitude and peace, we explore the darker, as-yet unknown parts of ourselves on a journey that can only be made alone.

After recognizing our personal strength, after taming our fears, we now understand that the next step of our journey requires that we use the courage and power we've developed to look at ourselves clearly, to examine our lives and make decisions based on both the darker and lighter parts of our souls.

We are in a transitional state, happy with our lives yet once again seeking. We open ourselves to be a conduit between the gods and the world of mortals, in hopes that we might learn more about the totality of existence. But by opening ourselves to the energy of the cosmos, we make ourselves vulnerable. Using our strength, we become weak. Using our weakness, we become strong.

The archetype presented by the the Hermit card leads us into a period of introspection, a time when we need space and peace. We look into the mirror and see not ourselves looking back, but a brief glimpse of the gods.

In our daily lives, the archetype of the Hermit can appear as a person. In this case, he might show up as a spiritual guru who sets us searching. He might sweep into our lives in the form of a metaphysical or philosophical book or television program that, once viewed, sparks off the restless need to journey within.

The Hermit might take the form of an event sparking a shift of attention to our priorities. He might come in the form of a mystical experience that turns our world-view inside out.

In my own life the Hermit has appeared, in various cycles, as a teacher who told me to question my beliefs and if they didn't hold up, throw them out; She slammed into my soul as the Earth Goddess, demanding that I remember who I am and what my spirituality entails; She arrived as Mielikki, the goddess I pledged to in 1992, claiming me for Her Priestess. The Hermit returned in a near-death experience in 1993, forcing me to examine my priorities relating to my writing and how important it is to me.

The Hermit becomes more than a feeling—it becomes a search through our souls to align the mystical side of our natures with the practical necessities of our everyday lives. We choose, through the Hermit, that which is truth for ourselves. We carry our lanterns to illuminate our search, and others sometimes believe we are inviting them for the ride.

While we cannot deny them passage, neither can we ease their way. Instead, we go about our journey and if they can keep up, they may find some answers in our wake.

The Spiritual Concept

In terms of spirituality, the Hermit becomes the element of mystical seclusion. The Hermit represents a solitary path, one that must be journeyed alone. When we enter into the Hermit's cave, we commit ourselves to the search—there is no going back. We are forever changed.

We can liken the archetype of the Hermit to the goddess Nephthys, Egyptian lady of dreams and hidden knowledge. She is also found in Demeter, searching for Persephone, who awakens the Spring and sheds light on winter's darkness.

The Hermit is embodied within Odin, on His solitary wanderings through Midgard; Adonis, the dying god who personifies solitude and sacrifice. We also find the Hermit in the form of Mithra, Persian god of the light who precedes the dawn.

The astrological sign of Virgo is connected to the Hermit, and we place the The Hermit within the Wheel of the Year at Samhain, alongside the card of Death. The Hermit represents internal transition, which always must precede the external transformations personified by the Death card.

The Card

Some common representations of the the Hermit include an elderly man wearing a cloak who carries a lantern. He is sometimes presented as an aboriginal shaman.

Guidelines for Use

In our ongoing journey through the major arcana, this should follow the meditation on Strength. You may also meditate on the Hermit during Samhain, or any time when you need to assess your spiritual path, when you feel the need for divine guidance.

Flowers:	myrrh, sage, gum mastic, sandalwood
Incense:	myrrh, sandalwood, sage, cedar
Oils:	cypress, benzoin, wisteria, chamomile
Crystals:	clear quartz, lapis lazuli, diamond
Candles:	white, indigo, purple

Meditation

Relax and get comfortable. Close your eyes and take three deep breaths.

long pause

You wake early in the morning, with dawn still a hint, a whisper against the eastern horizon. You slept the night on a ledge, next to the opening of a cave into which you are determined to journey.

At your feet sleeps the tiger with whom you traveled. A light flutter of breath tickles the cat's whiskers and you hear the wheezing of a faint snore. You gently stretch, quiet so you won't wake the sleeping cat, and then, with a quick stroke of its fur, you slip into the darkness.

long pause

The blackness swiftly descends around you, and you find it thick, palpable. Beneath your feet, the floor to the cavern feels firm, covered with a thin coating of sand. From somewhere, far ahead, you hear the faint sound of siren-song, a call so melodic, so beautiful, that you must answer. Cautiously, using only your inner senses to guide you, begin your journey through the darkness.

At first your steps are hesitant, cautious, like a child learning to walk. But as you continue, hands raised to guide you should you bump into a wall, you lose some of the hesitation, your stride becomes more natural, your steps decisive.

long pause

It seems as if you've been walking for hours when a gust of wind rushes by and brings with it the smell of moss and mold, a faint whiff of bonfire smoke. A chill passes over your shoulders and goose bumps rise along your arms and you suddenly understand the expression, "a goose just walked over my grave."

Occasionally your hands brush against the cavern walls, and the rock feels cool, almost wet beneath your fingers. As you use the wall for support and guidance, some insect, multilegged, races over your fingers and is gone before you can react.

long pause

The darkness seems impenetrable; you would think by now your eyes would adjust, but you can see no more than when you first entered the cave, and you have lost all sense of bearing. Your only clue as to direction is that the path seems to be sloping down, a gradual decline as you continue on your journey.

long pause

Now you hear a distant whispering, no more a siren-song, the rush of many voices left breathless by time. They converge in waves, riding the wind, one atop another until you can no longer make out individual words, just an incessant chatter.

long pause

You are descending rapidly now, more and more you have to use the cavern wall for balance. Once your foot slips on a loose rock and you nearly go tumbling to the ground, but then you catch yourself and continue along the path.

You begin to wonder just what you've gotten yourself into—you have no lantern, no food and water, your pack is next to the sleeping tiger. A hint of worry creeps into your thoughts and what started out a jaunt seems less and less a good idea.

long pause

And then, just as you are wondering how to return to the ledge, you notice a faint light in the distance. It stands out like a beacon and the light is so welcome that you find yourself hurrying toward it, not caring from what source it springs.

The slope is treacherous here and you slip and slide your way down the last stretch until you are standing level again, no more than twenty feet from the light source.

From where you now stand, you can see that the light is emanating from the center of a fountain carved out of stone. The water sprays with crystalline purity, lovely colors, all the rainbow. Within the fountain, you see creatures swimming, faerie spirits and animal spirits, spirits of the past and elemental spirits, all bathing in the tinted water.

long pause

Go over to the fountain and sit on the edge, watching the spirits at play. They seem familiar to you. In fact, you feel at kin with them, at home with their energy.

As you sit there, one of the spirits swims over to you and pulls itself out of the water. It will be your guide in this place. It carries a flat, broad mirror. Look closely at the spirit? Is it animal? Faerie? Human?

long pause

"Welcome," your guide says. "Welcome to the land of spirit. To understand this place, you must look into the mirror and listen to my voice."

It hands you the mirror and as you take hold of the beveled glass, you feel a longing deep inside, a desire to belong to this world for you can feel the strength and power inherent to this place rising around you.

Take the mirror and look into the glass. See yourself reflected in the light of the fountain. See yourself as you are in the daily world, not as you hope to be, not as you were, but as you are now. Do not judge, do not berate yourself, simply observe.

long pause

The image begins to change. Within the looking glass you see the dark part of your-self—perhaps represented as an animal or other entity, perhaps simply your image, but it contains your dark thoughts, your anger and envy, all of those feelings that you often try to repress.

Again, do not judge, simply observe. Understand that this part of yourself also holds your assertive drive, your competitive spirit. You would be a weak and indecisive person if you refused to accept this side of yourself. Look and see all the facets of what you might fear, of what you might strive to deny. To accept yourself as a whole person, you must accept how important this side of yourself is.

extended long pause—1 minute

Now the image ripples and changes once more, and you see the lighter side of your-self, the happy and joyful aspects of your nature. Within this facet of yourself, you find your compassion, kindness, and goodwill. But see that assertiveness is lacking, the drive that propels you to succeed exists within your darker side. Within this peace, you are content to just be, and within that contentedness, stagnation is often born.

Watch, but do not judge, this part of your spirit. Understand that it, too, is necessary for a holistic existence.

extended long pause—1 minute

Take three deep breaths.

long pause

As the image fades from the mirror, you hear a soft whisper in your ear. "Look into the mirror once again. See both the dark and the light sides of yourself and watch as they merge, blending into a balanced and centered individual. What color is your soul? What color is your spirit? Are you a rainbow, a kaleidoscope? Or is the color of your spirit a bright green? A brilliant purple? Look deep at the colors of your soul."

long pause

Within the mirror, you now see your most sacred of spaces. Within this place you are safe and protected. Here you find no danger of losing yourself, here you listen to your soul and know that you are hearing the truth as it is for you. You see a safe haven to which you may return any time you are feeling threatened.

Perhaps a grove deep in the forest; perhaps a meditation room . . . your sacred space might be an island, or a lake or riverside where Divine Energy resides. Perhaps you see yourself in the arms of the Goddess, or perhaps it is simply a comfortable chair within a cozy room. Look carefully and see what your inner sacred space looks like.

extended long pause—2 minutes

"Now close your eyes," your guide says. "Envision your sacred space again."

When you open your eyes you find yourself sitting, not in the cavern, but in the center of your sacred space. You may put down the mirror now and explore. Take your time to familiarize yourself with the terrain, with the furnishings or plant life or whatever is here. Listen, touch, smell . . . take a few moments to blend your energy with the energy of your sacred space.

extended long pause—2 minutes

You once again find yourself back in the cavern. Your guide hands you the mirror again. "Take this and carry it with you always."

As you hold the mirror, it begins to change shape, slowly transforming into a lantern. Within the lantern glows the colors of your spirit. Know that the only way you can ever lose this lantern is to lose track of it or forget where you put it. No one can ever take the lantern away from you.

long pause

"Anytime you have need," the spirit says, "you may return to your sacred space; it will be waiting, inviolate and sacrosanct. Simply sink into a quiet state and ask that you be in your sacred space. You will find your spirit there."

Now, it is time to return to the surface. Your guide shows you the path and the spirits wave as you begin to ascend the steep slope. With your lantern in hand, you find the cavern a much more congenial place, and the hike actually quite pleasant.

You soon reach the opening of the cavern. Your tiger is waiting for you, and as you hold the lantern up, you seem to be able to see the world more clearly.

long pause

The tiger noses the lantern. "I am part of your soul, too, you know," the cat says. "Now it is time for you to fully accept me into your heart. To accept that, although I belong to the dark side of yourself, I am not your enemy."

Embrace the tiger, for by now it has become a good friend. Feel its fur on your face, feel its strength shoring you up. The fear and pain it shoulders can wear you down, but only if you allow the feelings to fester, only if you deny their existence. When you accept your fears, then act to resolve them, they become strengths.

As you embrace the tiger, it begins to fade, turning into a vaporous spirit that flows into the lights of your lantern. As it blends with the colors of your soul, feel its strength and power flow into your body, flow into your will, and know that you have integrated an important part of yourself.

long pause

Now pick up your lantern and begin your journey back down the hillside. You feel lighter, happier than before. When first you journeyed up the path, you felt strong in yourself and confident in the outer world. Now you have recovered your inner self and so you are balanced, both spiritually and materially.

long pause

As you reach the picnic area again, notice that some of the hikers carry their own lanterns, you can spot them easily now. They are sure in their own path without forcing their views on others and the colors of their souls shine forth.

Still others have yet to find their balance and you discover, as you meander back to your vehicle, that you have developed a small following. These people seem to sense your surety; they are drawn to your light.

While you had no intention of leading the way, you realize that, in your wake, they might find the truths for themselves.

You must be cautious, however, that you do not allow them to drain your energy or to ask more than you can comfortably give. You are not prepared yet to take on the job of the Hierophant, perhaps you will never be summoned to that calling. So hold your lantern high and know that you are lighting your own way now—free from relying on others' energies.

Now, listen to my voice as I count from ten to one. You will awake refreshed and alert. Ten . . . nine . . . you are becoming awake and aware of your surroundings . . . eight . . . seven . . . six . . . hear the sounds around you . . . five . . . four . . . you will be fully alert and refreshed . . . three . . . two . . . one . . . take three deep breaths and when you are ready, you may open your eyes.

Suggested Exercises

1. Create your own sacred space in a private corner of your home. Place here all that you need to feel centered and balanced—perhaps crystals, incense, statues, a warm blanket, a favorite book or CD—only you can know what represents the sacred to you and only you can create a space that truly feels safe and secure.

2. Remember, there is a difference between honing your own sense of self and trying to lead others. Some people are natural born leaders, but they know how to help others find their own truths. You are not leading if you are telling another person exactly what to do for their spirit—it is a solitary journey and you can guide someone to their truths, but you cannot bestow the truth on another.

3. *The Thunder, Perfect Mind* is a poem that was found among the Gnostic texts discovered in 1945, near the Egyptian town of Nag Hammadi. *The Elemental Tarot* uses this poem to illustrate the energy of the major arcana. For the Hermit card, Caroline Smith and John Astrop assigned these lines from the poem: "In my weakness do not forsake me/do not be afraid of my power."

   These lines illustrate the duality of the spirit, the need for both light and dark, both strength and weakness. Meditate on this couplet and then look at yourself—what are your strengths? What are your weaknesses? How do they complement one another? Can you accept both as integral to your psyche? No one can be a Superman or Superwoman. We must do our best, then accept the limits that we cannot push beyond.

4. Plan a solitary outing to one of your favorite places. Take a lunch, a notebook or sketchbook—whatever you need and let yourself flow into your solitude. Focus on your thoughts, your needs, your connection with the world around you. Too often we get caught up in always needing to be with family, with friends, with your partner. Take some time to reacquaint with yourself.

Fate keeps on happening.

> —Anita Loos (1893–1981)
> *Gentlemen Prefer Blondes*

The Wheel

Visiting Lady Luck

The eleventh card of the major arcana is known as the Wheel (also the Wheel of Fortune). It is assigned the number 10.

The Wheel and Its Energy

The Wheel represents destiny, luck, fortune—all the forces beyond our control. There comes a point in life where we have done everything we can to ensure success and at that point, we have to let go and hope that the Universe smiles on us. We have ventured into the journey, deciphered our path in life, honed the necessary skills, applied them, sought out our inner light so that we are not focused solely on the material world . . . the next move belongs to the Universe, to destiny.

Everyone, at some time, has wished they could control everything happening in their lives. We all feel the need for things to go just right. It's natural to desire that our small successes will magnify and return multifold.

Once we have done everything we can, then we have the opportunity to call on the Universe, to ask for a boost of energy. Sometimes that boost takes a long time in coming, and if you haven't done your work in the first place, it may never come at all.

Other times, the shift takes on a dimension you never expected—the Universe kicks in like a dark horse and we stand there, thrilled by what happens, but rather confused by how it came about.

Still other times we do the work, we strengthen ourselves, we generously help our neighbors and everything falls into place in the order we hoped it would.

We must remember that destiny and luck, while not the same thing, are related. Destiny, we have more control over. But if we resist the evolution of our soul, of our lives, we muck up the works and then our luck shoots out the window and runs away. When we resist the pathway set before us (and some believe we set this path before birth, others believe the path is set for us by Divine Guidance), we interfere with our growth and find the going uphill.

The archetype presented by the Wheel leads us into a period where the unexpected is the rule, where serendipity and synchronicity reign. Within this phase of our journey, we find that, if we have truly followed our path, life sends us what we need and often much, much more.

The Wheel is not a card of ill-fortune, but a card of prosperity, of abundance (both in spirit and body), and of serendipitous events. Once the Wheel begins to turn, then nothing we can do will stop it, unless we turn our backs on the abundance that pours into our lives.

When we refuse to acknowledge our good fortune, when we give no gratitude or thanks where due, then the Wheel grinds to a screeching halt and we find ourselves tossed off the path, into a briar patch. Bad luck and ill-fortune exist, of this there is no doubt. But it does not come into play with the energy of this card.

In our daily lives, the archetype of the Wheel can appear as a person bearing gifts, as a promotion at work, as the unexpected winnings of fortune and money. It can be the culmination of both hard work and being in the right place at the right time. The Wheel is that sudden *I understand!* that leads to new discoveries and the production of masterpieces.

The Wheel might turn in your life when you find something you've been wanting (once, at the beach, I was telling my husband that we really needed a camera and two minutes later I found one, sitting on a piece of driftwood. Three hours later, no one had come to claim it, so I accepted it as a gift from the Universe); it turns when you are walking into a shop and find yourself singled out as their one-millionth customer. Lottery and sweep-stakes winnings fall into this category as well.

Or you might hear the Wheel creaking when you meet someone on a bus, start talking about how you need a new job, and lo-and-behold, they own a business and are looking for a new computer programmer (or whatever you do).

An artist might find the Wheel in a patron who sponsors them for a year of work . . . a writer finds the Wheel in a publisher or an agent. A nurse turns the Wheel when she carefully tends to an old man because she knows he's having a hard time. When he dies, he leaves her a large inheritance because she was so kind to him.

The Wheel exists beyond our control, we cannot will it into action, but we can set if off by our actions. However, once it begins to turn, we cannot stop it, nor can we control the direction in which it is rolling.

The Spiritual Concept

In terms of spirituality, the Wheel becomes the element of chance, leading to a new step in our destiny.

We can liken the archetype of the Wheel to the goddess Fortuna, the Roman goddess of fortune. We also find the Wheel in Kuan Yin, Chinese goddess of compassion and luck, and in Lakshmi, Hindu goddess of luck and love.

The Wheel is embodied within Jupiter, Roman god of fortune and prosperity; Bes, the leopard-skin-clad dwarf of the Egyptians who guards over women and luck; and in Ganesha, the Hindu lord of obstacles, fortune, writers, and thieves.

Let us place the The Wheel of Fortune, within the Wheel of the Year, at Mabon, along-side the Empress, for the Wheel represents abundance, prosperity, and the harvest from actions sown earlier.

The Card

Common representations of the the Wheel include a Wheel, often embodying the zodiac, sometimes spoked and other times not. Often you will find the outer circle of the Wheel contains a crocodile, monkey, and a Sphinx.

The Wheel is associated with the planet Jupiter.

Guidelines for Use

In our ongoing journey through the major arcana, the Wheel should follow the meditation on the Hermit. You may meditate on the Wheel during Mabon, or at any time when you feel the need to draw fortune and prosperity into your life.

Flowers:	peony, shamrock, mandrake, nutmeg, ginseng
Incense:	jasmine, almond, spice, sandalwood
Oils:	jasmine, olive, almond, high john, poppy
Crystals:	carnelian, green calcite, peridot, gold
Candles:	purple, green, gold, pumpkin

Meditation

Relax and get comfortable. Close your eyes and take three deep breaths.

long pause

You are sitting in your bedroom, preparing for sleep. The day has been difficult and you are tired and wishing that you didn't have to go to work tomorrow. A whole slew of things went wrong today and your supervisor is counting on you to resolve the issues in question. To make matters worse, you are up for a promotion and whether or not you receive it depends on whether you can solve this crisis.

As you look out of the window, you see the stars shimmering across the sky. The sight comforts you, the vast panorama reminding you of how insignificant our problems are in the face of such immensity as the universe. Still, the tension has crept into your neck and back. If there was only a magickal spell you could cast, or potion you could drink to immediately solve all of your problems.

Suddenly, from the northern quarter of the sky, you see a meteor go streaking past. The brilliant trail flames across the night, illuminating your entire room. Make a wish as you follow the shooting star—that tomorrow be a better day, that your fortunes pick up, that Lady Luck should smile on you.

long pause

Then, as quickly as you spied the meteor, it vanishes into the darkness. As you close your eyes, drifting into sleep, you wonder if anybody heard your wish.

Take three deep breaths.

long pause

The morning light slides through your window as you wake up and at first you panic, the clock tells you that you've overslept, but then you hear the phone ring, next to your bed. It's one of your coworkers. Your place of business has unexpectedly closed for the day and you don't have to come into work. You barely hear the explanation—it doesn't matter. The point is that you have the day off. When you replace the receiver you find that you have benefited from the extra sleep. Stretch out—work out what few kinks remain in your back.

long pause

As you dress, you feel something cold under your toe. It's a penny. "See a penny, pick it up, all the day you'll have good luck. See a penny, leave it lie, fame and fortune pass you by." The children's song runs through your mind and so you pick up the penny and slip it into your pocket.

When you get to the kitchen, you are prepared to grab a piece of toast or a banana, but instead find that some member of your family has made a wonderful breakfast, consisting of all of your favorites. Whatever you want to eat is sitting on the table, at the perfect temperature, and since today is a vacation day for you, you have the time to savor your meal. Take a plate and fill it with an arrangement of your favorite foods.

long pause

The newspaper is lying next to your place at the table and, with a sigh, you pick it up, expecting to read more bad news. But to your surprise, you discover that the headline is good news—some of the best news you could reasonably hope for. Think for a moment, if one major issue facing the world were resolved in a positive manner, what would you hope it to be? What would you like to see for the resolution? Envision the story that you would read in the newspaper. How would you feel? Would it impact your personal life in any significant way?

long pause

After you finish your breakfast, you decide to take a long walk. Open the door—since the autumn hit, the weather has been highly changeable, warm and sunny one day, cold and frosty another. Today you find the weather to be just right for your personal comfort zone.

Some of your neighbors are out in their yards, others seem to be gone to work. As you walk along, you come to a side street that you don't remember seeing before. Perhaps you were too busy to notice it, perhaps you just overlooked it. The street leads down a tree-lined lane and you see what looks to be a park up ahead. Turn onto the side street and stroll down the road. There seem to be no cars here, so you can wander along without worrying about traffic. Enjoy the walk, the weather is perfect for you. The trees, huge old cedars and firs, offer shade from both rain and sun.

long pause

A few moments later you come to what is, indeed, a park. There are swings here, and huge wooden jungle gyms, picnic tables and grills, even a convenient restroom area with water fountains should you get thirsty.

Wander around the park, play on the swings or jungle gym if you wish—they are sturdy enough for any adult—and take a little time to enjoy yourself.

long pause

After a while, you see a food vendor in the corner of the park. You reach into your pocket for money and find your old wallet instead. You thought you had lost this wallet months ago, but here it is, filled with cash that you don't remember having. The bills are stuffed into the wallet, far more than you need to buy a hot dog or roasted chestnuts or whatever the vendor is selling. He tips his hat as you place your order and wishes you a good day.

The food smells great. A picnic table nearby offers you a place to sit while you eat and as you are wolfing down the delicious snack, you hear a noise. Someone is standing at the end of the table, asking if it's really you.

When you look closer, you see this person is an old friend—one you feared you'd lost touch with and would never see again. Think through your life. If you could meet one person from your past—one person who mattered to you, who either influenced you in a positive way, gave help when you needed it, was there for you during the hard times as well as the good—who would it be? What would you say to them? Take some time to tell this person what you've wanted to say over the months or years.

extended long pause—1 minute

Reunions are sometimes strained when two people haven't seen each other for years, but are there any friends that you've left dangling lately? Any friends whom you've been ignoring? What can you do to change that? Friends are like lifelines, we don't realize how much we need them until they are no longer part of our lives.

Now your friend has to go, but you promise to call each other soon. As they leave, you decide to finish an errand or two while you are out and about. You have something to pick up from a department store that's not too far away and so you finish your snack and, with a brisk stride, head toward the main road again.

The department store is one of those multipurpose stores, they have food and toys and clothes and books, they have just about anything you want. As you walk through the doors, an alarm sounds.

At first you wonder what you did wrong? Are the police going to whisk you away, do they think you're some criminal? But as these thoughts go racing through your mind, a shower of confetti rains down on your head, along with a multitude of balloons. A huge sign unfurls from the ceiling.

"Congratulations," it says. "To our one-millionth customer!"

Several cashiers and the manager race over to your side. Flashbulbs go off and you realize that not only the whole store is watching you, but you're going to be on the local evening news, too. Smile for the camera!

You are awarded two prizes for being in the right place at the right time. The first is your choice of any gift from the store. Think about it for a moment, if you were given one gift right now, what is it that you would most like to receive? Perhaps your tastes are simple—a new outfit, a new set of cookware. Or perhaps you could use a complete computer set-up or a new car. What could you best use and enjoy right now in your life?

long pause

The second prize consists of two tickets to any place in the world. You can go anywhere, and you will be given a nice place to stay while you are there. If you could travel to any country, any state, for two weeks, where would it be? Why that particular place? What would you do while you were there?

long pause

Take a look at these two desires. Is there anyway you can, at least partially, fulfill these wishes? Often we treat ourselves last, giving to everyone else first. Can you comfortably pamper yourself? Can you give yourself gifts? If you have the extra money for these things, what are your reasons for not treating yourself to what you want? Are your reasons legitimate or are they based on guilt?

If you don't have the extra money, is there anything you can do to pamper yourself at home? Extra time for sleep? A special candlelight dinner for you and your partner instead of eating in front of the television? Can you assign your children some of the chores you always do in order to have a little extra time to yourself?

extended long pause—1 minute

You finish your errands at the store and make arrangements for your prizes to be delivered to your home, then decide to go visit one of your friends and tell them the good news. Their office is near your own and as you are walking in that direction, the answers to your work place dilemma suddenly pop into mind! They were right there for you to see, but you were too wrapped up in the problem to envision them clearly.

When you became focused on something besides your troubles, you were distanced enough to see the resolution. Stop in at your work place. Though closed for the day, your supervisor is there and listens closely to what you have to say. They concur with your findings, and within less than an hour, the two of you have worked out a way to implement your solutions. By the end of next week, everything will be back on track, no doubt about it.

long pause

You will visit your friend later—it's too late in the afternoon to stop in where they work, and so you decide to go home and tell everyone about the incredible day you've had. As you are crossing the street, you hear the squeal of brakes. Before you can react, you find yourself slammed to the ground, out of the path of an out-of-control car. The person who saved you managed to avoid getting hit, too, but they are shaken. You realize what a close call you had, and you also realize that this stranger saved your life by putting their own life in danger.

What do you say to them? How do you feel, knowing that you came so close to death? Will this change your life in some way?

long pause

Sometimes, when fortune saves us from danger, we don't realize until later just how the incident affected us. Other times, we know right away just how lucky we are. Has anything like this ever happened to you? If so, how did you react? Was another person involved in saving your life? Or did events just play themselves out so that you were spared? If this happened a long time ago, do you feel that it still affects your life?

If you've never had this happened, how do you imagine it would affect you? What changes do you think you might make in your life, if any?

extended long pause—1 minute

By the time you open your front door, you are more than ready for the day to end. It has been fun, but you also realize that fortune and luck can take their toll on you—good luck can be tiring, as well as wonderful. Sit down in your favorite chair. Your gaze falls on an end table where you find two things waiting for you—a message and a box.

The message is from your supervisor, who called to let you know you got the promotion. Think about your career, if you could advance ahead right now, what would you like to see open up for you? How would that advancement change your life? Would it bring you more money? More responsibility? Remember, any time you are given more to work with, greater results are usually expected. Think about the promotion or changes you would like to see in your career and ask yourself what your next step is toward achieving that goal.

extended long pause—1 minute

When you open the box you find a gift from your family to congratulate you. You find a beautiful charm carved from white and black onyx, a yin-yang symbol set in filigreed silver.

As you pick up the charm, something shifts. You are holding the black half of the charm. You sense that your day of fortune has moved on. Nothing will be the same as before—some momentous changes happened today. But fortune is a fleeting visitor.

We must take advantage of it while it showers blessings into our lives. If we let opportunities go by without notice, if we vacillate on our decisions, we often lose the chance to make any change at all.

Now, listen to my voice as I count from ten to one. You will awake refreshed and alert. Ten . . . nine . . . you are becoming awake and aware of your surroundings . . . eight . . . seven . . . six . . . hear the sounds around you . . . five . . . four . . . you will be fully alert and refreshed . . . three . . . two . . . one . . . take three deep breaths and when you are ready, you may open your eyes.

Suggested Exercises

1. Research all the different ways people use to call good fortune and luck to them—it's a fascinating study. Do you have any special charms or rituals to encourage luck to shine down in your life?

2. Good fortune often follows our directed focus. If we set the odds in our favor, fortune has an easier line to follow. If we buck the odds, then the path is tortuous. But remember, bucking the odds doesn't mean simply trying to achieve something difficult. If we have real talent for singing, acting, or writing, then the odds are not so bad should we aspire to a stage, recording, or publishing career. If we want to climb Mt. Everest and are out of shape, have asthma, and are afraid of heights, then we aren't doing much to help Lady Luck enter our lives.

3. Think about the times that the Universe has burped and landed a spot of good luck in your lap. Make a list of all the truly unexpected, wonderful things that have happened to you and keep it near for times when it seems like nothing is going right. Use it to remind yourself that yes, good things do happen in your life.

4. There exists a state of mind that I like to call surfing on the crest of the Universe. When we get into this state, it is easier to keep a streak of good fortune running. Hard to attain, harder yet to keep in motion, the consciousness required to achieve this states asks us to focus on every wonderful thing that happens to us through the

days and put all of the resulting excitement and joy toward our goals. I find this beneficial when I'm near to achieving a major goal and I need that last rush of energy to push it through—that last ounce of creative force required to manifest it. Usually I will achieve this state about two or three times a year. I can keep the energy running for about one or two weeks and during those brief periods, I find that amazing things happen in my life.

5. Generosity seems to attract good fortune. Try helping out where you can—out of your own desire to see others prosper—and you might be surprised by the rewards, both tangible and intangible, that you receive in return.

Part Three

Surrender to Fate:
The Search for Deconstruction

Justice is truth in action.

—Benjamin Disraeli (1804–1881)
House of Commons 2.11.1851

Justice

Balancing Act

The twelfth card of the major arcana is known as Justice. It is assigned the number 11.

Justice and Her Energy

First and foremost, Justice represents balance. What we resolved during our encounters with the Hierophant (intellectual work), with the Lovers (emotional work), with the Chariot (physical work), and with the Strength Card (spiritual work) we now balance within ourselves to create a holistic and centered state of existence.

Like the Librian scales, the scales of Justice balance precariously—a state achieved only through hard work and one that is difficult to keep.

The second major influence of Lady Justice forces us to examine our lives for miscarriages of action that disturb the natural harmony. Have we treated others fairly? Do our actions match our words? Do we honor our commitments? Are we looking at the world with eyes open, seeing things as they really are and not as we would like them to be?

The Justice card represents our ability to obey laws of behavior, to conduct ourselves according to the written and unwritten codes of society. This archetype is one of discipline, we come to it full of our lives because of the positive spin the Wheel has given us; but Justice, in no uncertain terms, puts us back to work. Since our lives have taken on an added growth and dimension, once again we are reminded (as we were with the Emperor) that strength, power and material fortune represent a certain level of responsibility.

The archetype of Justice includes the elements of self-discipline and control. We become bound in rules and regulations, we face the court, whether it be an actual courtroom or the judgment of our peers, and are held accountable for our actions. If we embrace honesty and truth, if we abide by the rules at this time, then we make progress in our journey. If we act underhandedly, lie, cheat, and break our vows, then our journey gets tangled in the mire.

During this phase of our journey, we find a certain harmony and beauty in the order that belongs to the archetype of Justice. Like a minimalist painting, or a room decorated in sparse whites, we find austerity refreshing.

This card also reminds us that Justice and her accompanying laws can be misused. For while the laws are built to protect the majority, often they ignore individual needs. If we are not careful, we might find that we trample our friends and our coworkers who play by different rules. We may judge them according to our beliefs, while forgetting that unwritten laws aren't formalized for a good reason—they cannot be applied equally to all.

The period ruled by Justice tends to be a restrained time. Within this phase of our journey, we become enmeshed in our own rules and beliefs, we advance through them and yet bind ourselves by their use. We blindfold ourselves to those people and events not existing within our sphere of existence; we limit ourselves to our own worlds. During the days of Justice, we tend to focus on our personal belief systems and, while we do not dismiss others as invalid, we tend to overlook or ignore that which does not comfortably fit into our reality.

During this time we may be unduly tied up with legalities, too, and legal matters of all kinds are indicated by this card.

In our daily lives, Justice can appear as a person whose approval we desperately want. She might be our supervisor or clergy or a mentor, someone to whom we hope to appear in our best light.

Justice may come into our lives as a tangible, visible reminder of the truth. She forces us to acknowledge hidden situations. If we have a secret child from a previous relationship, that child might show up on our doorsteps at this time. A criminal record we've been deliberately hiding—well, Justice will ferret it out for all to see. She is the lifter of secrecy, the opener of eyes.

Justice might appear in your life as an authority figure who inspires, who shows what a little self-discipline can do for our lives. She is the teacher who, while tough and demanding, turns our lives around. He is the mentor who inspires us to work long hours. Justice might be a political figure in whose campaign we become swept up; a magickal teacher who demands we study our arts if we are to learn from her, or a music teacher who convinces us that our talent is worth the will and discipline of daily practice.

We find Justice when we look at our lives and realize that, as wonderful as things have been going, we need a new lease on our work, a new discipline in our health, or we are in danger of growing lazy.

Justice exists as control within ourselves, and control by vote of the majority. During this period of time, we will have strong opinions as to right and wrong, and our judgmental nature will be at its highest.

The Spiritual Concept

In terms of spirituality, Justice becomes the element of cause and effect, leading to an understanding of how karma works in our universe.

We can best liken the archetype of Justice to the goddess Ma'at, the Egyptian goddess of justice, truth, and divine order. We also find her in Athena, Greek goddess who balanced wisdom and battle. She is embodied by the goddesses of sovereignty, whose blessings and rituals gave truth and legitimacy to the King of the Land, personified by the stories surrounding King Arthur and his court (especially during the pre-Christian origins of the Arthur-Merlin-Lady of the Lake myth cycles).

Justice is found within Tyr, Teutonic god of truth and law, who, like Athena, later added the dimension of battle to His sphere. We also see Justice in Yama, Hindu god of the dead who judges souls, and Vulcan, Roman god of the forge, also seen as a god of judgment.

Justice represents the astrological sign of Libra, and we place Justice, within the Wheel of the Year, at Ostara, alongside the Fool, for Justice represents a new beginning within the cycle, one of fresh insight, determination, and zeal of both action and belief.

The Card

Some common representations of Justice include a blindfolded woman holding a sword (the Ace of Swords) point down, between her hands. The balance scales are prominent on the card. The feather of Ma'at can usually be found on one side of the scales, with a weight on the other. Often the all-seeing eye of Horus (originally belonging to Ra) is found in the background. Ma'at was the only member of the Egyptian divinity allowed to use both of Ra's eyes. We also find representations of wisdom such as the owl or eagle.

Guidelines for Use

In our ongoing journey through the major arcana, this meditation should follow that of the Wheel. You may meditate on Justice during Ostara, or any time when you feel a need to draw clarity and truth into your life.

Flowers:	maple, holly, mistletoe, bay, aloe
Incense:	sage, carnation, copal, cedar
Oils:	rosemary, clove, carnation, frankincense
Crystals:	emerald, quartz crystal, turquoise
Candles:	blue, white, sea green

Meditation

Relax and get comfortable. Close your eyes and take three deep breaths.

long pause

You find yourself standing next to your bed. When you look down at the mattress, you see your body lying comfortably under the covers. As you watch, your chest rises and falls evenly, and you realize that you have projected astrally out of your sleeping self.

As you stand there, wondering what to do next, you hear your name riding along the etheric wind. Someone is calling you and the summons cannot be ignored. Step over to the wall and cross through the wood and plaster until you are outside, under the night sky.

long pause

You hear your name again, and find it easy to take flight, soaring up into the sky. You rise through the air, past the roof, past the trees, past the power lines. Into the darkened night you rise, higher and higher, floating easily on the updrafts.

long pause

The stars are shimmering overhead, they stretch across the horizon, dappling the night. You see the cloudy veil of the Milky Way as you continue to rise, misty wisps of galaxy trailing through the heavens. A slow sense of timelessness, of eternity, begins to permeate your soul.

As you float in the ether, a beam of golden light shines across the sky and you hear your name again. Turn in the direction of the golden light and follow its path.

long pause

As you enter the light, you find yourself propelled along, as if you were being sucked into the core of the gilded beams. Then, quickly, before you can stop yourself, you go sliding into the center of the light and through it.

The brilliant beams blind you with their intensity. Then, quite abruptly, the light disappears and you find yourself standing in the dimly lit opening of a long tunnel. A wind flutters by and your clothes go flying with it. You are left naked.

Again, you hear your name echoing up the tunnel, and you have to follow the call.

long pause

The walls and floor of the hollowed cavern are warm and dry, you see no sign of plant or animal life. As you continue through the shaft, your feet scatter sand that must have been here a thousand years.

The light remains constant; it must have some internal, natural origin. The walls glow a faint terra cotta, the dirt and compacted rock ruddy and clay-like in consistency.

long pause

The going is easy, for you are on a decline. As you pass through a particularly low-ceilinged passage, you come face to face with a woman dressed in a white sheath. She stands next to a bathtub of scented, soapy water.

"Welcome, traveler, on your journey to the truth of your soul and your life," she says. "Before you can pass through my gate, you must first cleanse your outer body, your *khat*. Please, bathe in my waters and be cleansed."

The bathtub is large and roomy, and as you sink into the warm suds, the scent of lotus blossoms envelopes you. Feel the bubbles dislodge any sand or grit that may have clung to your body, and let it float away, along with any physical tensions that have accumulated in your body.

long pause

When you are clean, step out of the tub. The woman gives you a towel with which to dry yourself, then allows you to pass through her gate, further into the tunnel.

After a while, you round a bend in the corridor. Now, you are confronted by a dark-skinned man wearing a white linen kilt. He is bald and carries a smoldering censor.

"Welcome, traveler, on your journey to the truth of your soul and your life," he says. "Before you can pass through my gate, you must cleanse your shadow self, your *khaibit*. Allow me to smudge you with sacred smoke."

Stand, with arms and legs spread, as he waves smoke around your body. You can feel the smoke eat through any negativity surrounding your aura, breaking up shadows that might be clouding your space. The scent of copal hangs heavy in the air. Then, a high, thin wind comes rushing through to blow the smoke and shadows away.

long pause

The man smiles and allows you to pass through his gate.

You continue along the corridor, feeling clean and light, and as you round another curve, you meet a woman dressed in a golden girdle and a white skirt. She is bare-breasted, and her hair is shrouded by a long white cloth, kept in place with gold and turquoise beads. She holds out a basket.

"Welcome, traveler, on your journey to the truth of your soul and your life. Before you can pass through my gate, you must prepare yourself."

Inside the basket you find a robe of white linen, with a turquoise scarab that fastens over the heart. Underneath the robe lays a golden chain belt, inlaid with cabochons of emerald. Dress in the robe, fasten the scarab over your heart, then link the belt around your waist.

long pause

The woman removes the basket and allows you to continue through her gate.

The incline is steep now, but you find steps have been cut into the tunnel floor and the passage, while not easy as before, is navigable. The robe is light against your skin, smooth and cool, but the scarab solidly anchors you. You feel more grounded than you have in weeks. The emerald belt jingles softly as you descend the stairs.

At the bottom of the steps, you come to a set of double doors formed from the ruddy clay, inlaid with turquoise and emeralds. As you approach, they silently swing open. Over the entrance, you see the words The Hall of Two Truths, and you realize that you are entering the domain of Ma'at, goddess of truth, honesty, and justice.

long pause

In the center of the room rests a set of scales; a balance. To one side of the scale, sits an Ammut, a creature with the head of a crocodile, the legs and forefront of a lion, and the rear of a hippopotamus. It waits silently beside the scales, watching you with calm, clear eyes. Sharpened teeth glisten from its mouth and you hope that it chooses to be your friend and not your enemy.

On the other side of the scales rises a tall golden throne, and etched on the headrest of the throne are twin eyes of Horus. In front of the throne you find a padded stool. Somehow, you know it is for you, and so you silently take your place there.

long pause

A sound from the far end of the hall alerts you. A tall woman enters the room. Dressed in a white sheath, in one hand she carries a scepter, in the other an ankh. An ostrich feather, dyed red, adorns her hair. You are in the presence of the goddess Ma'at.

The doors behind you rumble shut, when you turn to look, you see Ma'at again—she is both ends of the hall; you cannot escape without facing her.

long pause

Ma'at approaches the throne and steps up onto the seat. She lowers herself to rest on her heels and then removes the ostrich feather from her hair and flicks it into the air. With a whoosh, the feather rises and flies to the scales, where it rests on one side, tipping the balance.

"Before we begin, you may recite the prayer of the heart," she says. At first you don't know what she's talking about, but then the words come unbidden to your lips and you find yourself reciting.

You say, "O my heart which I had from my mother. O my heart which I had upon earth, do not rise up against me as a witness, do not speak against me concerning anything I have done." As you finish speaking, you realize that your prayer is not a prayer against the truth, but for clarity of vision concerning your actions.

long pause

Ma'at nods and points to the Ammut. "It would do you well to listen to me. I call you before me to weigh your life in progress, to ascertain the truth of your heart and your path. When you return to me, when your time on earth is over, you risk losing your heart to the Ammut, should your life be tainted with evil deeds and thoughts. So listen well now, that you might mend your ways, that you might abide by your ethics and avoid the loss of your soul."

long pause

She points to the empty bowl of the scales. "Place your heart on the scales," she says.

You wonder how you are supposed to do that, but then as you touch the scarab, you feel something pop into your hand. When you look down, a heart-shaped emerald glows in your palm. Within the emerald you see the spark containing your will, your actions, your thoughts, and the progress you have made in life. Place it on the scales and stand back.

With each question Ma'at asks you, the scales will tip, either in favor of your heart, in balance, or in favor of Ma'at's ostrich feather.

"Have you hurt anyone with a lie?" the Goddess asks.

Think to your life, have you ever told a lie that hurt someone? Did you confess, or did you hide your lie and let them continue to suffer? We are not talking of the simple white lies that smooth out social situations or prevent hard feelings, but lies that cause pain and suffering. How do the scales tip? Are they in your favor? If not, then how can you set the situation right? Or is it too late? What can you do to make up for any injustices your misspoken words caused?

extended long pause—2 minutes

Next, She asks you, "Have you hurt a friend, or betrayed anyone?"

Think to your life, have your actions ever resulted in the loss of friendship, in betrayal of someone who trusted you? Have you stolen from a neighbor? Slept with a friend's spouse? Promised to help out with a project and cancelled at the last minute, leaving the person in need? Remember, every person, from time to time, has hurt someone by their actions, but here we are talking deliberate sabotage. How do the scales tip? Are they in your favor? If not, then how can you set the situation right? Or is it too late? What can you do to make up for the injustices your misdeeds caused?

extended long pause—2 minutes

"Now," Ma'at says, "look to your life. You have much to be grateful for. But are you disciplined? Do you rest on your laurels, lazing away the days? Or do you have the self-control to continue working, to strive for a better life? Can you put aside your indolence and focus on the work that makes you a productive member of your race?"

Think about your recent months. Have you been too lenient with yourself? Have you let things go, let your focus wander? If you've had a string of good fortune, did you allow it to cloud your vision? Do you need to set a schedule, to infuse your work with a sense of wonder and excitement again? What can you do to keep yourself on track?

extended long pause—1 minute

Ma'at hands you back your emerald heart and you clutch it to your chest, feeling it slide back into your body. She smiles at you, not kindly, but with a just and fair gleam in her eyes.

She returns the ostrich feather to her hair and says, "Only you can truly judge your own heart. You know what resides in the secret recesses of your soul, and by that evidence, should you weigh your life. I am a reminder that truth is clarity. In that clarity, you may find a pristine sense of beauty and wonder."

long pause

"I am the scales of Balance," she says. "If you have too little or too much of anything, you are poorly connected to the cosmic order, to the Divine nature of the Universe. I am simplicity, and I am complexity. I am justice and I am iniquity. I am weakness, and I am strength. Go now, back to your body, back to your life, and search for ways in which you can balance your life according to the truth of your heart."

If you have anything you would like to say to Ma'at, do so now.

long pause

You find yourself in the tunnel outside the room. A great wind sweeps up and sucks you along the shaft, out of the cavern, lifting you into the air to carry you along.

Now you pass through the golden light, brilliant rays flashing from all directions. The great wind pushes you back into space, where the stars once again greet you in all of their beauty.

The wind whistles around you, carrying you down, toward the earth, past mountains, past trees, into your room and over your body, where it fades away as you rejoin your physical self and settle into your skin. You stir in your sleep and slowly begin to awake.

Now, listen to my voice as I count from ten to one. You will awake refreshed and alert. Ten . . . nine . . . you are becoming awake and aware of your surroundings . . . eight . . . seven . . . six . . . hear the sounds around you . . . five . . . four . . . you will be fully alert and refreshed . . . three . . . two . . . one . . . take three deep breaths and when you are ready, you may open your eyes.

Suggested Exercises

1. In a notebook, list the different areas of your life and whether or not you feel they are in balance with one another. Everyone will have one or two areas of major focus, but no one should allow any single area of life to rule their every waking moment. What activities can you tone down? What needs to be shored up? With an objective eye, examine your life and determine how you can bring it into balance.

2. I tried an interesting experiment some years back. I spent an entire week telling the truth—I told no lies during that time, and each night before I slept, I asked for guidance from the goddess Ma'at. It was much harder than I thought it would be. At times, I found myself remaining silent because I could not lie. Telling the truth would have complicated matters to an incredible degree. Until that time, I had not realized how integral to our society white lies have become. You might want to try this experiment, but be aware, if you begin it, you should see it through, especially if you ask Ma'at for guidance.

3. If you have hurt someone deeply through your actions or words, now is a good time to remedy the situation. The longer it goes on, the worse it's going to get. This is not

always an easy task to face, but in the end, you will be a better person for it. What's hard to accept is that there are some cases where we have hurt someone and nothing we can do will resolve the problem. We have to take responsibility for those situations and accept that we've caused permanent injury, whether mental, spiritual, or physical.

4. You might want to examine the judicial systems of different countries, to note their similarities and their differences. It can make for an interesting study.

Laissez faire, laissez passer.
Let it be, let it pass.

—François Quesnay (1694–1774)
attributed

The Hanged Man
Letting Go

The thirteenth card of the major arcana is known as the Hanged Man. It is assigned the number 12.

The Hanged Man and His Energy

At first, the energy connected to the Hanged Man seems severe and frightening to explore, but only if we look at the card in a superficial manner and don't dig into the underlying structures at work within this archetype.

True, the Hanged Man represents sacrifice, but much of the sacrifice is an illusion, for most often what we are called on to relinquish are habits and states of being that we need to release.

When we let go of something detrimental to our bodies or psyches, that sacrifice transforms into release and we are better for it once we emerge from the process.

When we encounter the Hanged Man, we are forced outside of our everyday existence. We have built ourselves a strong foundation, we have balanced our natures and just when it seems like everything should run like clockwork, here comes the Hanged Man to remind us that without constant evolution, stagnation takes over.

The Hanged Man is the guardian of our inner secrets, he delays our action, suspends life until we are able to gain a new perspective. With the Hanged Man, we move beyond ego, we relinquish our hard-won control and accept that, through the very success and strengths we've gained, we've also developed patterns and habits that must be broken if we are to continue our evolution of the soul.

Destructive habits are brought to the forefront, we learn wisdom through hardship. The hard work we invoked with Lady Justice now becomes a trial, we find ourselves swamped to the point where we have to back away, to turn and flee.

As we run from what seems like an overwhelming situation, we strip away the nonessentials, we lose our tunnel vision and race headlong to Yggdrasil, the World Tree. There we accept the bindings of the physical, in pursuit of Divine Sight. We chase our inner madness and follow it through the pain.

While we do not immediately resolve all issues brought to light by the Hanged Man, we challenge ourselves to face our limitations and boundaries, to sacrifice them at the base of the World Tree so that we too, like Odin, might discover the runes of knowledge and power.

When we enter this phase of our journey, we find that as we break habits and patterns, we set ourselves up for more chaos. This is not a phase that wraps up neatly, no tightly wrapped pretty packages here. The Hanged Man marks the beginning of a period of deconstruction, during which we tear down much of the façade we have erected during our growth.

This process continues on through the Tower card.

The Hanged Man is not an easy card to understand. He asks that we give and give, he steals that which we may think necessary for our happiness, but the process of understanding takes longer to grasp than the fleeting moments when we come into contact with him. The Hanged Man breaks our rules, he stomps on our fun and often we may curse the process, angry and frightened.

The period ruled by the Hanged Man tends to be a time of loss and sorrow, a time of confusion over just what's going on. Often we may hear ourselves asking, "Why me? Why did this happen to me?" or "Why did this happen now, just when things were going so well? I just got my life together."

We are, for the moment, blind to the long-term effects that this archetype plays out in our lives. If we weren't blind to the effects of this cycle, we wouldn't worry so much. And that worry is necessary, for we must use the sorrow and anger to advance our understanding of self-sacrifice, of loss and the good that can accompany it.

In our daily lives, The Hanged Man can appear as just about anyone who tramples our personal garden. He might appear in the form of our best friend who, with our spouse, betrays our trust. He might come in the form of a tornado that destroys our house and business or an accident that leaves us physically disabled. The Hanged Man is our supervisor who, out of the blue, fires us. We knew that we had some problems at work, but didn't realize they were bad enough for to lose our job.

The Hanged Man comes in the form of our doctor who tells us that unless we give up smoking, we're headed for lung cancer, or that we can no longer pursue our love of jogging and running because we have horrible shin splints.

Anytime we are forced to make major sacrifices in our lives, we can be sure the Hanged Man is at work. Even though these sacrifices might be our own choice, the Hanged Man is right there to ensure that the path isn't easy—no cold turkey, magickal releasings here. No, when we enter the realm of the Hanged Man, you can be sure the process will drag itself out so that we are spent to the utmost of our wills and abilities.

We find the Hanged Man when things have been at their best for a while; when, as wonderful as life seems, we need to remove ourselves from the overwhelming effort that goes into maintaining energy-expensive habits and destructive patterns.

The Spiritual Concept

In terms of spirituality, the Hanged Man becomes the sacrifice of the self for eventual greater good.

We find the Hanged Man within the god Odin, during his sojourn on the tree of Yggdrasil. In return for his pain and the sacrifice of one eye, he was granted knowledge of the runes. We also find the Hanged Man within the Roman god Saturn, who represents obstacles and limitations needing to be broken.

The Hanged Man can be found within the figure of Persephone, goddess of the Underworld. Through her descent into Hades' realm, She engenders the winter season, during which the world might rest. Her personal sacrifice allows the renewal of the land.

Let us place the Hanged Man within the Wheel of the Year at Lughnasadh, alongside the Tower, for the Hanged Man represents the sacrifice and destruction inherent within the season of harvest.

The Card

Some common representations of the Hanged Man include a blindfolded man (or androgynous person) hanging upside down, bound by one ankle from either a cross or an ankh. One leg will be bent across the other knee to form a triangle—he is not totally limited in his movement. The bindings around the other ankle represent limitations and patterns to be broken. Sometimes the Hanged Man will represent a specific person—as Odin or Arthur (once he was wounded and taken to Avalon).

Guidelines for Use

In our ongoing journey through the major arcana, this meditation should follow that of Justice. You may meditate on the Hanged Man during Lughnasadh, or any time when you feel a need to release limitations, overcome obstacles or break restricting patterns in your life.

Flowers:	comfrey, tobacco, rosemary, lavender
Incense:	sage, gum mastic, lavender
Oils:	lemongrass, sage, almond, rosemary
Crystals:	star sapphire, amethyst, ruby
Candles:	purple, black, indigo

Meditation

Relax and get comfortable. Close your eyes and take three deep breaths.

long pause

You are lying in bed, tossing and turning as you think about the day. Your life has been running smoothly since you became organized and focused; your successes have multiplied and the future looks bright.

But along with the sense of success has come an overwhelming feeling that you are shouldering a heavy load. The responsibilities of your career, the responsibilities of your home life and your spiritual life all seem to be piling one on top of the other and you cannot sleep for all the whirling thoughts in your mind.

long pause

As you snuggle under the sheets, trying to clear your head, you hear a whispering in the back of your thoughts—almost like a nudge. You sort your way through the mayhem crowding your mind and zero in on the energy.

The whispering becomes clear as you listen to it. The words are summoning you, and you feel the need to follow them. Slip out from under the sheet and quickly dress so that you can follow the call before it disappears.

You race out of the house and race down the sidewalk, through the empty streets until you come to the edge of the town. No one impedes your progress, no one stops you.

long pause

The night, while warm, is blustery and the air feels charged as if a thunderstorm might be on the way. A gust catches you up, propelling you forward and you trip over a tree root, sprawling on the ground.

As you lay there, you see, hidden in the undergrowth, a small path leading into the forest that boundaries the edge of the town. The whispering call is louder now, and as you pick yourself up and dust yourself off, it leads you down the obscured path, deep into the woods.

long pause

The path winds through the tangle of briars and huckleberries; ancient oak and ash trees silently watch your passage. You hear the muffled footsteps of animals lurking in the shadows and the glade suddenly feels menacing, a dangerous glen through which to pass.

As you push through the thicket, thorns snag at your legs and arms, you find yourself getting scratched by the brambles. Droplets of blood well up on some of the lacerations and the scratches sting as the air blows against them.

long pause

The thicket begins to lessen, then opens into a large clearing leading to a cliff face. The clearing reminds you of a quarry. Rocks and pebbles, none larger than an egg, cover the ground between you and the cliff, and they are slippery, quick to slide from beneath your feet.

Still the summons urges you on. There seems to be no way to avoid the rock-lined path, and so you cautiously step onto the pebbles, struggling to keep your footing as they shift and roll with every step you take.

long pause

Halfway across the clearing, your foot hits one of the rocks wrong and you lurch forward and are thrown to the ground. The stones make for a hard landing, as you sit up, you find yourself covered with painful and swollen bruises.

You begin to wonder if following this call is really worth it. By this time you are starting to get tired. But the whispering comes again and the siren-song lures you on. You push yourself off the ground and manage to cross the rest of the way over the rocks until you are standing at the base of the cliff.

A path leads up, it is steep and passes through sharp-edged rocks jutting darkly into the sky. Take a deep breath and begin your ascent. You have to use the stones on either side for balance and it's almost as if you were climbing the cliff face, rather than walking up a path.

long pause

Take three deep breaths.

long pause

The top of the cliff is in sight when you hear a noise from behind one of the rocks. A large cougar springs up onto the top of the stone and growls at you.

"What are you doing in my territory?" she asks.

You answer that you're following a call. The cougar snarls and, with a quick swipe, sends you reeling back against the stone wall. You feel blood dripping from your shoulder and see that the mountain lion has raked your flesh. She stares into your eyes, her gaze unflinching.

"You are far too flippant for your own good. You're certainly sure of yourself, aren't you? Think you're on top of the hill? Think you're beyond hardship? Think again," the cougar says. "This is my cliff, I am queen here, and you must receive my permission to continue."

long pause

At first you find yourself growing angry with the cat, how can she refuse you permission? You're successful, you're human, you've advanced through your journey this far and you don't like being told to humble yourself.

But then you gaze into her eyes and see the immensity of her power. She truly is Queen of the hill, these are her lands and you are but a traveler here.

Ask and receive her permission to pass through her lands.

long pause

Huffing, she backs away, allowing you to proceed. You wonder if she might attack you again, from the back, but she only growls and says, "Don't worry about it, human. I've given you my permission. My first attack came because you overstepped your boundaries, you didn't look for the signs that you were involved in something over your head and so you got hurt. Now you know better."

The top of the cliff is only a few strides away. As you pull yourself over the edge, you turn and see what a beautiful view it is from up here. You can see, far below, the rock-laden clearing, and the tangle of woods that leads back to the main road. But there is no time to rest.

Once again, the summons sounds, urging you on, and you turn to rush along the tall mesa.

long pause

The land up here is open to the sky. The night is dark, a waning moon glistens overhead, and you stumble into every hole and over every root that crosses your path. The nerves in your toes and feet are raw. Your clothes are bloodsoaked and in tatters. The thorn scratches and the cougar wounds have stopped bleeding, but they ache as you move along.

The plateau stretches for miles. Not far from you stands a dark, tall, twisted tree, writhing into the air. As you approach the mass of tangled branches and limbs, you notice that it is an ash tree, branches bare and stripped to the wind. A thicket surrounds the tree on three sides.

There is a pit at the bottom of the tree, a cavernous hole gaping in the ground. When you gather the courage to peek over the edge, you see only the blackness of the void, thick and inky, and you have to pull away when your stomach lurches. Who knows what unknown dangers might lurk within the hole?

long pause

You are very tired now, very sore, and so you rest on a stone next to the pit. As you are sitting there, you notice that a long rope dangles from one sturdy branch, ending in a noose above the sinkhole.

There is a rustling in the thicket behind the tree and a figure steps out. Dressed in a hooded brown cape, you cannot tell whether the figure is a man or a woman, and the voice emanating from the shadow-covered hood gives you no clue.

"Welcome to the World Tree," the cloaked figure says. "I am the Guardian of Secrets. I only reveal my truths to those who are willing to pay the price."

long pause

The Guardian's words intrigue you. You have come, following a call, and now you stand before one who might be able to give you an answer as to what the summons entails.

As if reading your thoughts, the Guardian again speaks. "You were called and you answered. The trail to this place is difficult, many embark on the path to the World Tree, but they give up when the journey gets rough. You have passed through numerous trials tonight, but if you should choose to understand the nature of this leg of your quest, then be warned, the night is young and you have not yet faced your greatest adversary. Think well before committing yourself to my hands."

The Guardian's words echo within your mind. You still feel the summons, there is great knowledge of your journey to be learned here and yet you know that this night will change you, will give you insights into yourself that you both need and fear to know.

When you have gathered your courage, for this is the only path through to the next leg of your journey, then tell the Guardian you are ready to be put to the test.

long pause

The Guardian waves one hand toward the rope. "Tonight you will go within and discover those traits that you must sacrifice, that you must ruthlessly tear out of your life. Delaying tactics, obstacles set up to sabotage you, fears that are but shadows in your own mind . . . you must face them down."

With a quick clap of the hands, the Guardian stands back. Six figures, all cloaked and silent, emerge from the bushes. Three to a side, they surround you and gently lower you into their arms until they are carrying you with ease over to the World Tree.

The Guardian affixes the noose around one of your ankles and nods. The rope tightens, then lifts you feet first into the air until you are hanging upside-down above the gaping pit. The six figures retreat into the shadows again.

long pause

"The rest of this night," the Guardian says, "you will hang, suspended from action, suspended with only your thoughts to keep you company. Listen well to the truth of your heart." Then the Guardian retreats, leaving you alone.

At first you can't believe that they left you alone like this. The ropes are not uncomfortable around your ankle, but you feel disconcerted, disoriented, and you think that there's nothing you can do to free yourself.

long pause

A rumble of thunder echoes across the horizon and then a flash of lightning rips the night sky asunder. Within seconds you are drenched as the clouds loose sheets of rain onto the thirsty earth. The pelting drops saturate the ground. The water pours down your body, from toe to head, and your eyes are filled with the racing streams so that everything becomes a blur.

long pause

Then, as quickly as the rain set in, it stops again and the clouds part, letting the moonlight shine through. Now muggy, the humidity and warmth combine to lull you into a waking trance. You become less aware of your body as you hang there, and when you look down at the pit below, you notice a faint light within.

A mist rises to surround the World Tree, and when you look into the void again, you see the swirling light of ten thousand stars spiraling, dim and distant. In their center glows an orb, a luminous pearl, and you know that it contains wisdom and knowledge and beauty. You reach down, into the pit, trying to grasp hold, but some unseen energy bars your path.

long pause

A deep voice rebounds out from the pit. "You cannot enter the halls of wisdom without a sacrifice. You must pay a price if you are to learn, to advance on your quest. You must discover what holds you back, what limits your vision."

Though you cannot see the questioner, you know that the being, whoever it is, can hear your thoughts. Think now, about your goals in life. What do you do to limit yourself? How do you sabotage your progress? Be honest with yourself. Take a moment to think about the self-imposed limitations that you allow to rule your life.

extended long pause—2 minutes

"What patterns must you break?" the voice asks. "What routines and structures have you built that impede your journey? Are they shoring you up, or do they prevent the free flow of your life?"

Once again, think about any destructive patterns that you have noticed in your life. Everyone falls into routine and sometimes that routine helps us, but other times it limits our visions, comforts without challenging. To continue to grow, we must break through the self-imposed obstacles that we use as crutches and risk the unknown. Take a moment to examine any patterns that you allow to impede your progress.

extended long pause—2 minutes

Once again you hear the voice. "Next comes the hardest trial. Are you willing to sacrifice, to give up those limitations and destructive patterns? Are you willing to take a chance, to risk breaking free of outworn habits? If so, then let them drop away into the void, into the abyss, to be cleared from your life."

Think now about what habits, patterns, and limitations that you have imposed upon yourself. Which are you willing to get rid of? Which are you willing to sacrifice for your growth and evolution? When you have decided on which habits and patterns that you're ready to release, then see them tumble into the pit, to be swept into the sparkling energy of the stars.

extended long pause—1 minute

As your limitations drop away, you find that you can reach in and grab the pearl. The gem rests heavy and brilliant in your hand, pulsing with a warm glow.

long pause

You wonder how you are going to get down, then it dawns on you that you have the power to free yourself. Only one foot is bound, and you can easily swing toward the trunk of the World Tree and drape your other knee over a branch. From there it takes but a moment, using the tree trunk as a brace, to pull yourself up until you are sitting on the branch. Then you untie the rope and jump to the ground.

long pause .

A shuffle in the trees alerts you. The Guardian has returned. The cloaked figure pushes the hood back and you find yourself staring into your own eyes. The Guardian is yourself.

"Well done. You have faced your limitations, you have identified your patterns and begun the process of releasing destructive habits. During the next leg of your journey, you will be called upon to undergo an even bigger transformation. For now, though, open the pearl and drink of the elixir within. You have won the right to self-knowledge."

long pause

You see that the pearl is hinged. When you open the top and lift it back, you find there a golden liquid within.

Your Guardian self vanishes in a wisp of mist, flowing into the liquid before you drink.

Sweet as honey, smooth as mead, the nectar slides down your throat and eases the discomfort you experienced this evening. The warmth of the liqueur rests your fears of change and transformation and you understand that you have awakened your courage and strength that have been hidden under the weight of fear.

For we only fear when we have something to lose, and you have come a long ways on your journey. You don't want to lose everything you've worked for.

long pause

A sweeping wind gusts around you, and in a swirl of warm air, you find yourself buoyed into the night and carried home. As you tumble into your bed, sleep overtakes you and you rest easy.

Now, listen to my voice as I count from ten to one. You will awake refreshed and alert. Ten . . . nine . . . you are becoming awake and aware of your surroundings . . . eight . . . seven . . . six . . . hear the sounds around you . . . five . . . four . . . you will be fully alert and refreshed . . . three . . . two . . . one . . . take three deep breaths and when you are ready, you may open your eyes.

Suggested Exercises

1. Honestly examine your limitations. Are they self-imposed? Do you sabotage your efforts? Are you afraid of change and so you convince yourself that you are comfortable where you are? Begin to analyze your routine and see if you need to make changes in order to evolve in your life, career, relationship, or whatever focus you are working on at this time.

2. Sacrifices of these natures are usually in our best interest—if we give up something that is detrimental to our health or lifestyle, whether emotional or physical, then the sacrifice is really an illusion.

3. Make changes slowly, if you decide to stop smoking, stop eating junk food, and start exercising all in the same week, chances are you'll fail because you are taking on too many changes at once. Be willing to give yourself time when deciding to tackle your bad habits. Face them one at a time.

4. If we must make a drastic change and do not have the time to implement it slowly, then try to make the transition as easy as possible by calling on friends for emotional support and by arranging the rest of your life to be as easy as possible during the transition.

5. Learn to differentiate between habits and patterns that can be changed, and those that are intrinsic to our personality. I'm very Type-A. I'd like to be more Type-B, but I realize that I'll never fully fit that category so I relax what I can and let the rest alone. My drive and ambition keep me motivated and moving.

6. Sometimes we are forced by outside circumstances to undergo major sacrifices—when a loved one dies, when we lose some of our mobility, when we are flooded out of our home, etc. During these times, we need to be as caring and gentle with ourselves as possible. These sacrifices may or may not happen for a reason, but we must accept our anger and pain, our feelings, and then work through them. We cannot repress our feelings and pretend that everything's for the best when it feels like our lives have been torn to pieces. Only after our emotions have calmed down should we look for any lessons to be learned from the situation.

Take, for instance, a twig and a pillar, or the ugly person and the great beauty, and all the strange and monstrous transformations. These are all leveled together by Tao. Division is the same as creation; creation is the same as destruction.

—Chuang-tzu (369–286 B.C.E.)
On Leveling All Things

Death
Transformation

The fourteenth card of the major arcana is known as Death. It is assigned the number 13.

Death and Its Energy

The Death card is one of the most misunderstood and feared cards of the tarot. Many people automatically assume that this card indicates impending physical death. In rare cases this might be true—I have had one such case. A client of mine had a heart attack the same night I read for him. The major focus card for the reading was Death, and the reading itself was confused and hazy—as if looking through a blurred lens. A few hours later, my client flat-lined for fifteen minutes, yet he managed to live through the experience.

But for the vast majority of people, the Death card represents transformation within a cycle—not transformation at the end of the lifecycle.

Death symbolizes a state of metamorphosis—the chrysalis of a caterpillar turning into a butterfly or moth. The archetype of Death indicates that we are ready for a major transformation brought on by the growth and evolution that we have accomplished during our journey.

We are ready to reap the harvest of our hard work—to make a significant leap in the progress of our lives. Only by sacrificing our self-imposed limitations through the energy of the Hanged Man can we now move into the realm of Death and accomplish that leap.

When we encounter Death, we can no longer turn away from the changes we know must take place. Just as the snake must shed its skin, just like the caterpillar must weave a chrysalis and transform into a butterfly, so we too must metamorphose during our lives.

These are not changes we can avoid—I liken the archetype of Death to the wheel of your life—once it begins to move, you can either take hold and ride it through, or you can resist and let it run over you. Either way, change is going to happen and there's nothing you can do to stop it. So you might as well make it as positive an experience as you can.

We undergo this deconstruction because we know that a more advanced state of consciousness/life exists on the other side. We are reborn, reincarnated within this same lifetime. The Death card represents endings and beginnings—and to allow that energy to manifest, we must first be willing to open up to the Hanged Man archetype so that we may detach and discard that which is outworn.

The period ruled by Death tends to be a tumultuous time, when our opinions and actions can change hourly. We are excited by these changes, but frightened too, for the unknown is frightening.

During this time period we may find ourselves throwing out all our old clothes—we want to look different. We might find that we have to face major changes in our relationships—a divorce or the decision to marry. We might find ourselves in the middle of a career change.

When we encounter these changes or urges to change, we aren't necessarily enthusiastic about accepting them; we haven't yet reached that point, but we know that we can no longer face ourselves in the same way again. It's time for transition and we grudgingly accept that fact.

In our daily lives, Death can appear as just about anyone or anything who catalyzes major decisions. It might appear in the form of a new job that entails moving across country. Or it might show up when we make a transition from having a moderate success to becoming a publicly-acclaimed professional, and now our world rips open. Or perhaps we are gay and finally find the courage and ability to walk into the open with our chosen lifestyle. The Death archetype can mark the beginning of menopause; the children leaving home.

Whatever Death signifies, you can be sure that, whether or not you're ready, here it comes—barreling around the corner.

We draw the Death card when things have been at a plateau for a while, when we need shaking up in our lives. Often the transformation is positive, though chaotic at the time of transition; sometimes the change can be traumatic but it will usually lead to a greater understanding of the self and of life's cycles.

A Spiritual Concept

In terms of spirituality, Death becomes the snake shedding its skin; the scarab beetle of the Egyptians.

We find Death within the god Hades, who rules the Underworld of the Greeks. We also find Him in Tuoni, the Lord of Tuonela (the Finnish Underworld). And Anubis, Egyptian god of the Dead, waits by the side of Osiris to judge the dead.

We also find Death within Ereshkigal, Babylonian goddess of death, known as the Star of Lamentation. She is also Tuonetar, who sits by Tuoni's side; and the Celtic Washer at the Ford, the water spirit who warns of impending death.

Astrologically, the Death card is associated with Scorpio. And where else within the Wheel of the Year would we place Death but at Samhain, alongside the Hermit?

The Card

Some common representations of Death include a skeleton robed as the Grim Reaper, carrying a scythe. On the card, we may also find such symbols of Death as the snake, the scorpion, the scarab, and the owl. With some cards we might also find a baby depicted, representing the complete cycle of life-death-life again (the rebirth/reincarnation doctrine).

Guidelines for Use

In our ongoing journey through the major arcana, this meditation should follow that of the Hanged Man. You may meditate on Death during Samhain, or any time when you feel a need for transformation and change.

This meditation calls for a drumbeat partway through, which is clearly marked. This beat may be prerecorded, or you may wish to work with a live drummer. If you choose the latter, I recommend that the drummer and guide practice the section together before the meditation to coordinate sound levels, rhythm, etc.

Flowers:	lily, posy, daisy, willow, rosemary
Incense:	copal, gum mastic, myrrh, lavender
Oils:	cypress, rosemary, poppy, lavender
Crystals:	lapis lazuli, obsidian, turquoise
Candles:	black, burgundy, purple

Meditation

Relax and get comfortable. Close your eyes and take three deep breaths.

long pause

You are standing on the path outside of your home. Once again, night has descended and you find yourself staring up at the stars. You had a dream, a dream that instructed you to hike into the woods to a clearing where you once picnicked during the summer.

The leaves are shivering on the trees, autumn makes its blustery sweep into town and you remember that tonight is Samhain Eve, the night of the ancestors. You've been so wrapped up in your work that you had forgotten until now.

It's too late to gather with friends, surely they've filled their Circles by now, and so you decide to follow your dream through and see what happens.

long pause

Children are out for All Hallow's Eve, and as you walk briskly along the streets you think about how little they understand what they are celebrating. So many of the old ways have been lost, so much knowledge repressed or destroyed. A little girl dressed as a skeleton runs by and you get chicken skin.

During the past few months, you've done your best to eliminate superfluous activity and wasteful habits. You've tended to that which is most important in your life—your health, your work, your spirituality, and those dearest to your heart. You've let go of those things that have pulled you away from your path and now it feels as if you're ready to make a leap, a jump in your evolution. But you aren't sure when or how it should happen.

long pause

The air is chilly against your skin, you are grateful for the warm jacket and extra blanket that you brought with you. As you pass another group of costumed children, you come to the edge of town, where a path leads to a gladed park. No one else appears to be walking this path tonight, you have the entire trail to yourself.

There are no lights here, and the moon is far from full. A thin crescent of silver shines wanly above you, with scarcely enough light to guide you along the well-trodden path. In your dream, you crossed into the clearing, and then the vision became fuzzy. Now, as you near the meadow, you begin to anticipate what might be waiting for you on this Samhain Eve.

long pause

The last of the autumn leaves come whirling off the huge old maples and oaks as a gust of wind catches them up and sends them spiraling into the air. You reach up to catch one, but the burnished leaf crumbles in your hand as you catch hold of it.

As you approach the meadow, you hear the sound of drums from beyond a copse of oak. You can see, through the barren branches, glimpses of flames crackling in the night. The scent of bonfire smoke comes wisping through the air to surround you and you find yourself curious as to who or what is in the glade.

long pause

The web of woven branches shakes with the sweeping wind. The gusts keen a shrill dirge as they rush through knotholes and cracks in the tree trunks. Step onto the leaf-scattered forest path. Your heels crunch against the frost-tinged leaves as you navigate the darkened glen.

A huckleberry bush sways to your left and you catch a glimpse of some small animal darting behind a yellowed fern. It might be a fox or a coyote, but it's difficult to tell in the faint light.

long pause

As you approach the end of the path where it opens into the clearing, you can smell the rising smoke, and you guess that it comes from apple wood. You quietly step into the shadows surrounding the glen.

Circled round the fire stand twelve people. One person wears a black hooded robe, another—a man—wears the hide and antlers of an elk. Still a third is clad in a silver gown and upon her brow shines a silver crescent headdress. Each person is costumed in a unique fashion, some aboriginal, some neo-Pagan, all obviously ritual dress.

long pause

They look up as you step out from the shadows. The woman in silver steps forward and says, "We have been waiting for you. You have come to a turning point, you have reached a time of transition. There is no going back, no stopping the cycle. You must accept that your life is transforming; that change brings with it stability; for only through change can we sweep away stagnation."

long pause

The shaman motions for you to enter the circle. "You can come to us of your own will. If you do not, we will, as instruments of the cycle, of the Gods, come for you."

Step into the circle, for you know in your heart that the cycle of transformation can only lead to enlightenment in your life and better you should embrace the inevitable rather than resist it.

long pause

As you step into their midst, two of the others lead you over to one side where they dress you in ritual garments representing the transformations now taking place in your life. These robes are different than your usual gear. Take a moment to examine the ritual wear and what it symbolizes.

extended long pause—1 minute

When you are ready, the Priestess motions you to her side. The silver of her gown sparkles in the bright light of the fire. She loosely binds your hands in front of you with a leather thong and guides you to the fireside.

"The ritual you are about to undergo will take you deep into yourself, into the core of your being," she says. "You will be asked to detach yourself from your fears, to look into the future and divine your coming path. With us you walk the path of the bat—for the bat is a symbol of death and rebirth. The ritual strengthens and tests your endurance. When you emerge from the night, you will be renewed, changed, and ready for transformation."

As she finishes speaking, she steps back and the black-hooded figure approaches. You cannot tell whether a man or woman hides beneath the cloak, but they carry a tall scythe and the blade glistens in the night.

long pause

You get a strange feeling from this figure, as if the person behind the robes is far more the stranger here than you. Without a word, they motion for you to follow, and you are led to the other side of the circle. The others part and you see that behind them a hole has been dug. Four feet deep and as long as your height, it gapes open, a fresh wound in the cool earth, waiting.

The hole is lined with a thin blanket and a small pillow. As sure as you know your name, you know what you must do. Step up to the edge and look into the freshly excavated pit.

long pause

Two men help you into the hole. As you cautiously stretch out, with the smell of moist earth thick in your nostrils, you see the Priestess standing to one side of the pit while the shaman takes his place on the other. He is holding a drum and begins to beat out a rhythmic cadence.

NOTE TO GUIDE: the drumbeat should begin here. It should not overpower your voice, but should be rhythmic and steady.

The other ritual participants drag a large tarp over the opening of the hole, and while it in no way interferes with your breathing, now you lay in complete darkness, unable to see anything.

long pause

You can hear the voice of the Priestess as she begins to speak. Her words echo with the sound of the drum, reverberating around you in your solitude.

Gaia, open your heart,
To one who comes seeking rebirth
Mother Bear, lead the way
Into the womb of the Earth.

Spirits of those who have gone before,
Ancestors, Witches, Midwives
Call up the magick, around let it spin
Transform the paths of our lives.

Into the darkness, alone we must walk
A vision quest for to seek,
Strong we must be, that we may see
How with the world we link.

So into the depths of the Earth
And into the depths of your mind
Go now, journey the quest,
To find what it is you must find.

The sour scent of the earth fills your nostrils as you lay in the darkness. You hear the rustle of wings, perhaps a beetle or moth scrabbling up the dirt wall, but you cannot reach out. With your hands bound, deprived of light and visual input, you find your other senses taking over. You begin to understand the freedom that can come through restriction. You are bound in body that your mind might fly.

Listen to the drumbeat. As you listen to the drumbeat, your breath falls into rhythm with the steady cadence. Let the drum take you deep into your heart, into your soul.

long pause

Take three deep breaths.

long pause

In the abyss through which it feels like you've fallen, you begin to see a faint light. It hovers above you, pale and shimmering.

As you watch, it grows, taking shape, and you find yourself staring into the glittering red eyes of a bat. The wings are black, far darker than the night, but they glow with an obsidian sheen, almost metallic.

The bat stares down at you, then lands on your chest and crawls up to look into your face. It gently bites you on your brow, where your psychic third eye resides. The teeth are needle-edged and sharp, you barely feel the sting of its nip.

long pause

With a feather-touch, the bat licks your brow and then vanishes. For a moment you wonder if it was even there, but then you begin to feel dizzy and you realize that it injected something under your skin. With alarming clarity, you slip out of your body, through your third eye, and go spiraling into the sky.

long pause

Surrounded by a swirling kaleidoscope of colors, in the center of the spiral, you see yourself, as you were when you were a baby. Now watch, see yourself transform through the important stages of your life.

Watch as you grow and change, and with each stage, remember how frightening and exciting those changes were. Each time you wondered if you were doing the right thing, making the right choices. Each time was a new transition, a rebirth into a new cycle of your life. Watch and remember.

extended long pause—3 minutes

Now see yourself as you are today, the sum of all of your changes and decisions. See yourself grow and transform from this time forward. In what potential direction can you see yourself heading? What might you become? See possible changes as they affect you and imagine what the outcome might be.

extended long pause—2 minutes

Next, think about the current events in your life. What transitions are you in the midst of? Do these changes frighten you? Are you worried that you might make the wrong choices? Remember, each step of the way is but one league of the journey. Even if you should make a wrong decision, you still grow through the experience.

For change sweeps away stagnation, which is the true slayer of the soul.

extended long pause—1 minute

NOTE TO GUIDE: *the drumbeat should end here. It should fade away gently.*

Suddenly you feel yourself sliding back into your body. You are cold and tired. The tarp rolls away and two of the ritualists pull you out and untie your hands. They shove a cup of hot tea into your hands and throw a blanket around your shoulders as they lead you to the fireside.

The Priestess sits beside you and, as you warm up, she says, "Remember your glorious ability to transform and be reborn within this cycle of life. Remember your strength in doing so. Do not be afraid of changes, embrace them, direct and focus them."

long pause

No one asks you of your experiences, for they all understand just how personal this ritual is. They lead you to the side and help you dress in your regular clothes, then you are taken to a nearby car where the Priestess drives you down a side road and into town. When you are in front of your house, she nods goodnight as you enter your door.

You are tired, so you pour a handful of aromatic salts into the bath as you fill it with hot water. As you sink into the tub, reflect on what you learned about yourself tonight.

Transformation is a natural part of life, and we are reborn many times throughout this life—first as an infant, then into early childhood, then as the growing teen who begins to see the world with different eyes. Remember your first job, your first love. Remember those heartaches which, at the time you thought would haunt you forever, but are now mellowed and long past. Know that whatever the change, you have the ability to make the most out of your circumstances.

extended long pause—1 minute

Now, listen to my voice as I count from ten to one. You will awake refreshed and alert. Ten . . . nine . . . you are becoming awake and aware of your surroundings . . . eight . . . seven . . . six . . . hear the sounds around you . . . five . . . four . . . you will be fully alert and refreshed . . . three . . . two . . . one . . . take three deep breaths and when you are ready, you may open your eyes.

Suggested Exercises

1. Make a list of all the major transitions you have undergone during your lifetime, and how you coped with each one. Then, when you are having a difficult time adapting to change, review your list for suggestions.

2. Try to see yourself as you are now, rather than having an idealized vision of how you think you should be or will be during some future time. There is nothing wrong with hoping and working for a change, but to lock yourself into one vision of how you think your path should be will block other positive events that the Universe might have in store for you.

3. If you are interested, look into the various animals that represent change and transition—snake, bat, and butterfly are three. Study the differing legends surrounding them.

4. Often, when we are about to undergo a major change, we will be struck with feelings of disorientation, panic, and melancholy. These are natural reactions to impending transformation. If we calm down and keep ourselves from doing anything to impede the progress now taking place, then we will be in a better frame of mind when that transition does take place. Use herbal teas such as chamomile or valerian to calm the jitters, take long baths or walk in the woods to soothe jangled nerves. During times like these try to limit your caffeine and sugar intakes so that you don't send yourself into overdrive, and be sure to get enough rest.

Keep to moderation, keep the end in view, follow nature.

—Lucan (39–65 C.E.)
The Civil War

Temperance
Fire and Water

The fifteenth card of the major arcana is known as Temperance (at least one deck lists this card as Art). It is assigned the number 14.

Temperance and Its Energy

The Temperance card is an ethereal stop along the Fool's journey. It wouldn't be difficult to mistake the inner peace of Temperance for the self-assurance of Strength, or the balance achieved through Justice. But when you examine the three cards side-by-side, you see that, while Temperance has elements of both the Strength and Justice archetypes, it goes far beyond either.

Temperance represents integration and synthesis of polar opposites—fire and water, male and female, light and dark, good and bad, and so on. Like the forging of

167

a fine, well-honed blade, the archetype uses the passion and fury of fire and the peace and tranquillity of water to strengthen your personality.

Representing a state of spiritual empowerment, Temperance moves the Fool into a state of inner peace that allows him/her to balance paradoxes, to bring joy and growth out of discontent. Unlike the balance of the Justice card, Temperance leads us to a place of regeneration rather than one of austerity and self-discipline.

With Temperance we enter a realm where we reflect on our lives and express feelings based on inner truths rather than on conventional expectations. Society may require a certain mode of action or belief from us; Temperance allows us to ignore those demands and to express who we truly are.

When we encounter Temperance, we may swing from one side of the pendulum to the other, but we will eventually come to rest in the center . . . we will find our median and come to a point of balance. This median may relate to paradoxical viewpoints, beliefs, and desires.

For example, I love both Washington State and the island of Hawai'i. I swing back and forth on my desire as to which state I wish to live in. I have yet to reach my point of Temperance on the subject. I know the advantages and disadvantages of living in both places, but still can't make up my mind. At some point, the pendulum will stop and I will have made a decision.

We may also find ourselves undergoing a sense of initiation, or enlightenment. During this time we may feel guided, through an outside Spirit Guide or the inner Spirit Guide (our Higher Self). The transformation we began through the Death card enters a new phase and we detach from that which does not relate to our inner journeys.

During this period we may find ourselves spending an inordinate amount of time with others of like mind. Temperance leads us to spiritual groups which mirror our own directions and beliefs. When we connect with others during this phase of the cycle, we tend to want a spiritual connection, a link based on beliefs. We may find ourselves partaking of one philosophical discussion after another.

When we encounter these shifts in consciousness, it feels like the world is opening up, like we've entered a new realm of existence that we knew was there, but weren't quite ready for. We feel regenerated, enthusiastic about our spiritual discoveries, and desire to work with others in order to create something greater than we might be able to as individuals.

For the Witch, this may mean joining a coven, for the metaphysical student, this may mean joining a study group. For the Christian, it points to a resurgence in church or Bible-study attendance. Whatever the spiritual path, we become, for a short time, zealots. We want everyone to feel as empowered as we do and, unfortunately, this can lead to a sense of misplaced righteousness.

In our daily lives, Temperance can appear as a Spirit Guide, as a guru, as our Higher Self suddenly raising his/her head. We might find Temperance in a metaphysical book or in a mystical experience that opens us up to the powers of the cosmos.

The archetype of Temperance can lead us directly to those *a-ha* experiences, which provide sudden enlightenment. We might undergo a physical initiation—such as the Reiki healing initiations—which open our psychic channels.

When we are within the realm of Temperance, we have to be cautious of running over others' beliefs. Too often, we refuse to see that enlightenment for one person may not signify enlightenment for another. I am a Witch, but that doesn't mean I believe the Craft is an appropriate path for everyone, even though it has been the right choice for me.

Temperance follows Death, for as soon as we have taken a step onto the path of transformation, we enter a new realm, and this realm happens to be spiritual in nature.

Our surrender to change and transition is the beginning, we now inhabit the calm before the storm. Once we reach a certain level of personal enlightenment, physical change must occur to mirror what has taken place in our hearts and souls. That physical change takes place within the realms of the Devil and Tower archetypes.

The Spiritual Concept

In terms of spirituality, Temperance becomes the initiator, the pathfinder who breaks through barriers and opens gateways for others.

We find Temperance within the goddess Artemis, the Huntress, who runs ahead and clears the path. We also find her in Nephthys, Egyptian goddess of hidden mysteries. She is also found in Inanna, who journeys into the Underworld, an initiation into the dark side of Her nature.

Temperance resides within Vishnu as Kalki, during the God's final incarnation-to-come. We meet him in Ptah, Egyptian craftsman god, known as the Opener of the Ways.

The Temperance card represents the astrological sign of Sagittarius and we can place Temperance within the Wheel of the Year at Imbolc—alongside the Magician. Imbolc is a time of beginnings, when we feel clean and pure, ready to take on new growth and challenges.

The Card

Most often we find an angelic, usually androgynous, figure represents Temperance. This figure may be holding a chalice into which two opposing liquids pour—often colored red and blue to represent fire and water.

Guidelines for Use

This meditation follows that of the Death card. You may find it useful to meditate on Temperance during Imbolc, or any time when you feel a need to for spiritual enlightenment and inner guidance.

Flowers:	damiana, mugwort, star anise, jonquil
Incense:	gum mastic, myrrh, sandalwood, honeysuckle
Oils:	honeysuckle, poppy, narcissus, gardenia
Crystals:	clear quartz, moonstone, aquamarine, iolite
Candles:	white, light blue, ivory

Meditation

Relax and get comfortable. Close your eyes and take three deep breaths.

long pause

You are sitting in your favorite chair. You've had a long day and the evening feels empty. You've read your newspaper, there aren't any books you currently want to read, and all the programs on television are reruns. You think about taking a walk, but the temperature gauge tells you that it's thirty degrees outside and dropping.

Everyone in your household has run off for the evening, busy and preoccupied. Even your pet ignores you in favor of the warm rug in front of the fireplace.

long pause

As you sit, restlessly looking for something to do, you hear a voice inside your head. "Get dressed and go outside," the voice says.

The night looks icy and you ignore the inner promptings for a while, until the insistent clamor drives you to the coat closet where you wrap yourself in a thick jacket, a scarf, gloves, hat, and boots. Thinking to yourself that you must be crazy, you slip your keys into your pocket and silently step into the snow-filled yard.

long pause

The smell of ozone hangs thick in the air, the sky is overcast with luminous clouds, and you know that there will soon be another storm. The sidewalk is covered with a thick sheen of ice and compacted snow, making it bumpy and difficult to traverse. A few cars slip past, their wheels crunching on the blanketed streets.

Your inner voice propels you to a nearby park. You have been here before, on the day when the Wheel of Fate rolled into your life. You met an old friend at one of the picnic tables. Now those tables are covered with snow and the only other inhabitants of this park are slumbering squirrels and a kitten huddled by one of the garbage pails.

long pause

The cedars and firs hang heavy, their branches weighing them down. The light from the frost-laden clouds has turned the park into a Faerie-land, and the layers of snow glisten like diamonds, frozen forever in an ethereal blue glaze.

Your heart soars at the sight—the pristine beauty of the night fills you with joy and you go running through the snow, laughing and playing like a child.

long pause

As you throw a snowball at a tree, you look up in time to see a white owl gliding by overhead. Its wings make no sound in the muffled night. The owl is obviously on the hunt. As you watch, it swoops down, barreling toward the ground. Then, before it crashes into the snow, the owl pulls up again, a rabbit struggling in its talons. You listen to the rabbit scream as the owl flies out of sight to eat its dinner.

long pause

The hunt sobers you and squelches your impulse to play. You clear a seat on one of the benches and sit down. The rabbit's cries reverberate in your ears and wrench open your heart . . . and yet . . . and yet, you understand that the owl was just hungry, that it followed its nature.

As you ponder the cycle of the hunter and the hunted, a queer excitement begins to steal over you. It's as if you stand on the edge of an chasm, and once you look in, you'll be privy to the secrets of the universe.

long pause

Dizzy, you follow the train of thought that is racing through your head. The chain of life . . . we are all part of the great chain . . . the fish eats plankton, the seal eats the fish, the bear eats the seal, humans eat the bear . . . when the human dies, they go back to the earth, back to the sea, and become food for microorganisms. The cycle is complete, the cycle moves on.

extended long pause—1 minute

You barely have a chance to take a breath when you see the kitten creep out from beside the garbage can. Time begins to speed ahead. She grows up before your eyes, turning from kitten to cat. The cat gives out a yowl as a male slips out from behind a tree and approaches her. They tussle and spat, then he mounts her and bites her on the back of the neck. After they mate, he rushes off. As if possessed by time-lapse photography, her stomach swells with kittens.

Again the dizziness sweeps through your head as she crawls up onto the table and gives birth. First one kitten works its way out of her womb, then another slides out, and a third . . . a fourth . . . a fifth. She cleans them, licking the birth fluid away from their eyes and nose, then bites the umbilical cord to sever their lives from her own. The kittens wriggle . . . one dies . . . the others seek her nipples and latch on. Life begets life. The cycle is complete, the cycle moves along.

Take three deep breaths.

long pause

Now look to your own life. How have cycles played an important part in your growth as a person? What cycles have you experienced that mirror nature's own? Have you borne children? Hunted an animal? Watched someone die? Been present at a birth? Think of the cycles that you've witnessed or participated in and how they affected you. What did you learn about life from being part of those universal patterns?

extended long pause—1 minute

Your mind now leaps ahead. As the ice-chilled air seeps into your lungs, into your body, the world becomes crystal clear. You know that if you just can reach out, you will become part of the Divine, part of the cycle of life. Take a deep breath and feel for your connection with the earth, with the plants and animals and other humans that inhabit this world and all that it contains.

extended long pause—1 minute

As you look around the frost-covered playground, you see a man standing in the shadow of the trees. The man steps out of the gloom and slowly crosses over to meet you. He appears to be wearing Native American dress, at first, but then his buckskins become a flowing robe and his features change and the man is now a woman.

She says, "I am your guide to your inner realms. I am your Higher Self, and I can appear in any form you wish me to take. Male or female, young or old, Native American or Celtic . . . my form and shape are up to you. Think now, of how you choose to see me."

Take a moment to find which image best fits your Higher Self. Remember, this figure is a part of you, so the image they take will also be a part of you.

extended long pause—1 minute

When your Higher Self has settled into a form that feels comfortable to you, you hear them say, "I am your link with the Divine, with the Gods. I connect you to the realms of

Spirit even as you connect yourself with the realms of the world. Through me, you experience magick and wonder and the knowledge that life goes on past the corporeal states. Take a moment to link with me, to find the connection we share, for I am both part of you and yet separate."

Take a moment to establish your link with your Higher Self—your Inner Guide.

extended long pause—1 minute

Now, when you have found the connection, your Inner Guide asks you several questions, each meant to strengthen your understanding of yourself.

First, your Higher Self asks, "Do you express yourself based on what you truly feel, or do you cover up your truths, bury them under layers of social conventions and expected answers?"

Think for a moment, about all the times you've expressed yourself as others expect you to, rather than on the truth of what lies in your heart. Can you express yourself openly? Can you be yourself when you are with others? If not, if your friends won't accept you as you as you truly are, then perhaps you are friends with the wrong people.

extended long pause—1 minute

Now again, imagine those situations where you have not asserted your right to your own beliefs. This time hear yourself speaking your truths. How do you think this will affect your friendships and relationships? Can you, in private, practice expressing yourself honestly until you feel strong enough to assert yourself with others? Take a moment to imagine what that would feel like.

extended long pause—1 minute

Next, your Higher Self instructs you to think about contradictions you might have in your life . . . opinions that don't mesh, dueling feelings or beliefs. Perhaps you find yourself pulled between two distinct possibilities.

Imagine those paradoxical feelings and thoughts, and first view them separately, each in their own space, giving each the validity that it deserves.

long pause

Slowly, superimpose one image of a belief or opinion onto the other. Try to see the points at which they do connect. If there are too many variances, then let them fall separate again, but if you examine them in detail, you should be able to find a few similarities.

long pause

Your Inner Guide tells you, "Eventually, with practice, you will be able to bring these polarity-based beliefs and feelings to a median point, where they will no longer pull you like a pendulum. You must simply allow them the time needed to sort themselves out, and keep looking for the similarities."

A bone-chilling gust of wind races past, sending shivers up your spine. Your Higher Self says, "You must go inside. The night is cold and you need warmth. But know that I am always with you, always inside, and you may call upon me whenever you need me."

Then, the image walks toward you and you feel the spirit meld into your body and become part of you, for in truth, your Higher Self is now and always has been a part of your spirit.

A sense of peace floods through your body and you know that this is what you've been missing. When you underwent your transformational ritual at Samhain, you knew that changes would soon follow. This feels like the next phase in this cycle.

extended long pause—1 minute

As you stamp your feet to warm them up, a flare of excitement and enthusiasm races through you. With all you have seen and experienced this night, it feels as though you have discovered the meaning of life. You've experienced the natural cycles and likened them unto your own life, and your inner sight and guidance feel so true for you that it crosses your mind to share this knowledge with others.

As you race along home, gliding over the ice as easily as you would traverse a dance floor, you see one of your neighbors. You stop him and try to convey all that you've learned, all that you feel you understand.

long pause

He shakes his head and says, "No, I don't see life like that at all."

Disappointed, you start to argue but then another truth strikes you—his truths are not your own. You understand the nature of life as it exists for you and you alone.

You could either continue the argument or let him have his own beliefs, whether or not you think he is wrong. If you reiterate your own position without invalidating his beliefs, then you have created a situation of tolerance, where you both can be right. The nature of the universe is subjective for each person.

Take a moment to restate your beliefs and to validate his belief system for him.

long pause

Your neighbor thanks you for your tolerance and waves good-bye as you head into your house. Those with whom you share your life are waiting for you in the living room.

Remember that you have given yourself permission to speak from the truth of your heart when you interact with them. While you know you must at times be tactful, you also know that from now on you must also be true to yourself.

long pause

Now, listen to my voice as I count from ten to one. You will awake refreshed and alert. Ten . . . nine . . . you are becoming awake and aware of your surroundings . . . eight . . . seven . . . six . . . hear the sounds around you . . . five . . . four . . . you will be fully alert and refreshed . . . three . . . two . . . one . . . take three deep breaths and when you are ready, you may open your eyes.

Suggested Exercises

1. Practice speaking from your heart when you are alone, especially if you have trouble expressing your beliefs and/or true feelings. Then practice with friends who you know will be supportive. When you have developed self-confidence, then tackle those who prefer that you share their opinions and world-views.

2. Examine the cycles of nature/life and your connection to them. Have you ever witnessed a death? A birth? Can you find a sense of peace in the way the cycles of nature work? There are many people who have a hard time with the violence they perceive in the natural order of things—that violence is often Nature's cleansing process, and it most certainly embodies the concepts of physical life/death. One must have death for life to continue . . . one must have life for death to become a reality.

3. If you haven't developed a sense of tolerance for those whose beliefs are different from yours, then now is a good time to do so. Remember, if you expect tolerance for your beliefs, you must give the same in return. Unfortunately, holy wars are still common today and it is tragic that a belief in the Divine can lead to murder and mayhem. If you have trouble with the precepts of a belief system, or you just feel that some of the actions of its followers are wrong, then you have a right to express your opinion. But you must then stand aside and let that person walk their own path, as long as they don't hurt others in the process.

4. When you are struggling with opposing opinions or desires, you first need to find the commonalties between the contradictory beliefs. Once you have discovered the similarities, you might find it easier to resolve the differences. Sometimes there will be no easy answer and you will be forced to make a choice. Other times, the situation will resolve itself as you discover the core of what you really want (which may be a third option altogether—there is always the chance that both opposing desires stem from the same core, and are simply differing manifestations of that wish).

Enter these enchanted woods, You who dare.

—George Meredith (1828–1909)
The Woods of Westermain

The Devil or Horned God
Leaping Over the Cliff

The sixteenth card of the major arcana is known as the devil (in some decks this card is known as Pan or the Horned God). It is assigned the number 15.

The Devil/Horned God and His Energy

The Devil/Horned God card is one of the few cards with two drastically different interpretations depending on which deck you are using. While I attempt to synthesize aspects of both interpretations into this mediation, let me first address how the card came to have such a dual nature.

First, during the early years of the tarot, Witchcraft and paganism were suspect and, to most people's minds, the Old Religions were thoroughly enmeshed with the Christian concept of evil. The Horned God of the pagans was expressly related to Satan and so the card was labeled the Devil.

As is well-known today, the image and foundation for Satan was plagiarized from the pagan gods of Nature, and the Church labeled Satan evil and perverse in their attempts to control the populace through fear. Their machinations worked to a large degree and only now are we reclaiming our gods of Nature as They were originally meant to be.

So, many decks today still connect the Devil card with the concept of evil and sin. They portray the archetype as being a slave to pleasure and debauchery, and the Devil is viewed as a puppet-master of those whom He influences.

However, there are a number of decks now appearing on the market that revert the archetype back to the god of Nature, to the god of Pagans and Witches. It is that archetype upon which I choose to focus in this chapter and so from here on out, I refer to the card as the Horned God.

The card of the Horned God is a card of challenge. When you encounter this energy, you know that chaos and ecstasy are not far behind. Perhaps this card represents the antithesis of the Justice card—there are few rules in the Horned God's game, self-discipline flies out the window. Here we have the energy of spontaneity, of impulsive action. Here we find our bedevilments plaguing us until we work through the fear and worries that we store inside.

This is not a card for cowards. Life in the realm of the Horned God offers intense challenge, a personal training ground where you must prove yourself. Temptations are rife, and this is the time in which to taste the fruits of desire. Here we find ecstasy of both body and soul and we may get our fingers burned in the process, but the experiences from this realm leave us stronger and wiser.

The Horned God represents a time period in which we must face our shadow-self, not to conquer or vanquish that part of ourselves, but to understand and integrate it into our everyday lives. For when ignored, the shadow grows in power. When given its rightful place, the shadow ceases to overpower and returns to its proper proportions.

Representing immoderation, the Horned God moves the Fool into a state of bliss and passion. This is the time when we leap over the cliff without looking down first, this is the time when the Fool picks up his/her backpack and returns to the open road. Discipline jumps screaming out the window when the Horned God knocks at our door—and we cannot help but let him in.

Much like the Celtic Ogham rune, Muin (Vine), this archetype represents a time when we release logic and reason and allow visionary states to enter our lives. We may exist in a blur during this time, we may indulge in mind-altering substances. This is generally a period when we revert to primal behavior—it's time to howl at the moon, to shriek from the top of a cliff.

Even when there seems to be danger in the road, we will not swerve because, when caught up by the Horned Lord's hunt, the chase becomes all. In this state of mind, all risks seem acceptable, we feel invulnerable. We are gods, or so we believe.

During this time, the Fool begins to hunger for the open road again, the town becomes too limited, the job too stifling. We are ready to break from our every day routine, we now see that we have outgrown parts of our lives. The Fool is ready for a new challenge, ready to take up the quest again.

The sense of inner peace and enlightenment discovered through the Temperance card becomes the springboard from which we dive. From the depths of our confidence and the nature of transition comes the desire to radically alter our course. We enter transformation by letting go of the familiar. In essence, we run off to join the circus and damned be anyone who warns us not to. Forget those potholes in the road—we're wearing blinders forged from the desire for metamorphosis.

During this time we may find ourselves acting in ways radically different than is our usual nature. Like a second childhood or a midlife crisis, the desire to kick off the shackles of responsibility overwhelms us. We find that our lives are suddenly turned upside down, and we like the feeling. No challenge becomes too difficult, no dare is left untaken.

When we encounter these wild pendulum swings, we embrace them and throw ourselves headlong into the fray. For, we reason, how can we be hurt when we are driven by spirit? When we are led by magick and passion?

We do not realize that, while this is a necessary phase of the cycle, it will inevitably lead to a fall. The Tower looms in the distance, but we can only see the forest in front of us and the panpipes are so seductive, the day so warm, that we overlook our shaky footing. We leap over the cliff, expecting water below—sometimes we splash into a warm ocean—other times razor-edged spikes lay in wait at the bottom.

In our daily lives, the Horned God can appear as our best friend suddenly suggesting that we skip the next two weeks of work and race off on the open road, no money in our pockets—"but surely something will come up to pay for gas and food." Or he may appear as a seductive new coworker who wants to lead us astray from our marriage, and since our husband isn't paying much attention to us lately . . . how can we resist?

He may come in the form of a chance path on a sunny day when we've got too much time on our hands and not enough to do . . . and so we go chasing merrily into the woods to meet the big bad wolf (who, as in the wonderful musical *Into The Woods,* wears a really hot leather jacket). He seduces us—off to pick flowers, we think—but we end up getting eaten alive.

The Horned God teases us, cajoles us, stares us down and challenges us to test our courage, to act on our boastings. On a moonless night, we stand at the edge of the forest and peer into the shadowed foliage, and his red eyes gleam out of the darkness, daring us to enter, if we have the courage. When we step into his realm, he chases us through the trails, his breath hot on our neck, as we realize we may have bitten off more than we can chew.

We shriek at the top of our lungs as he pursues us through the night, then just as we can run no more, we burst out onto the shore, where glimmering specks of phosphorescence sparkle on the sand and in the water. We are dancing among the stars.

The main problem we find with the energy of this card is that it has to end. No one can keep up such intensity for long. After a few months of moon madness, we must come back to our lives and see what's left.

We propel ourselves into other worlds, other realms, and have learned much. But then, as we slowly drag ourselves back into the town and see the shambles of our former lives, we enter the realm of the Tower.

When we are within the realm of the Horned God, we must try to remember that we have built a foundation for our lives and its unwise to throw away everything we've gained. It's difficult to give enough warnings about this card—the Challenger will sweep us up when he will and it's very hard to reason logically when in the grip of the Horned God.

But try to remember that there are ways to allow this power into our lives without destroying everything that is dear to us. When urged by some inner prompting to do something that could destroy a marriage, a friendship, a career, we must step back and ask ourselves, "What is the true core of my desire?"

Are we bored with our work? Do we want to change directions in our career? Do we need to put some sizzle back in our marriage? Does a friendship that was built on one set of interests need a new focus?

Sometimes we will go ahead and destroy those foundations, for not all structures are built on steady ground and they will crumble sooner or later. But make sure you aren't tearing down the castle when you just need to re-decorate.

The Horned God follows the Temperance card, for as soon as we have found inner spiritual strength and validated our own sense of self, we will be tested to see just how much faith we are willing to put behind our beliefs. How much do we trust our inner urgings? Where Temperance was the calm before the storm, the Horned God brings on the tornado and, like Dorothy, we're caught up in the mayhem and have just landed in Oz.

Now our physical lives engage the transformational cycle, matching what has taken place in our spirit.

The Spiritual Concept

In terms of spirituality, the Horned God becomes the Challenger, the Gatekeeper who dares us to enter the realm of vision and ecstasy and raging spiritual power.

We find the Horned God within the primal God-energy of the Witches. He is Herne, the Hunter, with glowing red eyes who watches from deep within the forest. He is Pan, the Piper, leading us into ecstasy, and Dionysus, the god of the vine. He is Bacchus, orgiastic reveler, and Oberon, Lord of Faeries, who lounges in flowered bowers. The Horned God is Coyote, nipping at our heels until we heed His presence.

The Horned God resides within Circe, seductive enchantress of the Greek isles; and Lilith, independent night-owl who needs no man's help. She is Mielikki, as Dark Huntress, who bids you creep with Her through the forest, a quiver of poisoned arrows slung across Her back.

This card represents the astrological sign of Capricorn and we place the Horned God, within the Wheel of the Year at Beltane, alongside the Lovers. Beltane is the rutting time, the time of passion and sexuality, and the Maypole represents the erect phallus of the Consort of the Goddess.

The Card

Again, we see the duality of meanings in the various representations of the card: Either we find the Devil as a traditional demonic figure, usually with a man and woman chained to him by puppeteer strings, or we find the Devil portrayed as the Horned-Goat god Pan/Herne. In the latter case, we often find symbols of sexuality on the card, such as an erect phallus.

Guidelines for Use

This meditation follows that of the Temperance card. You may also find it useful to meditate on the Horned God during Beltane or during any time when you are desiring dramatic change in your life.

Flowers:	valerian, wormwood, cannabis, galangal, mandrake, damiana, ginseng
Incense:	dragon's blood, vanilla, cinnamon
Oils:	violet, oakmoss, wormwood, patchouli
Crystals:	garnet, moonstone, peridot
Candles:	green, plum, burgundy, brown

Meditation

Relax and get comfortable. Close your eyes and take three deep breaths.

long pause

You wake at dawn on a cloudless day. Early streaks of tangerine color the pale blue of the spring morning. As you part the curtains and stare out of the window, you see that your neighborhood is beginning to wake, people are emerging from their houses, some in bathrobes to find the newspaper, others dressed for work, leaving before the traffic piles up on the freeway.

The pit of your stomach knots as you think about spending the day inside. Your job, once so interesting, has worn stale lately and you no longer find the thrill from your work that you once did. You aren't sure whether the problem is that you're tired of doing the same thing day after day, or whether you just need a break to get a new perspective.

long pause

As you look out into what is bound to be a beautiful day, you have the sudden desire to chuck it all—to run off to the beach or the woods and forget about your responsibilities. Before you can stop yourself, you grab the phone, dial your work place and find yourself babbling something about not feeling well.

Quicker than you thought possible, your day is cleared—free for whatever adventure awaits you. You stare at the silent receiver. The fib was easier than you expected. Your conscience pricks at you, but a glance back at the early rays of sun cresting the distant hills squelches any guilt you might have and you grab your bathing suit, keys, and backpack, and jump in your car. It's time for adventure—full speed ahead.

long pause

First stop, a grocery store, where you buy bread and cheese, fruit and pastry, and a clear, lightly-flavored water. Wayfaring food, you think. You toss the food into your pack and, stuffing a tape of your favorite wandering music into the cassette player, once again you speed out onto the open highway, letting Spirit guide your path.

As you zip along the road, you see an exit sign that points the way toward a park. What a perfect place to spend the day! As you turn onto the off-ramp, you can already imagine yourself lounging in the sunlight, letting the warmth soak into your body.

long pause

The ramp turns into a two-lane road, shaded by a thick stand of maple and cedar trees to either side. Eventually the drive turns into a parking lot and you find yourself at the park. There are a number of cars here; it would seem that other people had the same idea as you.

As you slip your pack on your back and grab your walking stick from the trunk of your car, you hear laughter in the clearing beyond the parking lot.

A group of brightly dressed people are milling around the park. You see a large pole with multicolored ribbons hanging from its top in the center of the grassy knoll and you remember that today is Beltane. With as much focus on your work as you've had lately, you forgot. It now seems that you've been directly led to a May gathering, and your heart leaps as you realize just how much you needed this.

long pause

A group of drums sits to one side, next to a fire pit that has been laid for the balefire. Vendors offer their wares—magickal oils and powders, candles and statues, daggers and wands. One woman is selling gauze skirts and shirts and drawstring trousers, and you see the perfect outfit there, in your favorite color. When you examine it closer, you find that the clothes are exactly your size.

Their prices are affordable and so, on impulse, you pay the woman her money and stash the clothes in your pack. Later tonight you will wear the garb, but for now you join the others who are swimming in the lake next to the park.

The water's exceptionally warm for this time of year, and so you change clothes, out in the open, at ease among others who are doing the same. No one looks at you in any way that makes you uncomfortable, and dressing out here is so much easier than looking for a bath house.

long pause

You wade into the lake, laughing as someone splashes you and welcomes you in with a loud hello. The water tingles over your body, it feels almost alive, and as you wade near the rushes by the shore, you think you hear a crystalline laughter from amidst the waving fronds.

When you look closer, you see the pale shape of a woman, almost translucent, gliding beside the shore's edge. She sees you watching her and, startled, ducks beneath the surface of the lake. No ripples mark her passage, and you realize that you've just seen a water sprite, perhaps an undine or a naiad.

long pause

When you have tired of playing in the water, you find a towel on the shore and dry yourself off. The sunshine soon dries your suit and now you dress in the garments you bought from the vendor. While the others seem friendly and welcome you into their midst, you sense a distance between them and yourself, and you realize that, as you've sought out your own path over the months, so your intense work and vision have taken you into a space that others cannot easily share.

The more introverted you've become, the more inner work you've done, the more isolated you now feel. As you think about this for a while, you see this state has both its benefits and its disadvantages. You have defined your spiritual path and tailored it to your personal needs, therefore it holds strong meaning for you. But the more specialized your spirituality has become, the more isolated you feel.

long pause

When you stop to think about this, you realize that you must retain a sense of individuality about your spiritual growth, and yet you want to reach out and connect with others in ways that won't compromise your beliefs. A nice balance, you think, but one that still leaves you feeling lonely at times.

And then, even as you are sorting things out in your mind, you look up into the eyes of a stranger whom, the moment you see them, is stranger no longer.

This person is someone you've known before, in a life long ago. They are attractive, seductively so, and by the look in their eyes, you know that they too seem to recognize you. Names are unimportant, only the fact that you instantly connect with them.

If you have a romantic partner, this is a terrifying feeling, for the intensity between this stranger and you grows with every moment. A flicker of fear races through your heart as you wonder if you've only now met your soulmate.

long pause

"I want you," they say. You realize that, given the right circumstances, this person is someone with whom you could willingly connect.

Their offer is real, and you must answer. If you are in a relationship, you must decide whether or not you will turn this person away. The choice is yours. Take a few moments to make your decision and act on it. Either you gracefully turn down their offer, or you accept and retire to one of the flower-covered bowers with them.

extended long pause—2 minutes

No matter what you've chosen to do, as soon as you act on your decision, they slip away, as if they've never been there. Disconcerted, you begin to wonder what they really wanted—did they mean you well? Did they bewitch you? Was there a connection between you after all?

Confused, you wander away from the crowd, for the gathering has lost its attraction. The wooded glen next to the park seems more inviting. A picnic table near the forest gives you a chance to sit down and eat your meal. You are hungry, the day has worn away quickly, and as you eat your bread and fruit, you try to sort out the strange encounter, but the events are too blurred and you truly do feel that you've been bewitched.

long pause

The afternoon has waned and the bonfire begins to blaze. The drummers pound away on their congas and bodhrans; the beats hypnotically in the early dusk. A group of dancers spins around the fire, their cries echoing through the air. As you pack away the last of the food, you spy a plaque on one of the trees standing sentinel over the trail. You meander over to the base of the tree to look at the plaque.

"Enter These Enchanted Woods, You Who Dare."

long pause

The moment you read these words, an odd compulsion overwhelms you. There is no help for it—you must run away into the forest, forgetting the drummers and the dancers, ignoring the fact that night settles over the area.

You take to the footpath, driven by an urge to see what lies deep within the glen. As you pass through the shadows of maple and cedar, alder and oak, the drums become muffled, the cries from the gathering fall away, and you sense that you've stepped into a different world.

long pause

A hush settles over the wood and you slow your pace. The feeling of magick and mayhem resonates around you. Faint green lights bob amidst the huckleberries, glowing orbs that flicker in and out of the trees. Some inner sense tells you not to get too close—this is a night of Faerie Magick and you don't want to get caught by the cunning folk.

The waning moon gives you little light and you can no longer see your hand in front of your face. A flicker of light from the will-o'-the-wisps occasionally glances off your face, but other than the Faerie lights, you have no guide, no sense of direction. Only your staff keeps you from falling, and you must trust in perceptions other than sight.

long pause

Still the urge to continue drives you on. Your feet become accustomed to the trail as you persevere, and you find that you can reach out with your psychic sense to keep from veering off the path into the ravines that you know line the right side of the trail.

The path slowly ascends. From a nearby tree, an owl's cry pierces the night. Somehow you know that, just ahead, you must round a bend. As you curve the trail, you feel eyes watching you from the hillside to your left. You turn, and there see a darkness far blacker than the night. It sucks light into itself, and right now it's drawing your attention. Your teeth chatter as you turn to slowly face the being you know lives within the ancient forest.

Out of the hillside, glow two crimson eyes. They stare right through you, into your heart, and you know that you are facing the Horned Lord, Guardian of the Forest, He who watches over the night.

long pause

Without a thought, your knees quiver and bend before the Hunter. You do not know how long you kneel before the hillside, but then, you hear a great laughter and both fear and excitement leap in your heart and you find yourself running into the darkness, down the trail, your feet barely skimming the ground.

You race through the trees, into the undergrowth, down a trail that leads to a beach near the far end of an inlet. The sand sparkles, shimmering with green and blue, yellow and pink phosphorescence. Every footstep kicks up a flurry of glitter and deep in your heart you know that you are dancing among the stars. The water glistens with this same faerie fire and you go wading in, letting the shining sparkles cover your skin.

Like a madness, the night embraces you, enlarges your soul, and you can no longer speak, only shout and shriek out your joy.

extended long pause—1 minute

The night wears away as you play in the water. As your senses slowly begin to return, you realize that you've been bored lately, that things in your life have gotten stale.

Tonight it feels as though you have entered a world of sensation and excitement, a world where magick grabs you by the throat and won't let go. If only this feeling could continue—if only every day held this intensity. If only life could change, and you could always be vibrant and brilliant.

But as you look into the sky, you realize that you forgot to tell anybody where you were going or when you would be home. Unwilling thoughts of responsibility creep back into your mind and you find yourself resenting the limitations they put on your actions.

long pause

You drag yourself to shore and begin the long walk back through the forest. Sore muscles remind you of how tired you are. How are you ever going to make it back to your car? But somehow, you find yourself back at the edge of the park, which now stands empty and silent.

A noise alerts you as you trudge along toward the parking lot, and when you turn back to look at the forest, you see, standing like a giant against the night sky, the Hunter Himself. Massive and masculine, with curving horns rising to the sky, His glowing ruby eyes shine down and you feel his laughter echo as you fall to your knees. If there is anything you wish to say to Him, take the time now and listen for his answer.

extended long pause—1 minute

The vision fades and you are alone again. As you step into your car, you find that your outfit smells like ocean brine, and you are covered with sand, clammy and uncomfortable.

But this day has changed you, and you don't look forward to going home. If you have a partner, you know they're going to be angry—perhaps rightfully so, depending on what your answer to your the stranger was. If you chose to accept the stranger's offer, how will you tell your mate? Even if you walked away, you now know that you can be tempted and it's not a comfortable feeling.

And the night—the night split open your soul and dazzled you with the primal force of the forest. How can you go back to your daily routine now that you've tasted the magick of the Forest Lord?

Confused and bewildered, unsure of what your next step will be, you only know that the activities of this night will alter your life and you wonder just what that will mean.

long pause

Now, listen to my voice as I count from ten to one. You will awake refreshed and alert. Ten . . . nine . . . you are becoming awake and aware of your surroundings . . . eight . . . seven . . . six . . . hear the sounds around you . . . five . . . four . . . you will be fully alert and refreshed . . . three . . . two . . . one . . . take three deep breaths and when you are ready, you may open your eyes.

Suggested Exercises

1. Sometimes we reach a point in our lives where it feels like we've boxed ourselves in. We need to figure out how to reenergize ourselves without impulsively destroying what we've created. Think of things that you like to do, uncommon activities you seldom allow yourself to pursue. When life begins to feel stale, take out your list and choose something to put a bit of sparkle back into your life. For one person this might mean sky diving, for another it's a day spent shopping, eating chocolates, and watching soap operas.

2. Spontaneity can be planned and still be fun. Set aside a day or two each month where you make no plans, have no schedule, where you can just take off and do whatever tickles your fancy.

3. If you want to include a friend in your exploits that's fine, but don't waste time discussing where to go. Simply call them, say "I'm going to . . . ," or "I'm going to do . . . ," and "Do you want to join me?" That way you still get to do what you want, but you've offered a friend the chance to join in the fun.

4. Sometimes these impulsive desires are telling you that you've gotten into a rut, that it may be time to switch jobs or reevaluate your relationship. You need to be cautious when you examine your feelings so that you don't ignore warning signs that point to disaster ahead in career or love.

5. Always remember, your actions will reap consequences, good or bad. Too often we act on impulse without understanding why we do so, without thinking about the laws of cause-and-effect. So next time you have the desire to run off and play, think about what might happen and then decide if it's worth the risk. Sometimes the answer is a resounding "yes" . . . other times we spot patterns of self-sabotage.

Die Lust der Zerstörung ist zugleich ein schaffende Lust!
The urge for destruction is also a creative urge!

—Michael Bakunin (1814–1876)
Die Reaktion in Deutschland

The Tower

Burning Your Bridges

The seventeenth card of the major arcana is known as the Tower. It is assigned the number 16.

The Tower and Its Energy

When we encounter the Tower card, we encounter the last stage of transformation in the third phase of the Fool's journey. Here we undergo the most traumatic effects of that change, here we truly understand the third part of the journey—we've driven ourselves to succeed (Justice), then sacrificed all that stood in the way of our goals (the Hanged Man). We've accepted Fate's intervening in our lives (Death). Then, when we've come to a place of enlightenment (Temperance), we cast caution to the winds and take the leap of faith—off the cliff (the Devil/Horned God).

189

Now we finish the third phase of our journey. We land at the bottom of the cliff, we cannot keep up the wild energy of the Devil/Horned God and the Tower crashes around our heads as we helplessly watch our lives fall apart (or so we think).

The Tower archetype comes into play when we have reached a point where we need to sweep away all that is built on shaky ground. A castle built on sand will fall at high tide. So too, if we have established foundations without thought to their stability, we must allow nature to take its course. For the Tower card represents a cleansing process; it clears the way for stronger growth.

While the Tower card symbolizes breakdown and dissolution, it also represents the chance to rebuild stronger than before. Destruction must take place before new creation—Pele covers the land with Her lava and destroys all in Her path, but at the same time, She enlarges the islands and creates new areas where life may take hold and grow.

So, in that sense, the Tower is a card of renovation. With the Tower we go through crises and traumas, we find our illusions shattered into a million shards, but we also regain a sense of self-awareness and we then rebuild on the sturdy bricks that are left after the storm has moved on.

We are liberated from shackles that do nothing to further our evolution as the Tower archetype moves through our lives. While the changes can be shocking and we lose all sense of security, we also begin to understand how rigidity cannot last in this world. For change is stability, as we discovered with both the Wheel and the Death cards, and the Tower only appears when stagnation has latched hold to some part of our lives.

The Tower card presents us with a chance to face up to chaos, to put our beliefs to a test. If we do not believe in our own strength, then the time spent in the realm of the Tower will topple our hopes and leave us crippled and broken. However, if we put into use the lessons we've learned since we began our journey, we find the inner will and confidence to continue, to know that our spirits cannot be destroyed by the seeming chaos raging around us.

We cannot hide from the Tower, it will seek us out no matter how much we try to avoid its energy. But if we understand that this is a natural process—Nature must regularly clean out her closets and that includes events that affect our lives—then we cease to blame others for the dramatic shifts that engulf us at this time. We still feel sorrow and confusion, but we understand that instability cannot last.

During this time period, we may find ourselves losing one link after another. The Tower generally appears as events in our lives rather than as people. This archetype may signify an impending divorce—when you or your mate has ceased to value the marriage, when one of you has found someone new or decided you want to experience life as a single person again.

The Tower can also be a natural disaster that destroys our home; or a senseless accident that leaves someone we love dead or maimed. We might find ourselves in the wrong place at the wrong time and end up paralyzed or disabled. The Tower might strip us of our career, or we might suffer a financial setback and lose our home and all of our belongings.

If the Tower comes in on a lighter note, it may indicate the end of a long-term friendship, the loss of a substantial amount of money, or the destruction of long-hoped-for plans. But whatever it indicates, we can be sure that this dissolution would have happened one way or another, because whatever has dissolved wasn't stable in the first place. What feels like loss is actually liberation from a situation that would have only grown worse as time went on.

When we let go of fear and face the unknown, when we are able to count the blessings we have left, then we begin to rebuild from the chaos. You can be sure that those things left standing after the Tower has played through are secure and can be counted on to withstand other storms.

I liken it to a brick house shattered during an earthquake. You sort through the mess, discard everything that broke, and scrub off the remaining bricks. Those bricks are tempered, and you can now use them to begin reconstruction, knowing that this time you have the experience and insight to built a stronger foundation.

For truly, when we first began sorting out our lives, during phase two of the journey (the Lovers through the Wheel), we weren't yet grounded in our own sense of spiritual development. We were focused on getting our lives in order and so it is both understandable and natural that some of the structures we first built no longer fit our evolution. Just as children outgrow their clothes, so we outgrow people and routines.

When we don't see this, when we are used to a certain routine, we tend to accept it as gospel. We now must look at the people and patterns in our lives with detachment; we must rid ourselves of "shoulds" and embrace that which is true to our lives now.

The Tower can be a frightening realm through which to pass; all our courage and self-confidence will be required to successfully navigate this time of destruction/creation, but once we are safely on the other side, we enter the fourth and last phase of our journey. The Fool becomes valiant, and through his/her bravery, achieves new spiritual heights and an understanding of the Universe.

The Spiritual Concept

In terms of spirituality, we find the Tower within Pele, Hawaiian goddess of both destruction and creation. We also find the Tower within Kali-Ma, who protects Her children even as She eats them. We also discover the Tower within the Furies, who seek justice through vengeance.

The Tower resides within the realm of Ares, Greek god of war, and Tlaloc, Aztec lord of the rain, who even as His nourishing waters fed the crops, demanded the hearts of children as sacrifice.

We place the Tower within the Wheel of the Year at Lughnasadh, next to the Hanged Man, for through this archetype we once again must sacrifice from our lives in order to achieve clarity of sight.

The Card

The Tower is usually depicted as a castle tower in the midst of crumbling. Blasted from the heavens by lightning, it topples to the ground in the midst of a cloud of smoke and fury. Often we see a figure falling from the Tower, and many times a dragon will be coiling around the structure, representing the powers of destruction, fire, and creation. If we search the card, we often find a symbol of new hope peering out from behind a brick or from one corner of the card—such as a flower or a patch of blue sky.

Guidelines for Use

This meditation follows that of the Devil/Horned God card. You may also find it useful to meditate on the Tower during Lughnasadh, or during any time when you feel like events are spiraling out of control and you aren't sure how to cope with them.

Flowers:	cactus, galangal, garlic, nettle
Incense:	dragon's blood, copal, pepper, tobacco
Oils:	dragon's blood, ginger, rue
Crystals:	obsidian, volcanic glass, carnelian
Candles:	rust, orange, red, burgundy

Meditation

Relax and get comfortable. Close your eyes and take three deep breaths.

long pause

You find yourself out in the woods, in a campground. Today is a lazy, late-summer day and you've taken a few days away from your work to relax. Ever since Beltane, when you raced off into the woods and met the Horned God, you've been uneasy, not sure of what consequences your actions engendered.

You know that Beltane night, wild as it was, shook up your universe but you still haven't seen the final results and you've been restless ever since then, almost uneasy.

long pause

Work has been rocky lately, you were spotted driving on the freeway when you called in ill on Beltane and so your supervisor knows you weren't sick after all. When you reported to work the next day, you found that you'd been censured on your employee record.

Your home life has also been tense, there's been a bit of discord between you and those with whom you share your house. Everyone seems on edge and you wonder just what is headed your way.

long pause

The wind rises, the air is charged, and it looks like a thunderstorm is rolling in overhead. The weather is muggy, humid, and you feel charged with that electricity which preceeds a storm.

A sense of foreboding begins to cloud your thoughts and you have the sudden desire to go home, to make sure that everything is all right. You begin packing up your tent and camp gear as the first flash of lightning cracks open the sky. A deep rumble rolls through the air, thunder so loud it hurts your eardrums, and then a sheet of rain comes cascading down to drench you and all of your gear.

You spend the next few minutes stuffing everything back into your car, then you speed off toward town and your home.

long pause

As you round the bend on the highway, your car lurches across the road. The ground convulses, great cracks appear in the asphalt and you screech to a halt under a stand of cedars. You scramble out of your car, grabbing only your backpack, as the ground shakes again.

An earthquake!

long pause

Lightning flashes across the sky, the rain blurs your sight, and you have trouble staying on your feet as the rolling earth finally comes to a halt. As you turn, one of the cedars breaks roots from the ground to go tumbling over onto the roof of your car, crushing the vehicle beneath it.

long pause

The thunder and lightning continue their show while you stare in disbelief at what used to be the highway. Cracked like an eggshell, no car could possibly navigate the broken pavement now. All traffic into or out of the town will have to be on foot.

You don't want to go near the car again for fear one of the other trees will fall. So you turn toward the city and begin to pick your way along the road, carefully stepping around the massive cracks and downed power lines as you go. Still in shock, you can't help but wonder what happened to your home.

long pause

The thunderstorm begins to recede as the town comes into sight. The rain's still coming down in sheets, but at least the lightning and thunder are moving on. Ahead, a maple tree lights up the sky in flames. It must be over thirty feet high, and the crown of fire quickly consumes the leaves and branches. The rain beats down—it will eventually quench the fires, but the tree is already blackened and scorched.

The first houses come into sight. Some have been spared, they don't appear damaged at all. Others are in shambles, shredded beyond recognition, a pile of toothpicks where only this morning someone's home stood. Fear knots at your stomach—in which condition will your home be? If you have pets or loved ones at home, are they okay? You would like to run, but there are so many power lines crossing the road that you know it would be dangerous for you to go racing through the jumble.

long pause

As you turn down the street leading to your house, you hear a scream from a badly-damaged trailer. A woman is caught in the rubble. You are the only one near—others are searching for survivors or trying to find their own loved ones. You run over to the pile of twisted metal and start tossing aside bits and pieces of the mangled mobile home.

Then you see her—the woman is caught under what once was a kitchen counter. You are able to free her without much effort—there are plenty of timbers and bits of wood around to use as leverage.

extended long pause—1 minute

As you help her from the rubble, you see that her ankle is hurt, probably broken or a sprain, and so she puts her arm around your shoulder while you help her hobble away from the damage. You sit her down on the sidewalk, away from any possible danger. One of her neighbors, a nurse, has noticed your efforts. She is on her way over to help right now. The injured woman thanks you and waves as you leave.

As you continue down the street, the ground suddenly rolls again—an aftershock!

This time you are thrown to the ground, and you skin your knees and elbows as you skid across the pavement. The tremor stops as quickly as it started, it wasn't nearly so violent as the first quake, but you find yourself anticipating the next aftershock.

long pause

The next corner brings you to your house. You quicken your pace to a trot, then a run. As you round the bend, you see your house—it isn't in shambles, but there may be heavy damage to several areas of the home.

You first assess that none of your family members were hurt during the quake. All loved ones, be they two- or four-footed, are all right. But now you must inspect the house to see whether the rooms are intact, or whether some might have collapsed.

Be aware that each room represents a part of your life.

The living room represents your social life, your interpersonal relationships between you and others. Inspect the living room to see whether anything has been knocked askew. If you can trust your friends, if you're happy with your social life, then the living room will be untouched. However, if anything is knocked asunder, or if the entire room has been disrupted, then you will know that there are shaky foundations shoring up your social life.

Look through the living room and determine the state of your social life. Your subconscious mind will recognize and identify the problem areas.

extended long pause—1 minute

Now go into the kitchen. The kitchen represents your family, your loved ones—any children you may have, your brothers, sisters, parents, and relatives. If the kitchen is intact then you can be fairly sure your family life is intact. However, if anything in the kitchen is upset, you will know that something in your family interactions is at odds.

Look through the kitchen and determine the state of your family life. Your subconscious mind will recognize and identify the problem areas.

extended long pause—1 minute

Next, move to the study. The study represents your career—where you're at with your work, where you think you should be going. If anything in the study has been shaken loose, then there's some turmoil in the area of your career.

Look through the office and determine the state of your career. Your subconscious mind will recognize and identify the problem areas.

extended long pause—1 minute

On to the bedroom. The bedroom represents your love relationship, or lack thereof. Look through the room—if anything is out of place, then you know that some area of your relationship is out of kilter. Or perhaps, if the earthquake hit this room hard, it may mean that your relationship or lack thereof is putting a strain on you.

Look through the room to determine the state of your love life. Your subconscious mind will recognize and identify any problem areas.

extended long pause—1 minute

Your next stop is the altar table kept in an alcove. On this altar are images and items relating to your personal spirituality. Take a moment to examine the altar and everything on it. Is everything in order? Has anything been knocked over? If something is out of place or broken, then it may mean that some areas of your spiritual path are built on shaky foundations. You may need to examine your beliefs to see how they relate to you as a person today.

Look over the altar table to determine the state of your spiritual life. Your subconscious mind will recognize and identify any problem areas.

extended long pause—1 minute

Now peek into the bathroom. The bathroom represents your private side, the side of yourself you keep hidden—the secret joys and secret shames that are yours alone. Your dreams and goals and hidden motivations reside in this room. Look around. Has anything been disrupted? Is everything in its proper place? If not, then perhaps your perceptions and hopes aren't properly aligned to the person you are.

Look around the bathroom to determine the state of your psyche. Your subconscious mind will recognize and identify any problem areas.

extended long pause—1 minute

For your last stop, return to your bedroom and open the doors to your closets. These closets represent your fears and inner demons. While everyone has them, sometimes they are out of proportion. Are your closets a jumble now? Are they so full that the earthquake knocked everything into one big pile? Or are your fears and worries sorted out enough so that they remained firmly on the shelf when the earthquake hit?

Look through your closets to determine the state of your inner fears. Your subconscious mind will recognize and identify any problem areas.

extended long pause—1 minute

Now you have assessed your house. How much overall damage did the earthquake do? Are the foundations stable, or are you going to need to completely rebuild? Begin clearing away the clutter. Make sure you examine each piece to see if you can dust it off for rebuilding, or whether it's useless and should be discarded.

You may be fortunate, your life and your house may be built on secure foundations. Or you may find that many of your assumptions and your relationships were built on shaky ground. You must also remember that sometimes, as we evolve, we outgrow a relationship, a belief, or a career even as a baby outgrows their crib.

There's no shame in finding we need to revamp our perceptions of life. What was true for us yesterday may not be true for us tomorrow.

So look through the damage to your house. What can you save? What should you discard?

Before you can rebuild, you need to clear away the dross, that which is now trivial and unimportant in your life. Take a few moments to sort out that which you can safely keep in your life, and that which has run its course.

extended long pause—2 minutes

Now that you have cleared away the superfluous, look at what's left. These are the secure foundations that make up your life. Perhaps you will need to renovate entire sections of your routines and relationships. Perhaps you only need to fill in chink-holes that cracked under the strain of the quake.

What has been left standing are those things, beliefs, and people into which you can safely put your trust. They make up the support network for your life. Know that they will be there for you when the going gets rough.

long pause

Your subconscious mind can see the signs when you begin to build on shaky ground, but your conscious mind may not want to accept the truth. Each time you add a room to your house, you must ask yourself—does this room detract from the stability of my house? Is it built on a secure foundation?

In the same vein, each time you accept a belief or person into your life, you must ask, does this belief or person add to my life or detract from it? Can I trust this friend, can I rely on this belief? If tomorrow an accident left me paralyzed, would my friend be there to help me? Would my belief desert me if I found myself in trouble?

long pause

While it is better to perform this sorting-out process before an accident or emergency, we often leave it until the last minute. We are, after all, only human. So now, look over your house and begin to make plans for rebuilding. You may have a long task ahead of you, you may have to drastically restructure your life. Or a few days of good hard work may take care of the weak spots.

long pause

Now, listen to my voice as I count from ten to one. You will awake refreshed and alert. Ten . . . nine . . . you are becoming awake and aware of your surroundings . . . eight . . . seven . . . six . . . hear the sounds around you . . . five . . . four . . . you will be fully alert and refreshed . . . three . . . two . . . one . . . take three deep breaths and when you are ready, you may open your eyes.

Suggested Exercises

1. Examine the various areas of your life with a detached eye. You might want to have a good friend who doesn't have a hidden agenda help you. Make a list of those areas in your life that feel shaky and try to determine just why they feel unstable. Often we can prevent the flow of problems into our lives if we will analyze our motivations and desires before we give into them.

2. If the Tower manifests in your life through a divorce, a traumatic incident or accident, or an ongoing series of disasters, it can be an indication that you aren't listening to your intuition. I always tell my tarot clients and magickal students, intuition is *not* what you feel, *not* what you think—for head and heart can lie. Intuition is a little voice in your gut that says, "I know . . . " "I know I'd better not get involved with that person . . . " "I know this deal sounds too good to be true . . . " "I know that I'd better not go for a drive tonight because the road feels too dangerous . . . " Listen to your intuition, it will usually lead you to safety.

3. If we grow up in chaos, we learn it as a natural state of life. We must break childhood patterns that were perpetuated by dysfunctional parents. Remember, a family can be chaotic and still love you. Love may not always provide the stability and security we need in our lives. If you are in a codependent relationship, the fact that you love your partner doesn't mean the relationship is a good one. Love must be mature, game-free, clear, and honest to truly benefit and enhance our lives.

4. In the event of disaster, remember the practical before the metaphysical. Call the police, the ambulance, the fire department when necessary. If you are in an abusive situation, GET OUT! If you are held up by robbers, give them your money and save yourself. Try to keep your wits about you. Magick and metaphysics are important, but you must remain grounded and you must take practical steps first. Okay?

Part Four

Metamorphosis:
The Search for Spirit

*L*ook at the stars! look, look up at the skies!
O look at all the fire-folk sitting in the air!
The bright boroughs, the circle-citadels there!

—Gerard Manley Hopkins (1844–1889)
The Starlight Night

The Star
A Clear Inner Life

*T*he eighteenth card of the major arcana is known as the Star. It is assigned the number 17.

The Star and Its Energy

When we encounter the Star card, we encounter our intuitional self. As we enter the fourth and last part of the Fool's journey, we bring to this phase a self that has gone through trial and test . . . through fire and ice . . . we have built our lives, then torn away the excess, stripped ourselves to only those foundations that securely reflect our true natures. Temperance has given us a sense of inner peace which now asserts itself fully. We come charred from the Tower, but strengthened by truth. We have put our houses in order and now we take the leap into the celestial/universal consciousness.

As we begin the fourth phase of our trek, we seek the cosmic well from which to purify and cleanse ourselves. We are not ashamed of our ashes—the Tower crumbled so that we might liberate ourselves from outworn patterns, but now we want to wash away the grime and emerge radiant in our clarity.

The Star archetype comes into play when we have cast away our masks, when we wear only our true faces, when we live our lives in honesty. We cannot touch the stars if we are mired in the swamp. With our house/life built on a firm foundation, we now ascend the hill and soar into the heavens, seeking like-minded friends and connections. With our own lives set in order, now we reach out to help others.

The Star card symbolizes self-esteem, self-confidence, and self-trust. By listening to our intuition (again, the voice inside that says *I know)*, we navigate with a new sense of security. We know who we are, and we follow the guiding light of our inner spirit in order to make celestial connections. Filled with a new sense of hope and harmony, we become pioneers. We open ourselves to the universe, we journey through the gateway, and so become travelers in a wider sense of the word. We no longer need healing for ourselves, so we set about healing the world.

We have come through our traumas with scars, but scar tissue is often stronger than the original flesh, and so we have empathy for others while still retaining a sense of detached compassion. Because we exist in this state of alertness and peace, so the universe often sends wonderful surprises our way. We may also receive unexpected enlightenment—answers that were hard to find yesterday suddenly cascade into our lives.

During the time of the Star, we may find ourselves volunteering to help others, we may devote our time and money to charitable causes, or to group efforts rather than to our own individual needs. Groups like Amnesty International, the American Civil Liberties Union (ACLU), Safeplace, Mothers Against Drunk Driving (MADD)—all of these fall under the influence of the Star archetype.

Star periods tend to sail along without hitches. We may find that our intuition, our psychic abilities are heightened. We may also find our minds racing, sleep may drag its feet because we have so much we want to think about.

The Star card presents us with opportunities to expand our horizons, to give back to the world rather than take from it. When we donate our money or time with a generous heart, we find ourselves rewarded in unexpected and delightful ways. One might liken the Star card to the Celtic Ogham rune Uilleand (Honeysuckle). When you reach the core of your journey, you find hidden treasures awaiting within. But if you take the journey simply to find the treasures, they will disappear and you're left with crumbs in your hands.

The Star strikes like lightning and when it appears in our lives, we must make use of the highly charged energy, for it can just as quickly vanish.

Coax the Star and she will hide herself, but turn to your problems, face them head-on, and the Star will be waiting for you around the next corner—she will leap out and carry you on her shoulders for a while. Just when you're too tired to stand, she lets you drink from her water jug and your energy returns tenfold.

When the Star appears in your life, she may come as a blazing comet, streaking through your conscious mind to wake you out of your trance.

Or you may find her in the blink of an eye—she is elusive. Seldom appearing as a person in your life, she sneaks up on us and then pounces with an enthusiasm hard to ignore. When we're in her embrace, we feel liberated from the cares of the world. We're on a natural high!

The Star can be a book that opens our eyes, a sudden shift in perception brought on by a mystical event, by watching a movie, by listening to a speaker, by experiencing life in someone else's shoes for a time. Because our lives are clear of instability, because the Tower has stripped away the veneers and illusions, we can experience the energy of the Star with full clarity and joy.

She is harmony, inner peace, the spring wind gusting on the mountain, the feeling that we can soar. Through the Star we are purified, clarified, washed clear of all cobwebs. The Star brings new experiences into our lives to rejuvenate and renew us.

The Spiritual Concept

In terms of spirituality, we find the Star within Nut (or Nuit), the Egyptian star goddess. She is also within Venus, the Evening Star, Roman goddess of love and spring time. And you may seek the Star in Arianrhod, Welsh goddess of the Silver Wheel, whose castle—Caer Arianrhod—lies in the starry skies.

The Star resides within the realm of Uranus, the Greek god of the skies, and within Enlil—Sumerian lord of the heavens.

The astrological sign of Aquarius is connected to the Star, and we place this card within the Wheel of the Year firmly within the element of air.

The Card

The Star is usually depicted as the Aquarian water bearer, kneeling between the night sky and the Earth. A woman (or being) pours water from either a waterfall or the heavens into a stream on the ground. You will find other star-like images surrounding her, and the card will often have depictions of crystals and gems scattered on it.

Guidelines for Use

This meditation follows that of the Tower card. You may also find it useful to meditate on the Star during the spring time, or whenever you feel the need for clarity, intuition, and hope.

Flowers:	white rose, citron, lemon verbena
Incense:	lavender, lemon, rose, primrose
Oils:	lavender, lemongrass, mint, camphor, rose
Crystals:	star sapphire, celestial quartz, celestite
Candles:	white, silver, pale blue, lavender

Meditation

Relax and get comfortable. Close your eyes and take three deep breaths.

long pause

You have come on vacation to a small island, where you find yourself pleasantly left to your own devices. Your family decided to stay home, so you have the freedom to wander at leisure, enjoying your solitude as you traverse the empty beach. You carry a simple walking stick and your backpack for your journey today.

While the island is rather empty, for most visitors choose to come here during the peak summer months, you feel no lack for company—indeed, you are relieved not to have to put up with hordes of tourists and interruptions.

long pause

As you meander along the beach, white sand warms your feet and filters through your toes. Unmarred by any rocks or hidden twigs, this beach is one of the purest you've seen. The sand lies in a long belt along the seashore. Here and there a crab scuttles by, and occasionally you see the body of a jellyfish washed up by the tide and stranded.

The ocean rolls in to kiss the shore, cresting in waves. Seafoam sprays across the sand and then pulls back again, leaving a clean slate in its wake.

long pause

Off to one side of the beach lies a fern-shrouded path. It leads through a stand of palm trees and wild orchids, on into a patch of ti plants and anthuriums. Wild ginger twines around the scrub trees, and fragrant perfume from the tropical forest wafts down to catch your mind and set it sailing.

As you follow the footpath, you find yourself ascending a slight grade. The trees are thicker here, but you don't feel closed in like you might in a coniferous forest. The light plays off the leaves as a remarkable sense of peace descends to cushion both your mind and body. The gentle ambiance of the late afternoon warms your heart and you find yourself both relaxed and incredibly aware. You can hear the rustlings in the undergrowth, but no sense of panic or warning alerts you and you know, instinctively, that you are safe.

long pause

Here you have the time to think about the past months. The earthquake rattled your senses, it took you a while to recover from the stress, but now your house is rebuilt, stronger than before, and you find that your life has followed suit.

You have straightened out any problems with your career and your relationships, you are more content than you have been since the very beginnings of your journey.

Now you find that your thoughts are turning outward, you yearn for connection with like-minded people and yet, in your heart, you know that those connections will come in their own time. Their absence is noticed, but does not overwhelm you. You have begun to understand the cyclic nature of life and you know that when it is right, these new friends will make themselves known.

long pause

As you continue along the path, you find that the foliage is beginning to open out. The trail has led you upward, at an easy but steady slope. As you step out of the jungle, you see that your path now leads to a mountain, and you realize that it is one of the mountains you used to see in the far distance when you were first on your journey.

You have come across the sea only to find the quest before you again.

Narrow but sure, the path leads to a ridge where the sides of the jungle fall away to reveal soaring cliffs below, covered with thick vegetation. Ravines, deep and chasmed, shore up the sides of your path and far below you see the ocean—a splash of aquamarine tinting the canvas of the world.

long pause

As you watch the distant water crest onto the beach, you return to your journey.

Now you begin to think about your vacation. When it is over, you must return home, return to work. The time spent on this little island will recharge you, reenergize your batteries, so to speak. By the time you are ready to leave, you will be looking forward to your job again, to seeing your home, to returning to your daily routines.

You will board your plane happily, for your heart is rooted elsewhere and to there you will return.

long pause

The ravine is so steep that it leaves you dizzy when you peek over the edge. As you pass over the ridge, you see the path leads to a bowl-shaped lea higher up the mountain. An ancient crater, you think, now filled with grass and scrub brush and the lulling rush of the wind.

The sun is low in the sky as you crest the ridge and peer into the grassy caldera. To one side of the bowl sparkles a pool, fed by the cascade of a tinkling waterfall. The water flows out through an underground river, toward the ocean, you suppose. Liquid crystal, you scoop up a mouthful of the warm water and drink deeply. The taste of sunshine lingers in your mouth.

As you wash away the dust from your climb, you notice that although the evening is still warm a tang in the air predicts a chilly night at this elevation. With relief, you think about your backpack, with the sweater and blanket you thought to bring.

long pause

You spread out your blanket and set your dinner atop the light quilt. Bread, cheese, fruit . . . whatever suits your fancy . . . you had the foresight to pack exactly what you now desire to eat. Enjoy your dinner, washed down with large sips from the crystal pool.

long pause

The light begins to fade. Here in the tropical climes, twilight is brief and quickly gives way to night. Put on your sweater and lean back to enjoy the evening. There are no dangerous animals here, that much you know, and you have neither heard nor seen any person this day, save for at breakfast when fellow travelers wished you well for the day.

As the last rays of sun slip out of sight behind the ridge, darkness surrounds you and the stars begin to shimmer into view. There are so many! Here, away from the street lamps and city glare, you watch as a panorama of light glimmers down on you. It's as if some giant from the sky grabbed up a handful of jewels and tossed them across the velvet night.

long pause

How vast the universe is, and how beautiful. You begin to enter that state where all your problems, all your worries seem but a pinprick on the head of a needle compared to the infinity stretching above you. Everything drops away, tonight there exists only you in connection with the celestial heavens.

And yet, however small you are in the proportion to the universe, you know that, in your own way, you are an integral part in the order of things. You are a link of the great chain, a component of the force that binds this universe together. Your connection is strong and you can draw upon the energy of the cosmos for help or comfort whenever you may need to.

extended long pause—1 minute

You find yourself thirsty again, and so take your cup over to the waterfall. As you reach out to allow the water to fill your vessel, you suddenly see something streak by. You look up, your hand still under the splashing stream, in time to see a meteor flash across the sky. Then another, and another goes zooming past!

long pause

Now you recall—it is the second week in August, and you are witnessing the Perseids meteor shower. This should be the prime night for viewing, and you have one of the best spots in the world from which to watch the meteors streak through the night.

A reflection from one of the meteors shimmers against the surface of the water in your cup and, with a swirling sensation, you realize that you can drink in the essence of the stars. Raise the cup to your lips and drink.

A shiver of light races down your throat to fill your body. Gold and silver droplets tingle into your fingers, into your arms and legs and toes and stomach. The star water washes through you, pure and clear, crystalline as a vase. Look at your hand—you can see tiny sparkles of light emanating from beneath your skin—you are a child of the stars.

extended long pause—1 minute

Your hair raises as if caught up by the wind's fingers and, with a whoosh, the breeze laughs and sings its way into your thoughts and then out again, taking with it all the negativity, stress, and tension you may be holding onto.

long pause

You feel like laughing. As you open your mouth, the sound racing out of your throat catches you unaware—it is the clinking of golden coins, the splash of the waterfall, the echo of silverware on china—and the melody of your laugh makes you laugh again, for joy.

You raise your eyes to the stars once more. The meteors are thick now, streaking, whistling, racing across the sky to meet their fiery destiny. The shimmer of lights reels across the heavens until you, too, begin spinning. You twirl and spin, whirl and dance under the stars, drunk on starlight.

long pause

With such beauty as this, can there be anything but hope? Your heart soars with inspiration, you feel as if you could move mountains, end wars, build worlds. Let your mind soar, just what possibilities could you bring about if you reached out to touch your potential? What powers reside within you? What strengths lay untapped? What dreams and wishes could so easily come true if you only opened yourself up to them and gave them room in your life to manifest?

extended long pause—2 minutes

Everything in your world seems incredibly clear, you can see miles ahead and years into your destiny. Your intuition is racing, and you hear that little voice inside guiding you, telling you what you need to know about people and situations and places.

Take a moment in your joy to greet that voice, to reach out and connect with your Inner Guide. Welcome its help into your life, carve out a niche in which it may reside. For this guide is your lifeline, your ticket to sail ahead, to leap mountains, to race the wind and return safely. Everyone has this knowledge, if they would only take the time to learn. So greet your inner voice and listen to its clarity.

extended long pause—1 minute

Now you feel an urge to lay down on the grass next to the pool. As you stretch out, the Earth hums beneath your body. The stars sing overhead. Slowly, you begin to sense a harmony between them, a rhythm that connects and coils around itself, twisting this way and that . . . slithering up your spine like a sensuous serpent, rolling under the ground in a web to catch up those who can hear the call, who can follow the pattern.

And you know that this rhythm is the heartbeat of the universe, composed of all life forms, of all beings great or small, from the largest sun to the smallest white dwarf and all creatures in-between. Listen now, to the harmony and cadence, to the music of the spheres. Listen and learn, let its melody soak into your heart, let the bass shore up your body . . . listen as the universe performs its concert tonight.

extended long pause—1 minute

As you lie there under the swirling cosmos, you find your eyes closing.

Take three deep breaths. As you exhale, the energy of the star essence retreats back into the heavens, leaving a trail of glittering dust to remind you of your connection to the celestial order of life, and then you close your eyes and drift into a deep slumber beside the pool.

long pause

When you wake, it is morning. The sun gleams over the horizon and you realize that you slept atop the mountain all night. You can remember your experiences, though they seem distant, like a rare dream.

A part of you feels sad, as if you'd found an exquisite jewel and then lost it again, but another part of your heart knows that you didn't lose anything, you simply returned to your grounded body, and that is where you need to be. One cannot continue to dance among the stars when trying to work their way through life.

You sit up and find, in your lap, a beautiful orchid. Brilliant white, the edges of its petals are rimmed with silver and when you inhale, the scent sends you reeling back into the night sky.

long pause

Your intuition tells you this orchid will never die, will never fade and pale. And should you ever drop it or lose it, the flower will return to you when you ask. Take the orchid and pin it in your hair, then rise and gather your things. It is time to leave the mountain.

Tomorrow you will return home from your vacation, and though it sorrows you to leave the beauty of this island, you know that exciting people and events await you in your future.

long pause

Now, listen to my voice as I count from ten to one. You will awake refreshed and alert. Ten . . . nine . . . you are becoming awake and aware of your surroundings . . . eight . . . seven . . . six . . . hear the sounds around you . . . five . . . four . . . you will be fully alert and refreshed . . . three . . . two . . . one . . . take three deep breaths and when you are ready, you may open your eyes.

Suggested Exercises

1. Spend a night outside watching a meteor shower. The Perseids occur every August, check your local almanac. Try to reach out for your connection with the cosmos, let your everyday life fall away as you focus on the stars and the streaking meteors. You may find that your problems seem less worrisome afterward.

2. Practice not only grounding energy, but calling it down from the stars, in much the same manner that you draw it up from the core of the Earth. Mingle the two energies together for a sense of balance.

3. Spend an entire day focusing on your intuition, do everything it tells you to, heed every warning, every urge (as long as you aren't urged to commit some act of violence). At the end of the day, take stock of how you feel about listening to your inner guidance. Sometimes it's hard to accept that we know what our best choices are—we are accustomed to giving that power to others, especially in the psychic community.

4. Learn something about astronomy. It can be fun when you recognize constellations and different stars. Buy or borrow a telescope and see for yourself what other galaxies look like. Visit an observatory and learn how the astronomers make their discoveries.

5. Study astrology, the mystical side of star science. The moon has an effect on Earth. If all the universe is connected by a vast force or energy, why shouldn't other planets and stars affect us?

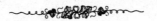

White in the moon the long road lies,
The moon stands blank above;
White in the moon the long road lies
That leads me from my love.

> —A. E. Housman (1859–1936)
> *The Welsh Marches*

The Moon
Initiation and Hidden Dreams

The nineteenth card of the major arcana is known as the Moon. It is assigned the number 18.

The Moon and Her Energy

When we encounter the Moon card, we delve into our psyches, past our conscious thoughts, past the subconscious, into that core of power that lies at the heart of magick and initiation. The Moon seems a simple card, but within its seeming simplicity lay the seeds of a complex process. With the Moon, we touch upon our cosmic destiny—with the Sun we will bring it forth into the world.

Like the Empress, the Moon is a feminine card—but here the Moon reflects the immense power of the Goddess as a whole, rather than Goddess as Mother.

Creatrix, Destroyer all rolled into one, we hold the Triple Goddess in our sights when our gaze raises to the night sky. We see the Maiden as the moon waxes, the Mother when she comes into full play, and the Crone when the moon dips into its waning cycle. All three converge at the time of the new moon, the gestation of the Maiden/Mother out of the destruction of the Crone. Life into death into life.

Considered to be the primal egg from which the world hatched, the Moon gestates with the energy that will become the Sun. To give birth, she dips below the world as night retreats and allows the dawn to emerge in all of its glorious, expansive brilliance.

Once within the realm of the Moon, we discover the cyclic nature of the world. We see cycles of fallowness and fertility, ebb and flow. Even as the ocean's currents flow in constant motion due to the influence of the Moon, so do the tides of life.

On another level, we find a link between the Moon card and the Celtic Ogham rune of Mor, or the Sea. For the ocean represents the primal mother, the Goddess in all of Her power, and so the Moon is linked to the element of water. Connected to water through its influence on the tides and to women through an influence on menstrual cycles, the Moon represents, in the majority of belief systems, the ultimate nature of femininity.

Strong and luminous, cyclic and ever-changing but always immortal, the divine nature of Woman is reflected in the glow of the moon.

The Moon also encompasses the world of visions and of dreams. When we sleep, we often leave our bodies in order to learn lessons and/or help others. For many, the dreaming world is as real as the waking world. Is it any wonder that the aboriginal concept of the Dream Time is as real to the shamans as our own sense of reality is to us? They travel to the Dream Time in spirit to work their magick/medicine.

When we enter the realm of the Moon, we often find ourselves dreaming vividly, active to where we wake exhausted. We may also find it difficult to stay awake, for if we practice the psychic arts and don't allow our minds enough time to journey inward (through guided meditations, meditation in general, or self-hypnotic trance work), the body will shut itself down so that the spirit can fly free into the Dream Time.

The Moon archetype enters our lives when we have accepted our intuition, when we've sought out our spiritual quest and, having found the path, committed ourselves by oath, blood, soul, and word.

The Moon offers us initiation into the mysteries of the divine, of magick. We must embrace this energy in order for it to manifest in our lives. For we have traveled this far on the Fool's journey and are now responsible not only to ourselves and our families, but to the world.

We have developed power and influence, and must use it wisely. The Star gave us the intuition with which to navigate through the coming years, now the Moon offers us initiation into the realms that allow us to fully use our psychic powers.

We will become, through the Moon card, the Priestess who greeted us during the beginning phase of our journey.

And yet, the Moon is a stern Mistress. Because we are no longer the simple Fool we were at the beginning of our journey, far more is expected from our efforts. When we misstep, when we falter, we are taken to task. The child must be guided away from danger and folly. The adult should know better and act accordingly.

The Moon represents all things hidden, all that which is not yet ready for observation, for scrutiny. For if we expose that which the Moon obscures, then we might influence the outcome and therefore defeat our destiny in the process. At times, the Moon shines light on the trail as we navigate the ethereal realms. Other times, she turns her back and we stumble in the dark.

In your daily life, you will find the Moon speaking to you through dreams and guided inner journeys. During these periods, your dreams will be vivid to the point where you might wake wondering where you are. They will hold images both mystical and seductive, in which you may often find your shadow self appearing center-stage.

For to accept the shadows of your persona makes room for the lighter side to exist. Deny one and you reject the other. Polarities, again . . . and polarities cannot exist with one side of the equation missing.

Enter the realm of the Moon and you move toward committing yourself to a spiritual path—if you are a Witch or pagan, this might mean making the decision to pledge yourself to a specific god or goddess as a priestess/priest, (see my book, *Dancing with the Sun,* for more information on dedications and pledges to Deity). Or, if you belong to a coven, you might feel ready to move on and form your own.

If you happen to be Christian or Jewish, the Moon archetype might inspire you to enter the seminary where you will study to become a minister or a rabbi. For a Buddhist, the monastery will beckon. If you have less of a religious bent, the Moon may simply clarify your spirituality so that you have little doubt left as the nature of your beliefs. However, one of the important things to remember about the Moon archetype is this: everything is still happening at an internal level.

This is not the time to tell others of your decisions, for there are still plans and events that must occur before you can manifest your ideas/dreams. The Moon brings us mists and shadows and the dark of the night and it is all too easy to stumble on the path if we feel that others are watching us.

We must focus all our energy into navigating the Dream Time if we expect to succeed. This is, perhaps, one of the most dangerous cards for we have come so far that, if we trip up, we lose so much.

The Moon enchants us, like the Goddess she represents. The glowing orb rolls through the heavens, calling to us in the night . . . "Come run under my light and taste my silver ambrosia."

Unlike the Star archetype, whose energy is lightning fast, the Moon cajoles us, taps us on the shoulder, beckons like a siren from an island in the sea. Like the wolves, we cannot shield ourselves from her power. We are caught by her magick, hypnotized by her beauty.

The Spiritual Concept

We discover the Moon within Luna, Roman goddess of the moon. We also find her in Selene, the Greek goddess of the night, and Aradia, daughter of Diana and Lucifer.

The Moon shines from within the Hindu god Chandra and the Japanese god of the Moon—Tsukiyomi. We also find the Moon within the Egyptian lord Horus, whose eyes are the sun and the moon.

The astrological sign of Pisces is connected to the Moon, and we place this card within the Wheel of the Year firmly in the element of Water.

The Card

The Moon is usually depicted as the actual heavenly body, but after that, the variations are so numerous that it's difficult to create the sense of an average background for the card. Some of the more pervasive images included in the different decks include wolves or dogs, twin pillars or standing stones, waterfalls or the ocean, salmon, scorpions, lizards, and various water-related plants.

Guidelines for Use

This meditation follows that of the Star card. You may also find it useful to meditate on The Moon during the autumn months, or whenever you feel the need to connect to the core of your spirituality.

Flowers:	willow, poppy, lemon balm, trillium, water lily
Incense:	jasmine, sandalwood, almond
Oils:	lemon, lotus, jasmine, camphor, poppy
Crystals:	moonstone, clear quartz, silver, black onyx
Candles:	white, silver

Meditation

Relax and get comfortable. Close your eyes and take three deep breaths.

long pause

You are sprawled in a hammock out under the golden glow of a late-September afternoon. The weather is not yet inclement, and you find yourself continually nodding off as you swing between two huge maple trees.

Occasionally, one of the first leaves to turn color breaks free and comes drifting down to land at your side. You brush it away, not really caring whether or not the burnished leaf stays in the hammock with you. Lately you've been so sleepy, so tired. Your dreams have been a vivid mishmash of images, you can remember scenes and characters, but the visions have been so complex that you find it difficult to remember any particular dream in its entirety.

long pause

Dozing, you drift in and out of consciousness. Then, a force grabs hold of your thoughts, your mind, and drags you down, deep into the ocean. You struggle, but cannot break free. The energy is too strong, and you must dive under the waves, follow it downward.

Down, it pulls you, down . . . and you find yourself plunging headlong, as you dive into the depths of your psyche, under the surface with its currents and eddies. Down you swim, further and further, until the sunlight disappears from the glimmering expanse above you.

long pause

Past your conscious thoughts you race, past your daily concerns, into the depths of your subconscious where all of your hopes and fears reside. Let go of all your thoughts for the mundane world. Let them flow out of you like a stream flowing from the inside of an iceberg.

Hidden from light, hidden from darkness, past shadow and clarity, like an arrow loosed from the bow, you fly through the depths, your aim straight and true.

long pause

Never quavering, never wandering, you descend through all the masks, all the guilt, all the pride, all pain and joy. Every hurt, every slight now seems meaningless. All of your pride and will, all of your shame and sorrow, flow away into the currents surrounding you. You descend beyond the depths of emotion, beyond the depths of the conscience, deeper and deeper you swim.

long pause

All thoughts of the surface slowly disappear, all concerns vanish as you submerge into the hidden reaches of your soul.

Take three slow deep breaths.

long pause

Far in the distance, you see a glowing sphere of silver and white. Luminous, she hangs in the center of this ocean that is your mind, suspended, waiting, full with the promise of destiny and greatness.

Now you focus your entire attention on the sphere. You are drawn to her much as a moth is drawn toward a burning candle. Her pull enthralls your heart with siren-song, beckoning you. Whispered entreaties cajole you on. If you do not reach out to take her in your arms, your heart will break and you will never recover.

long pause

And then, you reach out to touch the surface, and find that your hand penetrates the orb. You pass through the outer layer of the glittering egg and into the center, where a faint radiance shines from a core of liquid silver. The dripping argent smells sweet, citrus . . . much like lemon ambrosia, and you are suddenly hungry and have the irresistible desire to taste it.

Hesitant, you place a drop of the silver on your tongue. The flavors of lemon and mint fill your mouth, then explode into an icy blast as the liquid silver pours down your throat.

long pause

Take three deep breaths.

long pause

Slowly, from deep within your core, you feel an odd sensation begin to travel through your body. The ocean quakes, you sense a change in the currents around you, movement where there was no movement, stillness where the waves once crashed against the shore.

As if you are deconstructing, you break apart to blend into the primal soup that surrounds you. Thought begins to waver, your sense of self becomes blurred as you meld into that vast consciousness that makes up the universe.

extended long pause—1 minute

For what seems like a thousand years, you swim in the universal mind, then . . . a spark catches the faintest periphery of your vision . . . and another. Quickly now, synapses snap and crackle around you, waking you out of your slumber, urging you to rise.

Life blossoms within your soul; evolution is taking place right before your eyes. The primal spark of consciousness glimmers, then begins to grow. Even as you rouse yourself, you feel an urge to break out of this glimmering orb into which you sank, into which you aimed your direction.

long pause

As you press against the sides, the urgency grows. You must break through the shell surrounding you! You hammer on the sides of the orb, which have now become hardened.

Nothing happens and a sense of panic begins to race through your mind. You must be free! Using both hands, you pound against the brittle shell—again and again, your fists drive into the walls.

long pause

A faint crack appears against part of the luminous curve and, like a broken mirror, spider webs out, a lattice of fractures that race along. Thin cracking noises splinter the silence. Then, one last blow to the center of the break and the orb cracks, the primal egg splinters and you are free.

long pause

As you emerge from the egg, you find that your body now emanates a delicate luminosity. You are radiant. As you swim back through the waters, up into the realm of your subconscious, you once again encounter your worries and fears, your hopes and dreams. But now those worries seem distant, they no longer hold power over you, and your hopes and dreams have transformed into goals. You know you will achieve them in your lifetime.

long pause

Once again you swim on, upward, through the currents and eddies, into the conscious layers of your mind. Here you hear the rustle of scurrying thoughts, once more feel the hustle of daily matters. But now, these thoughts seem focused, organized. You have achieved a sense of perspective on them.

long pause

As you break from the foaming waters of your mind, you see that you are near a long, sandy shore. You step out of the water, dripping seaweed. There, some twenty feet from the water, stands a woman. Dressed in the colors of twilight, she wears a crescent moon on her brow and you once again recognize your old friend, the Priestess.

She silently hands you a towel. You dry yourself, then dress in the sparkling robe of silver that she holds out for you. All this while she speaks no word, simply watches and waits.

long pause

When you are clothed in the silver robe, she holds up her left hand and calls out in a loud voice. "Earth," she cries, and the leaves from the undergrowth near the shore rustle. You see a spirit, cloaked in moss and ivy, emerge from the undergrowth. The elemental stares at you with glowing green eyes and creeps to her place in the north.

long pause

Once again, the Priestess holds up her hand and calls out. "Wind," she cries, and the breeze whistles as a gust of air sweeps past. You see a spirit, cloaked in feathers and spider silk, soar in from the sky. The elemental lands in the east. She stares at you with brilliant lavender eyes.

long pause

A third time, the Priestess calls out her summons. "Fire," she cries, and the sands part as a spirit, cloaked in glittering flames of green, gold and orange, rises from beneath the shore. The elemental dances into the south, and stares at you with flaming red eyes.

long pause

The Priestess raises her hand to the ocean and calls out. "Water," she cries, and the sea begins to foam and churn as a spirit, cloaked in seaweed and ocean foam, rises from beneath the waves. The elemental flows to her place in the west, eyeing you with flickering blue eyes.

long pause

The Priestess motions for you to join her in the center of the circle. She kisses you on both cheeks. "Welcome back to my world, Fool who no longer plays the fool. You are nearing the end of your journey. Before you can pass on to fulfill your destiny, you must be initiated into the halls of the wise ones. Will you accept responsibility for the powers that you have developed within yourself?"

And you know that to retain your power you must pledge responsibility for what you may wreak in this life. Be the results good or ill, you alone are responsible for your actions and your words. Pledge your oath of responsibility for that which you perpetrate.

long pause

She bids you to hold out your left hand. When you do, she links a chain of silver around your wrist. Then she bids you hold out your left leg and proceeds to link a chain around your ankle.

"Be aware, that you are chained and unchained, bound and free. As so you bind yourself to your power and your will, so too that power shall set you free."

long pause

As the chains touch your skin, you become aware of just what responsibility your spiritual path brings to you.

You cannot shift the blame to others for your mistakes, you cannot expect to say "I'm sorry" and have all your errors wiped clean. You must live with the results of your actions, and this is the most solemn weight of all in this path you've chosen. You carry the weight of your deeds and yet . . . you also carry the freedom of your deeds.

The Priestess anoints your forehead with an oil that smells of freshly turned earth and lilacs and patchouli. She takes you by the hand and leads you in front of the Earth Spirit.

"Behold," she says. "The Spirit of Earth. You now have the will and power to command this element to attend your rites and rituals. But look into the eyes of Earth and know just how far her power extends, and how if you misuse or abuse her, she will turn on you and devour your body."

long pause

Look into the eyes of Earth and see her in all of her power. The ivy twines at the roots of the oak. The moss clings to ancient trees in the northern forests. The palms sway gently against the sand on the tropical islands. The rocks and mountains and crystals and caverns slowly evolve, slowly weather, only to return to the earth where they are buried deep. Look into the eyes of Earth and know this element.

extended long pause—1 minute

The Priestess anoints your forehead with an oil that smells of lavender and mint and rosemary. She takes you by the hand and leads you in front of the Wind Spirit.

"Behold," she says. "The Spirit of Wind. You now have the will and power to command this element to attend your rites and rituals. But look into the eyes of the Wind and know just how far her power extends, and how if you misuse or abuse her, she will turn on you and devour your mind."

long pause

Look into the eyes of the Wind and see her in all of her power. The clouds race across the sky before a thunderstorm. The hurricane rocks the coastal areas, pounding with gale force winds. The fresh breezes clear the mind and cool the body on warm spring mornings. The wind catches up all negativity, spiraling it to the sky and beyond, clearing the path for new thought. Look deep into the eyes of Wind and know this element.

extended long pause—1 minute

The Priestess anoints your forehead with an oil that smells of dragon's blood and pepper and carnations. She takes you by the hand and leads you in front of the Flame Spirit.

"Behold," she says. "The Spirit of Fire. You now have the will and power to command this element to attend your rites and rituals. But look into the eyes of the Flame and know just how far her power extends, and how if you misuse or abuse her, she will turn on you and devour your spirit."

long pause

Look into the eyes of Fire and see her in all of her power. The bonfire crackles on a chilly autumn evening, sparks shooting to the sky. The lava pours molten, down the side of the volcano, flowing toward the sea. The green fire sparkles in the woods on Midsummer's Eve. The golden sun shimmers on desert sands, heating your body until you must dance the ecstasy of life. Look deep into the eyes of Fire and know this element.

extended long pause—1 minute

The Priestess anoints your forehead with an oil that smells of camphor and spring rain and hyacinths. She takes you by the hand and leads you in front of the Water Spirit.

"Behold," she says. "The Spirit of Water. You now have the will and power to command this element to attend your rites and rituals. But look into the eyes of the Water and know just how far her power extends, and how if you misuse or abuse her, she will turn on you and devour your heart."

long pause

Look into the eyes of Water and see her in all of her power. The river tumbles through the valley, carrying rocks and stones with it on its way to the ocean. The pool in the grotto lies still, its surface a sheen of perfect glass. The rain pelts out its rhythms on the roof, lulling you into a melancholy exploration of your sorrows and your joys. Look deep into the eyes of Water and know this element.

extended long pause—1 minute

The Priestess anoints your forehead with an oil that smells of sunlight and moonbeams and star-shine. She bids you look into the sky at the moon and stars. "Behold," she says. "The Universe in all its glory. A million suns, a thousand moons . . . galaxies beyond counting. You have the will and power to call on this energy to attend your rites and rituals. But look into the glory of the Universe and know just how far her power extends. If you misuse or abuse her, she will turn on you and devour your soul."

Look up at the panorama extending above you. Moons wheel around planets wheel around stars. Galaxies run wild, careening through the cosmos, colliding and merging, expanding and deconstructing. The force that holds all things together sparkles around you, within you, deep within your heart where you drank in the ambrosia of the heavens. Look deep at the celestial consciousness and know that you are of it and yet separate.

extended long pause—1 minute

Now the Priestess and the elementals stand back. The Priestess smiles, rather a sad smile, and says, "Welcome to my world. You now are one of the wise ones, you now possess the answers which you so long ago came to me seeking. You have discovered the truths of your life, through your quest. Now it is time that you went into the world and shared your knowledge. Your material needs are met, your emotional needs are satisfied.

"Now you must let Spirit guide you that others, just starting out on their journeys, may seek you out. You will not give them answers, but help them discover their own truths, so as I and all of my companions have aided you. Good journey, my friend. You are nearing the end of this cycle, but there are three more realms through which you first must pass."

long pause

The Priestess and her elementals turn as if to go. If you wish to say something to her, do so now, and listen for her answer.

extended long pause—1 minute

As she disappears into the undergrowth, you feel a strong pull to lie in the sand. You curl up on the warm beach and let the gentle breeze guide you to sleep. When you awake, you are back in your hammock.

Now, listen to my voice as I count from ten to one. You will awake refreshed and alert. Ten . . . nine . . . you are becoming awake and aware of your surroundings . . . eight . . . seven . . . six . . . hear the sounds around you . . . five . . . four . . . you will be fully alert and refreshed . . . three . . . two . . . one . . . take three deep breaths and when you are ready, you may open your eyes.

Suggested Exercises

1. Spend eight weeks observing the elements and the phases of the moon. Each week, focus on one of the elements or the phase the moon currently resides in, and try to make a spiritual connection to how that element or moon phase affects you. It is important to remember that each person will come to a different understanding of the elements or moon cycles, and that everyone's view is valid—for their own lives.

2. The Moon archetype represents a period of time when we are going through a form of rebirth. Examine some of the various myths and legends surrounding the concept of spiritual rebirth and see if any of them resonate with your life.

3. Try to be present at the birth of an animal or a baby. Watch the expression of astonishment when the newborn enters the world. We go through much the same amazement when we journey through a spiritual initiation.

4. If, like myself, you are a Witch (or if you consider yourself Wiccan), interview various Witches who pledged themselves to a specific deity/deities. Having been someone who once worked with any deity who struck my fancy, then pledging myself to Mielikki and Tapio—who set definite boundaries on the other Gods I can and cannot invoke—the difference of going from one state to another is like jumping over a chasm. Not better, not worse—simply very different.

The Sun

Expanding Your Horizons

The twentieth card of the major arcana is known as the sun. It is assigned the number 19.

The Sun and His Energy

The Sun is a brilliant card, leading us out of the realm of our psyche (the Moon) into the conscious realm where we are alert, aware of everything going on around us. The Sun provides us with unlimited energy, life force, and growth. Through this archetype, we touch on our connections with the rest of the world, we form partnerships and learn how to collaborate. Teamwork becomes all-important when we enter this realm.

The Sun represents all things exposed. No shadows are left hidden, no cobweb can withstand the cleansing power of the Sun. Here secrets come to light, motivations are held up for inspection. In return for the freedom and movement that this archetype brings to us, we pay with a lack of privacy.

Like the Emperor, the Sun is a masculine card—but here the Sun reflects the grand and generous power of the God as universal, rather than as absolute leader. Here the masculine energy accepts help, and evolves into a democracy rather than a monarchy. The Sun puts everyone to work so that everyone might have time to play. While the periods foretold by the Sun card are busy and active, they are also fun, full of laughter and joy. Here we have the quilting parties, the barn raisings, the brainstorming sessions in which a great deal of work is completed in the guise of an informal gathering.

Considered to be the eternal source of life-energy, the Sun pulsates with creative, vibrant power. He beams down on the world with his smile, albeit sometimes his brilliance can scorch the land and then suffering follows (again, indicating the need for polarities. The balance plays out here in the dance of the Sun and the Moon).

Once within the realm of the Sun, we enter the heart of success, of achievement. For within this cycle, we grow, teach and expand our awareness to encompass community success, community as a living organism. We emerge from the womb of the Moon, from our initiation, ready to put our power to use for the good of the many.

The Sun indicates robust health, champions of the downtrodden, honesty and truth, harmony of action. Within the Sun archetype, we find the Egyptian symbol of the ankh—representing fertility and life force. Here we discover powerful motivation to work for our causes, we are stimulated by active and inquisitive minds who come together to solve problems.

Brilliant, embodying strength and generosity, the divine nature of Man is reflected in the glow of the Sun.

When we enter the realm of the Sun, we often find ourselves joining organizations and clubs, making connections in the world that combine both business and charity work. Groups like the Lion's Club, the Eagles, the Elks, and other fraternal organizations tend to fall under the rule of the Sun, although not all among these groups will be conservative or made up of older, middle-class Americans.

The Sun enters our lives when we been traveling on a firm spiritual path, when we have our own lives in order and know where we're going. We've survived suffering and pain. We have come through self-doubt into a place where we are sure of our choices. Now we take the powers that we have mastered, that we've accepted responsibility for, and put them to work in the world around us.

The Sun offers us a chance to change the world, to do good for others, and leave a memory. We embrace generosity and work toward world harmony because we, ourselves, have evolved. We enjoy our own lives and so we want others to enjoy theirs. We are no longer struggling on a material level because we've harnessed our intuition and we've mastered our trade. Now that we are secure, we reach out to give others a helping hand.

We use intuition (from the Star) and our influence or power (from the Moon), to make changes in an unjust world.

In your daily life, you will find the Sun speaking to you through invitations to participate in public events and gatherings—perhaps educational, perhaps charitable. You will find yourself itching to make progress, filled with energy and creative ideas that can expand the boundaries of what your group deems possible.

You will discover a new well of inspiration, and you may find yourself acting as a mentor or motivator for others. You do not necessarily become a teacher through this archetype, but you are looked upon as role model.

Enter the realm of the Sun and you move toward committing yourself to the elimination of injustices and suffering. Perhaps your focus will be in a specific area (women's rights, racial discrimination, religious freedom, help for the disabled), or you might turn your attention on more global problems—overpopulation, the environment, human rights. Similar to the Star card in this respect, you take these concerns a step further and begin to act on them, rather than just making yourself aware of them.

Where the Moon was internally based, the Sun leads you out into the world. It's time to use your voice, to make known that which you are planning so that others will hear your call. The Sun inspires us, heals us, spurs us on. We do not doze in the shadows here, nor do we spend hours focused on our inner guidance. We have heard the call and now we answer.

The Spiritual Concept

We discover the Sun within the Egyptian god Ra. We also find him in Helios—Greek god of the Sun who is the brother of the Moon goddess Selene. The Greeks also attributed Sun energy to Apollo, muse of light and music.

The Sun shines from within the Japanese goddess Amaterasu, and the Australian aborigine Sun goddess, Knowee, who continually carries Her torch through the sky.

We place this card within the Wheel of the Year firmly in the element of fire.

The Card

The Sun is usually depicted as the actual Sun, but, like the Moon, the variations are numerous. Some common images included in the different decks are lions, eagles, the ankh, two children dancing in front of the sun, roses, and the Egyptian winged disk—a symbol of success.

Guidelines for Use

This meditation follows that of the Moon card. You may also find it useful to meditate on the Sun during the summer months, or whenever you feel the need to increase your connection to world concerns.

This meditation calls for a drumbeat, which is clearly marked. This beat may be pre-recorded, or you may wish to work with a live drummer. If you choose the latter, I recommend that the drummer and guide practice the section together before the meditation to coordinate sound levels, rhythm, etc.

Flowers:	sunflower, marigold, acacia, daisy
Incense:	tangerine, copal, frankincense, cinnamon
Oils:	orange, heliotrope, bay, cedar
Crystals:	orange calcite, yellow topaz, citrine
Candles:	orange, gold

Meditation

Relax and get comfortable. Close your eyes and take three deep breaths.

long pause

The sky is brilliant blue on this warm, sun-filled morning. You have been invited to a garden party and ritual, and now you stand in front of the path leading to the host's backyard where the gala is supposed to take place. The faint strains of guitar music come strumming out of the lattice-work fence. Covered with a blanket of ivy and moss roses, the fence runs along the path, and as you follow the trail, you come to a gate.

As you step into the yard, you see a vast meadow of green, dotted with patches of fox-glove and trillium, daisies and columbine. A row of sunflowers stand sentinel against one of the hedgerows, and one side of the yard ends at the edge of a pond, big enough for swimming and fishing, but not large enough to be called a lake.

long pause

White wicker lounges and chairs stand out against the verdant background. You see several picnic tables, all but one are covered in food. People mill about the yard, talking, and the low hum of their conversation fills the air along with the droning of bees and the call of robins and grosbeaks.

Your host is sitting at one of the picnic tables, along with several men and women that you recognize. They are community and neighborhood leaders, and you know them because you belong to some of the same organizations they do. They wave you over and you cross the lawn.

long pause

The picnic table is covered with brochures and pictures. You recognize pamphlets from several charity organizations, as well as several international groups concerned with the protection of the environment, endangered species, and so on. Your host bids you to sit down and look through the leaflets.

Flip through several that catch your eye. What do they concern themselves with? What do you think is most pressing in today's world? Which groups and causes do you find yourself most interested in taking an active part in? Take a few minutes to leaf through the brochures and decide which causes stir you to action.

extended long pause—1 minute

"We need people to organize events, to sponsor workers, to speak at functions about these concerns," your host says. "We were hoping you might be interested in helping us." You find your interest piqued and you agree to take several of the brochures home to read at length. You also agree that you will pass extras out to people who couldn't make it to the gathering today.

Your stomach rumbles and you wander over to one of the tables. Every imaginable picnic and finger food is here, plate after plate of breads and cheeses, fruits and pastries, salads and meats. Fix yourself a dish of your favorite goodies.

long pause

You see a group of people you don't recognize. They are sitting beneath one of the large maple trees, eating and laughing. Drawn to them because of their laughter, and the fact that they are sitting in one of the best places to both enjoy the warmth of the day and the shade, you meander over and sit down on the periphery of the group.

They introduce themselves. One is a woman who runs a shelter for battered women; another organizes transportation to work for those who can't afford a car, but don't live near the busline. A short, stocky gentleman spends several hours every week gathering petitions to save the Endangered Species Act.

Still another is the secretary for a natural disaster relief society. They all have careers, they work to support themselves and their families, but each person seems to feel it necessary to take on unpaid and often overlooked tasks in order to make the world a better place.

long pause

"We may not always agree on politics or the best way to go about something," says one of the women, "but we do all agree that action must replace rhetoric."

Just then, your host rings a loud bell and calls everyone over to the edge of the lake. "We're going to start our ritual of empowerment to spur us on, to give us the motivation to continue making a difference."

He asks everyone to think of a specific cause they wish to represent for the ritual. It should be a concern that you know something about—both the problems and potential solutions. Take a few minutes to think of a cause that you wish to represent in the ritual.

extended long pause—1 minute

Your host says that there are supplies on the central table. You are to make a mask that represents the problems leading to your concern. The masks are to be attached to a handle so you can hold them up, and all the materials should be flammable. They will be burnt as part of the ritual. Go over to the table and look through the supplies until you find what you need to make your mask.

Take a few moments to design a mask. You find that your creativity allows you full rein on this task, and the mask you design perfectly fits the image you envision.

extended long pause—1 minute

When you have finished your mask, you once again join the circle. A large fire has been kindled in the center, and your host and his wife stand to either side of the blazing flames.

"We are here to burn away the obstacles leading to a better world," your host says. "We are here to make our promises of action and to pledge ourselves to the creation of a tolerant, loosely knit community of concerned individuals. Together we can make a difference. Together we can network and link up so that our various resources might join together and become stronger."

long pause

His wife steps forward and says, "First, we identify the problems. Each person come forward, show your mask and identify it by name, for only in clearly naming our enemies can we seek to understand them, to enlighten them or, if they refuse to listen, to destroy them."

One by one, each person steps forward and holds up their mask. As they do so, you hear them call out the names of grave problems facing this world.

One person waves a mask of a beaten woman. "Domestic abuse accounts for half the murders of women in this country," he says.

Another holds aloft a mask of a tiger. "The tiger is in danger of extinction. Poaching, and those who buy from the poachers, account for the deaths of hundreds of these endangered cats yearly."

Then a third steps into the circle. Her mask shows the face of a starving child. "Children starve because there's not enough food. People crowd their lands. I stand for the overpopulation problem."

Still another strides forward. He carries a mask of a dying man. "AIDS runs rampant. Research is underfunded, women with AIDS are ignored, opponents of birth control preach that their children should not have access to condoms. Ignorance breeds death."

One by one, each person steps forward . . . the issues seem overwhelming . . . each piling one atop another. Finally your turn comes. Step into the circle and speak about the cause you are concerned with.

extended long pause—1 minute

Your host holds up his hands after everyone has spoken. "Now," he says, "we must speak of what steps have been taken, what successes have been met."

Once again, people step into the circle. The woman standing for domestic abuse says, "Domestic abuse is no longer a hidden issue. The government is speaking out on it. Billboards advertise crisis lines. Shelters provide a haven for women seeking to escape their attackers."

Next you hear, "The abuses of the governments against their own policies are becoming known. Magazines are spreading the word of the tiger's plight. Environmental groups donate money to help fund protected reserves."

Think of what successes, even partial ones, that you've heard of regarding your issue. Every positive step is a step in the right direction. Take a moment to tell the others what has been done to rectify the problems.

extended long pause—1 minute

When everyone has taken their turn, your host once again takes the center of the circle. "All well and good," he says. "But there is much work left to be done. We do what we can on an individual basis, then link our deeds with those of others. Together, we can make a difference. We can overcome the problems facing our planet, our environment, and our society. Step forward, pledge yourself to action. What will you do to make a difference?"

long pause

As the others take their turns, think about what you can do to help. Perhaps you don't have time to volunteer, but do you have the money to make a contribution? Or can you afford a few hours a week to make phone calls, pass out leaflets, speak at a conference, put on your grubbies and go out to clean the oil off animals at the sight of a spill?

Think about what you are willing to do. Everyone alive owes a debt to this planet, for the Earth sustains us. We have a responsibility to our fellow travelers, we have all faltered and we've all had someone help us. Now it is time to give back.

Step forward now, and make your pledge.

extended long pause—1 minute

[NOTE TO GUIDE: the drumbeat should begin here. It should not overpower your voice, but should be rhythmic and steady.]

A drumbeat begins to echo through the yard. The host motions for people to begin circling the fire. A chant, so low that you almost can't recognize the words, grows as the pace hastens. These words echo as you follow the drumbeat, as you circle the flames.

Mother of the Earth
Daughter of the Drum
Father of the Sun and Sky,
Strengthen now our voice
Let us make the choice
Let the world hear our cry.

Pain and suffering overwhelm
This world on which we live
Problems scattered everywhere in sight,
But if we take a stand
Combine our power, hand-to-hand
The world will tremble with our might.

May beauty flow within our hearts
May wisdom grow within our thoughts
May our spirits soar aloft like birds,
Our abundance, let us share
And to those in need, give care
May our actions always fit our words.

As the chant dies away, each person—in turn—throws their mask in the flames, burning away obstacles. The masks flare up as they meet the fire's kiss, and you can feel the power raised through the chant release and spiral into the sky. You know that the energy is speeding toward solutions to the problems the world faces.

When it comes your turn, cast your mask into the fire and watch as the flames burn it into ashes.

long pause

[NOTE TO GUIDE: *the drumbeat should fade out here. It should fade gently, not end with an abrupt halt.*]

Once all the masks have been burned, everyone joins hands around the fire. The glow of the flames reflects the glow of the sun, and you feel energized, hopeful. While you see the reality of the problems facing our world, you also see, around you, the solutions. The answers lay in the hearts of you, your friends, and every person on this planet.

long pause

The circle opens and people return to their picnic. Now everyone gathers in specific groups, each focused on one or two issues. You join them, optimistic that, together with others, you can make a difference in this world.

Now, listen to my voice as I count from ten to one. You will awake refreshed and alert. Ten . . . nine . . . you are becoming awake and aware of your surroundings . . . eight . . . seven . . . six . . . hear the sounds around you . . . five . . . four . . . you will be fully alert and refreshed . . . three . . . two . . . one . . . take three deep breaths and when you are ready, you may open your eyes.

Suggested Exercises

1. Get together with friends and plan a ritual similar to the one in the meditation. The ritual should be kept on an optimistic note. It can be overwhelming when we think of all the problems our world faces, but we have to remember that people are making a difference, one person at a time, and that if we each contribute what we can, then we've at least made an inroad on what are very critical issues.

2. Research charities and organizations before you donate your time or money to them. Make sure that they stand in accordance with what you believe. Sad to say, there are many fraudulent companies trying to pass themselves off as legitimate. Be sure that you don't get taken in by a good line.

3. When we begin to reach out to the world in this manner, we often find ourselves overcommitting at first. Try to limit your participation so you don't get burnt out and quit altogether. Take it slow until you are prepared to make more sacrifices. Then expand the causes you work for or organizations you donate your money to.

4. Sometimes, when we are just trying to get by, to make a living, we don't have extra time or money to give to others. There's no shame in this. It's a fact of our society that sometimes, especially in single-parent households, there's just not enough to go around. But you can still help out in little ways. Call your Congressmembers when an issue arises in your community . . . sign petitions . . . try to keep abreast of the concerns facing our world, if only to educate yourself for when you do have more energy to devote to the subject.

The day after that wedding night I found that a distance
of a thousand miles, abyss and discovery and irremediable
metamorphosis, separated me from the day before.

        —Colette (1873–1954)
         Noces

Judgment
Reflection and Metamorphosis

The twenty-first card of the major arcana is known as Judgment (sometimes called Aeon or Karma). It is assigned the number 20.

Judgment and Its Energy

We are close to the end of our journey. Two more realms exist through which the quester must pass. The archetype of Judgment represents the concept of karma. Primarily a reflective card, Judgment leads us into an analysis of our perceptions, observations and our insights. We must reflect on all that we have undergone during the past cycle, from the starting point (the Fool) until now, so that we might have a clear picture of where we stand before we enter the realm of the World and close our journey. Now we must look back on those who harmed us, on those we harmed, and perhaps not forgive, but at least release our hold on old grudges and memories that may still haunt our thoughts.

Judgment represents the promise of renewal. With this card, we rediscover what we have lost sight of. We link all lessons learned through this cycle, examine the whole for any missing components, and then step through into the realm of the World. Judgment is our last chance to make things right, to put our lives in order.

An androgynous card, Judgment reflects impartial observation. We must not allow emotion to interfere when we examine our progress. While we cannot return to the previous phases of the journey—for we have come too far on the path—we can, perhaps, fill in the gaps. For our quest nears its end, for good or ill, and everything we have learned, everything we have done, now culminates. We are almost ready for a new quest, but before we can begin as Fool again, we must identify all that we have gained, and perhaps lost, within this current cycle.

Judgment stands aloof, watching us, forcing our attention to our deeds, our words, our actions. Cause and effect rule this realm. For every action, there is an equal and opposite reaction. Do unto others as you would have them do unto you. What you do returns to you three times over. Here we find the moral code of the universe. Here we place all we have learned on the scale and see whether it balances.

Judgment indicates acumen, clear sight, an attempt to be fair and just. We discern between good and evil, quality and shoddiness, truth and falsehood. We judge, even as we ourselves are judged.

It is important to remember, however, that most often, we project judgments based on our own acts, based on what has happened to us. Remember that no absolutes apply to the entire universe, no statements that stand as truth for everyone. We learn that our judgments are biased, and cannot help but be. As detached as we believe we are, we will always have some reason behind our opinions.

Within the Judgment archetype, we also find the symbol for Pluto, a planet of transformation. Until we examine our lives and the results of our actions, we cannot take the last step in our journey. We are striving toward metamorphosis, but first we must strip away our facades and look ourselves squarely in the mirror.

When we enter the realm of the Judgment, we often find ourselves at the verge of life-transforming decisions.

These decisions will catapult us into a new journey, where once again, we become the Fool. We may decide to move half a world away. We may reject all we've believed and turn to a new spiritual path. We may turn our backs on our family and leave behind everyone we've ever known.

At other times, Judgment may influence us to take what we've developed from this cycle and substantially alter it.

A writer may go from writing fiction to nonfiction. A computer programmer may leave a large company to open her own consulting business. A teacher may quit the school system to teach training seminars in a corporation. But in order to make these momentous changes, we must first assess all we have done, and all skills we have developed.

In your daily life, know that you will feel Judgment approaching. Perhaps you are content, but you begin to anticipate a change and yet you don't know what that change is going to be. Or you grow restless once you've succeeded at a major goal, and know that it is time to take on a new challenge.

Or perhaps an event or a person will force you to reevaluate your life. However, unlike the Tower card, Judgment does not lead us to panic. We are too wise and sure of ourselves for that. No, we almost always recognize the need for change because we feel it in our souls. Within the realm of Judgment, we plan for change, welcome it—no untoward roofs crashing in our heads here.

Enter the realm of the Judgment and your insight crystallizes. If you break commitments, if you walk away from people and organizations, it will be because you sense dissolution coming; you know it's inevitable in the evolution of your life. There are no spontaneous and foolish acts in this realm, every movement is deemed necessary. Use the intuition of the Star card to take action as required.

Judgment is an esoteric archetype. Neither active nor passive, the energy bides its time and enters your life only when appropriate. You may not be able to explain to others why you are leaving the group, why you are moving to the southern hemisphere, but in your heart you know that it's the only course for you to take. Your physical quest has remained still for a time, during which you have journeyed far with your spirit. Now your body must follow suit and so you undertake the process of metamorphosis, knowing that you are doing exactly what you need to.

The Spiritual Concept

Judgment is often embodied by Gods of the Underworld, and so we discover the archetype within the god Pluto, and the boatman Charon, who ferries souls across the river Styx.

We find Judgment within the goddess Hecate, who stands at the crossroads of the world. She is also within the cauldron of Cerridwen, through whence dead warriors pass and are renewed to life.

We can place this card within the Wheel of the Year at Yule, alongside the Hierophant.

The Card

Judgment is usually depicted as an androgynous, angelic figure, often with wings or a brilliant aura. This figure will sometimes be holding a trumpet or horn. At times we will also find the feather of Ma'at depicted on the card, or the figure of the child-god Horus.

Guidelines for Use

This meditation follows that of the Sun card. You may also find it useful to meditate on Judgment during the Yule, or whenever you sense a major life transformation approaching.

Flowers:	pepperwort, mistletoe, pansy, comfrey
Incense:	myrrh, patchouli, musk, gum mastic
Oils:	anise, poppy, cypress, musk, patchouli
Crystals:	bloodstone, clear quartz, lapis lazuli
Candles:	indigo, dark purple, black

Meditation

Relax and get comfortable. Close your eyes and take three deep breaths.

long pause

You find yourself on the side of a mountain. One of the tallest near your town, you have often looked at the craggy peak, thinking that someday you would climb it. But never before have you felt propelled to journey here.

Early this dawn, you were called to the journey. You packed your rough-weather gear and said your good-byes, then set out. A hint of intuition tells you that this climb will have a life-transforming affect and, although you don't know what it is, or where this trail will lead you, you know that you must answer the summons.

The mountain is covered with snow, the wind howls around you with gale strength that shakes the cedars. It rushes through the barren wood, moaning like a banshee.

Everyone told you it was a foolish idea to traverse the cliff side in a storm, but you paid no attention. You only knew that you must come to the mountain and climb. Some inner urge drove you here, now you must see the journey through, even though you are putting yourself in danger.

long pause

The cedars and fir hang heavy with the snow, caught under the weight of their crystalline blankets. They guard the trail in this muffled winter world, and you must slog through, using your walking stick for balance. Three feet of snow on the ground tug at your legs each time you take a step. Time after time you go cascading face-first into the icy powder; time after time you rise and return to the journey.

long pause

The sky is overcast, hazy with that winter-white sheen that always predicts snow. A hint of ozone confirms your suspicions and you wonder just how long it will be before the white flakes begin to fall again.

A hawk goes winging by, on the hunt. What can it hope to find up here in this desolate country? Mice, perhaps, or a rabbit. You trudge along, slowly making your way up the trail, and soon you begin to slip into a waking dream.

You begin to flash back to memories of your journey. How much you have learned in the months . . . years . . . since you began the quest. Think over your choices in this cycle. What have you learned about yourself? What skills have you developed that you never thought you could acquire?

Remember when you were at the beginning of your quest, without care, without direction? How far you have come, and how wise you've grown as you've traveled through the different realms. Take a moment to examine the difference between the way you were when you first embarked upon this cycle and where you are now.

extended long pause—1 minute

The wind catches you off-guard and sends you careening to the ground. You look up just in time to see the flakes begin to fall; it's snowing. They are thick, huge and sticky, and falling fast. Wet snow, heavy snow. Soon the inches will begin to pile up, and for the first time, you wonder about the advisability of coming on this trek.

You look around for some sort of shelter. You brought a light tent with you, but it would be nice if you could avoid setting it up just yet. You wanted to be farther along on your journey before breaking to make camp.

Ahead on the trail, another twenty minutes of hiking away, you see what looks like the opening of a cave. It's right on the path, you won't have to go out of your way to reach it, and so you decide to keep a move on. You pick up your staff and use it to force your way up the hill, toward the cave and safety.

long pause

About twenty yards below the cave, the trail steepens abruptly. The snow on this part has hardened into a sheen of ice. You think it might be easier to turn around and go back, but when you look down the path, you see a huge old fir tree lean dangerously across the trail, then come crashing down, its fall muffled by the thick layer of snow. There is no going back, you know that. In this weather, you could neither go around nor scramble over the tree. You must go on, you have no choice.

As you struggle up the icy slope, working your way ahead inch by inch, you find your thoughts turning to all the struggles you've encountered and overcome on your journey. Think of the fears and doubts you used to have, and the self-confidence you now possess. Think about how ineffectual you once felt, and how competent you now have become.

extended long pause—1 minute

You've progressed so far on your journey, through some difficult odds, and now you can put that determination to use on this patch of the ice. As you've done before, you now grit your teeth, take a deep breath and force yourself along the trail.

long pause

To your relief, you find that this last thrust of effort pushes you beyond the icy patch, and you now climb toward the cavern with ease. The snow is lighter here, due to the outcropping of stony rock that overhangs the path.

You start to rush toward the cave when your training stops you. Focus for a moment on your inner voice. Your intuition is alert, your subconscious aware. Reach out, seeking an answer as to whether the cave is safe.

After a moment you sense that, yes, the cave is safe. You may enter without worry. With a last look at the snow, which is starting to pile up now, retrieve your flashlight from your backpack and enter the cave.

long pause

At first you feel overwhelmed by the darkness. In contrast to the silvery light from outside, you find that you can barely see. But the flashlight penetrates the gloom and soon your eyes adjust and you begin to make out the contours of the cavern.

You are in a large room. Several ledges buttress against the walls, almost like windowseats in a house, and they promise a wide, if solid, place for you to stretch out and relax. Stalagmites thrust up from the cavern floor, stalactites jut down from the ceiling.

One of the sculptures formed by dripping minerals is so unearthly, so exquisite, that you wish you could take it with you, but you know that to disturb such beauty would probably destroy it.

long pause

You are too tired from your climb to further explore, but from what you can see, the cave looks safe enough. Sit down on one of the stone ledges and take off your pack. You need to rest. There is food in your pack, and water, and you even thought to bring spare socks and a thermal blanket, to guard against getting unduly chilled.

As you dry yourself off and eat, you begin to think about how the different adventures on your journey have changed you, how they've prepared you for new experiences and unexpected events. You've found that you have the strength to cope with stressful situations, and you've also found that you can trust your own intuition.

long pause

You've learned that intuition is not what you think, and it's not what you feel, but an inner voice that says, "I know." Every day that you've listened to your inner guide, you've added more strength to your self-confidence and self-reliance. And while you've had teachers on this journey, you now understand that you have been your best teacher, your own guru.

Think now, to your intuition, and how your hunches and premonitions have proved true in your life. Take a few moments to think about the times that you've trusted your intuition and been glad of it.

extended long pause—1 minute

After you eat and change your socks and dry out your clothing, you want to rest. Lay down and close your eyes. Take three deep breaths as your body relaxes against the stone bed.

long pause

You find yourself standing beside your body. Once again, you realize that you are journeying in your sleep. A noise in the darkness makes you turn, and you see a shining figure step toward you. At first you're not sure whether it is a male or a female, but then you see the hint of breasts under the rose-colored robe and realize that you're facing a woman. She has golden wings, and her eyes glow with a brilliant golden light.

At first you think, an angel? Could it be?

Then, in answer to your unspoken question, she says, "I am not an angel, not the way your kind thinks of them. I exist within the astral realm. I am known by many names . . . guide, deva, angel, avatar . . . but tonight, I come as your guide. You must review your journey, for you are almost at the end and before you can enter the last realm—the realm of the World, you must ascertain whether you have done everything you needed to do."

long pause

She bids you to review your life. Your journey has wrought many changes in the past months . . . years. You have undergone trial and transformation. You have been student and become teacher. You have formed friendships and dissolved relationships.

You have raced under the night in a mad frenzy, you have disciplined yourself to the point of asceticism. Now you must seek your inner guide, you must look over the lessons through which you have passed.

long pause

"I will ask you a series of questions," she says. "It is not me whom you shall answer, but your own self. So think upon each question and then answer silently, for only you can truly judge your progress."

The first question she asks is, "Have you done the best you can, considering all circumstances? Can you truly look back and say that you did what you were capable of, given the time, the environment, and your state of being?"

Think now, and answer to yourself.

extended long pause—1 minute

The second question: "Do you feel you have evolved? If you still feel lacking, is there anything you need to do to shore up that which you believe to be weak?"

Think now and answer to yourself.

extended long pause—1 minute

Her third question: "What do you feel was the ultimate purpose of this journey? When you started out, you knew not where you were going, but now look back. Can you see purpose to your travels and lessons? Can you sum up what you believe to be the core of your quest?"

Think now and answer to yourself.

extended long pause—1 minute

Now, she says, "You have reached a turning point in your life. This journey is almost ended, a new one will soon begin. You must release all grudges and hurts accumulated during this phase of your life if you are to go on to new quests and adventures.

"I do not ask you to forgive those who harmed you, although you may if you wish, but you must put the past behind you and learn from it, grow from it . . . let it go into that space where it becomes memory and nothing more.

"Think about your grudges you carry, the old heartbreaks and anger and sadness, and let it go. Let it flow out from your heart and sink deep in this mountain, to be transformed by the earth and washed clean again in the fires of the Mother."

She waves her hand and a hole opens before you, in the floor of the cavern, and you can sense that it drops to the very core of the world.

long pause

Take time to examine any grudges you are carrying within you, for they weigh you down and prevent the free flow of your life. Let go of useless anger and shame that you've faced, but not discarded.

Once you face a problem you must cast it away, for to carry it further is to carry deadweight. See the old grudges and hurts as dull gems, no longer of any worth. Pick them up and cast them into the hole, to the center of the earth.

extended long pause—2 minutes

When you have finished, the woman steps aside and points to the back wall of the cavern. You see a passage leading up.

"There lies your path. Wake now, gather your things, and leave my realm, for you have one last league of the journey to traverse, and it is time for you to go."

If you wish to say anything to the spirit, do so now and listen for her answer.

long pause

You find yourself sinking back into your body, and then you wake. Gather your things together, hoist your pack on your back, and step into the passage that the woman pointed out to you.

long pause

The corridor leads upward, with rough steps hewn into the mountain. With your staff they are easy to ascend and you find yourself counting as you climb. Ten steps . . . twenty . . . thirty, and still they ascend.

Forty steps and you continue to climb . . . fifty and your legs start to get tired. You shine your flashlight up the passage and see no end in sight yet.

Sixty . . . seventy . . . eighty . . . you feel like you will never reach the end of this passage, and then, before you can react, the batteries in your flashlight die and darkness surrounds you.

long pause

As you stand there, barely breathing, not sure of what to do, a glimmer flickers from above. You blink a couple of times, trying to decide if the light is your imagination, or if you really see it. Finally you realize that, yes, you do see a faint light shining down the passage.

Your staff braced in one hand and the cave wall against the other, you feel your way up the last steps . . . ninety . . . the light is growing brighter . . . one hundred, and you stand on a ledge with two exits, one facing to your left, the other toward your right.

long pause

Light streams in through both exits and curious you peek your head out of the left one. You see a vast panorama of snowy peaks. You recognize, far below, the path up the hill which you ascended.

You pull your head back in and turn to the right, but a sudden rumble behind you makes you jump and you move just in time to avoid being caught by a cave-in. A flurry of dust settles as, coughing, you examine your situation.

The exit to the left is blocked, as is the passage through which you just ascended. Your only option is to leave through the opening to the right.

long pause

As you poke your head through, you see sunlight gleaming down on a valley that slopes gradually down the mountainside. In the center of the valley, you see a gazebo, adorned with leis of gardenias and ginger, plumeria and hibiscus.

Laughing children race around, shrieking with joy. Near the gazebo stands a cluster of adults. They talk, watch the children, arrange food on blankets for a picnic.

As the sun rises above the crest of the mountain ridge, one of the men looks up and sees you. He beckons you down, to join them. With a deep breath, you step out of the cave and enter the realm of the World.

Now, listen to my voice as I count from ten to one. You will awake refreshed and alert. Ten . . . nine . . . you are becoming awake and aware of your surroundings . . . eight . . . seven . . . six . . . hear the sounds around you . . . five . . . four . . . you will be fully alert and refreshed . . . three . . . two . . . one . . . take three deep breaths and when you are ready, you may open your eyes.

Suggested Exercises

1. Examine different times in your life when you feel you were near the end of a cycle. Did you take time to examine how the cycle had affected you? Did you manage to tie up as many of the loose ends as you could? If we leave too many things unfinished, our next journey, or cycle, will be affected. When you near the end of a major transformation, always try to clear up any lingering problems, grudges, doubts, so that you are free to move on.

2. If you have a hard time ascertaining how a certain period in your life affected you, perhaps you can ask a friend to help. Sometimes we need to take stock of our progress, so that we can remember past mistakes and avoid them the next time. This is part of recognizing harmful patterns; especially when it comes to love relationships and self-sabotage that prevents success.

3. Remember, you don't have to forgive someone who wronged you, but neither should you allow the grudge to poison your thoughts. Put the hurt aside—if you have truly let go, then you won't think about it very often, and you won't let it taint how you treat others. However, it is also important to learn from harmful events so you can try to avoid getting caught by similar situations in the future.

The longest journey
Is the journey inwards
Of him who has chosen his destiny.

—Dag Hammarskjöld (1905–1961)
Markings

The World
The End of the Journey

The twenty-second—and last—card of the major arcana is known as the World (or the Universe). It is assigned the number 21.

The World and Its Energy

We have reached the end of our journey. As we enter the realm of the World, a cycle passes and a new one prepares itself to be born.

The World represents the culmination of our quest, the end of the road. When we leave the realm of Judgment, we leave knowing that, for good or ill, there is nothing more we can do. We step into the World and—if what we have learned is not enough, then too bad—there are no paths back. If we have passed through the cycle in optimum form, we should feel very balanced about leaving our quest. We have done our best and, in our hearts, know it's time to move on.

The World represents omega into alpha . . . end into beginning. We break through the final walls, destroy all limitations and find freedom on the other side. We have left behind a cycle of structure and learning. Free from structure, for we have evolved to where self-discipline is a part of our hearts, we no longer need schedules to continue our growth.

The World represents regeneration. The land is renewed, we are dancing in tune with the Universe. This means that we are precisely where we need to be. As we look around this new realm, once again we discover that we have entered the realm of the unknown. We stand on the threshold of change, the eve of a new quest.

As Fool, we have completed the circle. Much like the concept of reincarnation, the last part of the cycle is also outside of that cycle. While our souls have evolved, our conscious mind must return to the Fool's naïveté so that we do not interfere with the next set of lessons. Yet, as we embark upon our new journey, we are wiser than before. We just may not realize it.

The World archetype becomes a symbol for unity, for the whole of existence. We see the macrocosm reflected by the microcosm. As above, so below. Here we live out the energy we discovered in the Star card, here we link ourselves to the cosmic voice and become one with creation.

The World teaches us nothing, but allows us to exist in our true states, linked together with others on a spiritual plane. We do not enter this realm to learn, but to explore a state of joy and unity and rest before we once again take to the road.

Much like the Summerlands of the Celts, the realm of the World gives us a respite from action, while at the same time preparing us for our next sojourn.

When we enter the realm of the World, we find ourselves in a resting state, a period of peace and contentment. We have just seen a major transformation take place in our life experience, now we take some time to enjoy our new world before we take stock and throw our packs on our back to explore it.

But we cannot move on until we've thoroughly absorbed the impact of the journey through which we've just passed.

In your daily life, you will greet the World with relief. It may come as a vacation after a major change, or as a period of adjustment in which you remain relatively free from commitments. You know that soon you will be busy again, throwing yourself into the new state of your affairs, learning new skills, accepting new challenges, but for now you just want to relax.

Enter the realm of the World and you find yourself walking on the beach, in the woods, sitting on the grass in the sunlight . . . letting your mind drift over the events of the past few months as you examine the changes that they have wrought in you.

You have come to the end of a long road and now you look back with wonder, amazed that you managed to make it through some of the trials that befell you. You know that you struggled, you know that you persevered, but from where you are now it's difficult to even remember the beginnings of your journey.

You are no longer the person you were when you stepped into the tarot shop, when you set foot on the path, and yet, as much as you've evolved, you know enough to realize that someday, perhaps weeks—perhaps months or even years—from now, you will once again cross into the realm of the World and look back on yourself as you are this moment, with a new wonder in your heart. It is the nature of the cycle. It is the nature of life.

The Spiritual Concept

Let us look for the World within the Goddess complete, the Great Mother who encompasses both Earth and Moon, land and sea, brilliant day and velvet night. She is nameless, this Goddess, but we feel Her presence everywhere and She listens to our heartbeats as we walk across Her body.

And we turn, too, to the God of Nature—the Horned God who is also Sky God. He is cyclic, as is the Fool's Journey, and yet He is always Consort of the Lady, be the year waxing or waning, fertile or fallow.

We place this card at the center—the hub—for the World not only represents the Wheel of the Year, but also the Wheel of Life.

The Card

This is perhaps one of the most varied cards in the deck. I have seen the World represented by everything from a dancing figure in the middle of the Universe to the Worm Oroborous; from Yggdrasil, the World Tree, to a picture of the Earth herself.

Guidelines for Use

This meditation follows that of the Judgment card. You may also find it useful to meditate on the World whenever you have reached the end of a long, tiring journey or cycle. In this case, use this meditation only after you have dealt with any traumas or lingering doubts during those journeys or cycles. The World meditation is also appropriate for inclusion in a ceremony honoring the transition of a loved one or friend from life into the arms of death.

Flowers:	rose, lotus, jasmine, peach, cedar
Incense:	frankincense, pine, lemongrass, musk
Oils:	rosemary, jasmine, rose, peach, musk
Crystals:	nautilus seashell, pearl, aquamarine
Candles:	blue, green, teal

Meditation

Relax and get comfortable. Close your eyes and take three deep breaths.

long pause

You are standing in a cavern. To your left and behind you, the exits have been blocked by a cave-in and you know you can never dig your way through the tangle of rocks and dirt. You have only one direction in which you can turn.

You peek through the exit to your right, into a cascade of sunlight. It shimmers down through a valley that lies in what looks to be an ancient volcano crater. The hills of the valley are steep and ridged and covered with patches of verdant foliage. Within the center of the valley, sits a gazebo, adorned with leis of gardenia and ginger, plumeria and hibiscus. Behind the gazebo, you see an ash tree reaching toward the heavens.

Laughing children tumble through the grass, shrieking with joy. Near the gazebo you see a cluster of adults. They talk, watch the children, arrange food on blankets for a picnic. As the sun rises above the crest of the ridge, one of the men looks up and sees you. He beckons you down. With a deep breath, you step out of the cave and enter the realm of the World.

long pause

As you lightly trip down the hillside, a group of children comes running up to meet you. One of them carries a lei woven of roses, and she drapes it around your shoulders and gives you a peck on the cheek. Her smile is brilliant, her eyes filled with happiness. You have the feeling that even though you are a stranger, these people will welcome you into their midst and treat you as one of their own.

As you look around the valley, you see now that the people come from all races and backgrounds. Caucasian, African, Asian, Polynesian, Mediterranean . . . all ethnicities are represented here and no one seems to care. The children play together, the adults intermingle, and not one furrowed brow is seen, not one unkind word heard.

long pause

They lead you over to the gazebo and offer you a place to sit. "Rest," they say, "and eat. Enjoy yourself. Our valley is overflowing with abundance. We have food and drink, we have blankets if you are tired, and games should you desire entertainment. Make yourself at home, enjoy your stay with us."

As you look around, you see every conceivable food that you might want eat. Every drink for which you might find yourself thirsty. Decide what you want to eat and fix yourself a plate of food.

long pause

Huge pillows and blankets clutter the floor of the gazebo. In one corner you see a row of books, the titles blank. As you examine one, you see that the cover has a space on it in which you may write. A quill and inkstand rest on the shelf next to the books and, as you watch, one of the women sits down beside you. She scribbles something on the cover of another book, waits a few moments, then opens it and begins to read.

At your inquisitive look, she says, "Whatever you wish to read . . . all you need do is write the title on the cover and the contents will appear on the blank pages. When you've finished reading, write "The End" on the last page, and the book will once again become blank."

Try it. Pick up the quill and write the title of your favorite novel on the cover of the blank book in your hands. Then open up the pages to find the story.

long pause

There seems to be no schedule here. People sleep when they're tired, eat when they're hungry, play and talk when they wish. There are games of all kinds inside the gazebo, and the weather never varies, but maintains a consistent temperature somewhere in the mid-70s. You are neither cold nor hot, and so the days drift by in a comfortable haze.

As you relax from your long journey, you begin to explore the valley. One day you see, behind the ash tree, which stretches so far into the sky that it looks as if it might very well hold up the heavens, a purple tent staked into the grassy floor. Banners of green and gold wave from the center of the tent. At first you think you might go over to see what's in there, but then one of the valley people calls you back and you turn, with just a hint of reluctance, and join the others for a game of riddles.

long pause

A few days later, you notice that the make-up of the people has changed. A man whom you were eating lunch with only yesterday has disappeared. Two new women have joined the group. You don't remember seeing the man leave or the women enter the valley. When you ask the others about it, they shrug and turn away, uninterested.

Still some days later, you remember the tent and return to where it sits behind the tree. Again, you feel a gentle urge to see what lies inside, but once more, you are called back to the party and so you leave it for later. There is no rush, you think, no hurry.

long pause

Your days continue in the same pattern for awhile, the sun rises and then the moon, day and night slide past . . . the seasons do not vary. Occasionally a man or woman leaves or enters the valley, but you don't know how they managed it. There seems to be no way in or out save for the blocked passage through which you first arrived.

Then one morning, you wake to find the slightest tang of autumn in the air. You mention the chill to the others, but none of them notice. The days grow steadily colder, and still no one else but you pays any heed to the weather.

Finally, when the blankets in the gazebo are barely adequate to keep the cold at bay, you wake one morning with the knowledge that you must visit the pavilion behind the ash tree. Today you explore, find out what lays behind the fluttering tent walls.

long pause

No one pays you any attention as you meander over to the tent. This time no one distracts you. A faint quiver in your stomach alerts you to the fact that something exciting is about to happen, something new.

As you enter, you see a table in the center of the tent, with a chair on either side. To your left, you see a small altar. You take a quick peek, but your intuition tells you these are sacred objects and so you keep your hands to yourself.

Atop the white linen tablecloth rests a vase filled with daffodils, bright yellow and fragrant with their spicy scent. A large wooden pentacle sits in front of the vase, and on the pentacle, a prism. It separates the rays of sunlight filtering in from the tent flaps into rainbows that dance around the room.

long pause

A stick of rose-scented incense gently smolders to the left of the pentacle, ash falling into a copper holder. To the right sits a bowl of water scented with rosemary and lemongrass.

The scene is familiar, you have the feeling you have been here before. The room begins to swirl and shift as a woman enters from the back of the tent. She wears a gauze dress, lavender with a stippled pattern etched in gold. Gold hoops peek out from beneath her hair. A golden pentacle rests at her throat.

You notice a touch of silver intermingling with the ginger brown of her long curls and her eyes are ancient with knowledge and wisdom. She smiles to you and bids you welcome and when you hear her voice, you remember. Pythia—Lady of the Oracle.

long pause

In one quick flash, you remember your journey, every step of the way, from the beginning when you stood in front of a small tarot shop and wondered if you should go in!

Pythia smiles. "Welcome back," she says. "We meet again, fair Fool."

Welcome back? you think. But you have not returned to where you first began. You say as much, but she waves away your protests.

"Don't you remember I told you that you can never go back to where you were . . . to who you were? Every event, every person we meet, changes us. We can never recapture what we once had. We must evolve and continue to grow."

long pause

She places a crystal ball on the table. "Look deep into my crystal," she says.

As you stare into the sphere, you see yourself, once again dressed in the garments of the Fool. You understand how the journey is never truly over, but only paused while we rest and refresh ourselves. We may end cycles, we may leave people and places behind, but we continually quest after knowledge of ourselves and the world in which we live. Books and teachers have their limitations. We can only learn on a heart-core level by experimenting, by experiencing . . . we grab up our pack and set out on the journey.

extended long pause—1 minute

When Pythia sees that you understand all of this, she removes the crystal ball and lays a deck of cards on the table. "You are rested," she murmurs. "You have replenished yourself. Now it is time to pick a card."

In your heart, you know she speaks the truth. The last part of any cycle is recovery and rejuvenation. And now that you have rested, it's time to move on . . . time to pick a card and start new again.

You will take with you all you learned from this journey, the lessons will not leave you in times of need. But there are new experiences which call your name and its time to continue.

Reach out and pick a card. When you turn it over, you see the Fool.

long pause

Pythia motions you to stand. "You have your supplies, you have your courage. Come then, and let me lead you to the door."

You follow her out the back of the tent where you find yourself facing the ash tree. A door into the tree, hidden from view by the canvas of the tent, opens and she stands back, smiling.

"Be of stout heart. The path lies ahead. Good luck and good fortune to you. We will meet again, someday, somewhere. Be watching for me."

Then, before you can react, she pushes you through the door into the tree and you find yourself facing a set of stairs leading up. As you ascend the wooden steps, you know that there is a door, just ahead waiting, and it will lead you into a new world of experience.

long pause

Now, listen to my voice as I count from ten to one. You will awake refreshed and alert. Ten . . . nine . . . you are becoming awake and aware of your surroundings . . . eight . . . seven . . . six . . . hear the sounds around you . . . five . . . four . . . you will be fully alert and refreshed . . . three . . . two . . . one . . . take three deep breaths and when you are ready, you may open your eyes.

Suggested Exercises

1. Research the various afterlife scenarios of different faiths. Many, especially those which espouse the doctrine of reincarnation, hold that the afterlife is a place where the soul may rest and rejuvenate before its next incarnation. Examine how that aligns with the concept of the World card in the tarot.

2. If you've gone through a metamorphosis in your life, you'll probably need some time to relax and unwind before attempting any new projects. Try to schedule your work or home-life so that you can take a few days' vacation after you've made a major move, either on the home front or career-wise. This will allow you to gather your thoughts, clear your head, and relax your body.

3. The World card represents unity, regardless of race, age, gender, religion . . . I propose that we think about creating World Day celebrations among our various communities. Of course, you will want to be cautious of inviting someone you know to be outwardly hostile. There are people who aren't advanced enough to let go of their anger, and they can only spoil the intent. However, if enough people join together to celebrate the joys of life, without focusing on a single race or religion, then we can begin to foster dialogues and increase tolerance in our society.

It is art that makes life, makes interest, makes importance, for our consideration and application of these things, and I know of no substitute whatever for the force and beauty of its process.

—Henry James (1843–1916)
Letter to H. G. Wells, July 10, 1915

Afterword
The Creation of Guided Meditations

And so, we come to the end of the journey, out of the woods into the sunlight. But wait, is that another forest up ahead, lurking in the shadows of your subconscious?

There will always be issues for you to face, there will always be problems in life. You can utilize the tarot for these, both in a divinatory sense and as a guide. You might want to try writing your own meditations sometime, perhaps based on the major arcana, perhaps based on the minor arcana. In this chapter, I have attempted to explain the process I go through when I'm writing a guided meditation in hopes that it will help those of you who would like to try your hands at this.

While I cannot give you a formula, I can help set parameters that might be useful to you in attempting to forge your own set of meditations.

I would call the process I went through when I wrote these guided journeys akin to trance work, although the research was very analytical. To create the meditations in *Tarot Journeys,* I first assembled all the tarot decks I own. Even though I know the meanings of each card intimately, I went through every booklet and book that came with the decks and jotted down the highlights and the unusual approaches each deck had to the interpretations of the cards. After eliminating the redundancies, I made a list of the information I had gathered.

Then I researched the gods and goddesses appropriate to the cards. I focused on what energy the card had and looked for deities whose attributes corresponded to the particular archetype. I didn't really consider astrology or numerology or anything like that in making these choices, but solely based it on the relevance of the god or goddess to the energy of the tarot card being examined.

I found *The Tarot Handbook* by Angeles Arrien a great help in exploring some of the symbolism found in the imagery of the cards. *The Witches' God* and *The Witches' Goddess,* both by Janet and Stewart Farrar, and *The Ancient and Shining Ones* (now titled *Magick of the Gods and Goddesses*) by D. J. Conway were wonderful references for researching the attributes of the deities.

After this, I compiled a list of incenses, crystals, oils, and other materials that matched the energy of each archetype. Some of this I could easily figure out from my years in the Craft, but I did use several books to help me when I was stymied. I used Scott Cunningham's *Encyclopedia of Magical Herbs* for some of my flower, incense, and herb correlations.

Once I had this information organized, I was ready to begin the more intuitive research for my writing.

I removed all the major arcana cards from each deck and arranged them in order, from the Fool to the World. Then, when I was ready to begin, I took all the cards for the particular meditation I was working on and began to study them. I work at my desk in my office, which also contains my ritual gear, so I felt that this was as close to sacred space as I could get. Since I view all of my writing, metaphysical or not, as a spiritual act, for me this was the ideal working environment. Not to mention that, as a professional author, it makes little sense for me to write somewhere other than my office and desk.

I lit a stick of incense germane to the archetype and let myself drift into trance and examined the imagery of the various interpretations, calling on the spirit of that particular archetype to help me discover the deeper meanings and symbolism that might elude a casual glance. I noted all my impressions in writing, so I wouldn't forget any of them, and added these to my lists of interpretations.

After this, I was ready for the actual writing. I let the information about the card mull around in my head as I searched for a quote that I felt encapsulated the archetype and the cycle of life that it signified. This would allow me to focus on the quote as a symbol for the chapter, constantly reminding me of the energy involved. I have always found books that used this process seemed to hold a little something extra for me and loved reading the gems that the authors had dug up.

While some of the quotes were ones with which I was familiar, for others I thought about the major energy the chapter/card would encompass and then used *Bartlett's Familiar Quotations* and the *Oxford Dictionary of Quotations* to search for passages relevant to the topic. After I had my quote and wrote up the first part of the chapter, discussing the Fool on this particular part of his or her journey, I came to the meditation.

A guided meditation will have several goals. One, it must help lead the reader/student into a trance state, so it has to flow smoothly, not be abrupt or jarring in language. Second, if the meditation is for more than the individual, it must speak directly to the students without assigning gender or age or status, and therefore must be worded so that it can be applicable to many people rather than just to one group.

A third consideration is the lesson, or goal that you wish to impart to your students. You must allow for a thorough examination of the issue being addressed in order to achieve maximum benefit. I don't know how many "guided meditations" I've seen that are mere skeletons and generally not specific enough to be of much help at all. So you will want to write your meditation longer than you think you might think is necessary. Get into detail. As with fiction, involve all senses—sight, hearing, touch, taste, smell. Paint a vivid picture with the words in order to immerse the student fully in the experience. Consider the guided meditation an interactive story. Much like a spiritual video game, only the mind is the screen and the words are the program.

I always start my meditations the same way, with the same words, for several reasons. One, consistency helps the student automatically start sliding into a familiar routine, in this case for trance-work. The other is that the first words direct the student to calm down, to close their eyes, and they promote a "settling down" period.

Every time I come to an important point in a meditation, I incorporate a long pause, in order that the student might have time to process the images and what those spark off within themselves. I also keep a lot of dream symbolism and general metaphor in my mind when I write meditations since I am speaking to the subconscious. For example, tigers are seen as embodying strength, lions embodying leadership, the moon as hidden mysteries and feminine energy, the forest as the subconscious. This is where a smattering of psychology will come in handy, but you can do just as well by reading books on dream analysis and studying the works of authors like Joseph Campbell and Jung.

As far as the actual wording of the meditation, well, writing has as many approaches as does everything else in life. When I'm writing guided meditations, I "see" the action internally and describe the surroundings, I follow the journey as it's laid out for me. There's no magic template, no magic formula fill-in-the-blank guidelines I can give you—if I were to do so, it would be stiff and wooden and so like every other meditation that you wouldn't get any benefit whatsoever out of the exercise.

All I can do is try to point you in the right direction. Your meditation will have a beginning, a climax where the student must either answer a key question for themselves or examine the "big" issue of the archetype you're working with, and then a resolution. With *Trancing The Witch's Wheel*, each meditation was separate within itself. *Tarot Journeys* builds on each meditation because it's comprised of many small journeys within one long journey.

So, in a sense, you must consider the next meditation along the road, and the one behind you, when you write a series of guided journeys in this manner. You must keep yourself effectively in the past, present, and future and weave together a concept for where you want them to lead even before you start. I laid out an outline as to the most important lesson each card would be encompassing, just a two or three word description. Then I went from there. As I finished each meditation, I would think about the next one, where and how it would pick up from the last, and where it would lead to. And so, I followed the breadcrumbs into the woods, only I was the Witch rather than Gretel, and I slowly wended my way through the labyrinth of the major arcana.

When it came time to formulate the suggested exercises for the chapter, I thought about what lessons were being learned, and what one might be able to do, without involved instructions or guidance, to amplify and exemplify the journey just passed through. I tried to think of simple things that related to either the action or the thought processes presented in the meditation and play off of that.

Now, if you want to try writing your own meditations based on a particular need you have, I list here some suggestions on what cards might be applicable to certain situations. It is my hope that with these guidelines and suggestions, you can find your own voice and create something individual and meaningful to you. After all, that is what all of my books espouse—the necessity to find your own path. I present my view, my vision of the world in hopes that it might spark off your own internal senses so that you can tailor your spiritual journey to your own needs.

Blesséd Be, my friends, and remember, we must all journey into the woods in order to discover our inner strengths, face our inner demons, and revel in our deepest and most passionate feral selves.

Suggested Cards for Specific Situations

You will be able to think of more card correspondences for various situations on your own once you are more familiar with the tarot.

Swords: intellectual matters; school, education, communications
Wands: energy, passion, vitality, creativity, physical strength and health
Cups: emotions, the psyche, spirit and inner guidance
Disks: material world, physicality, manifestation, career

Beginnings and New Cycles: the Fool, Aces

Intellect, School, Education, Communication: the Magus, the Hierophant, Ace Swords, 4 Swords, 6 Swords, 8 Wands

Love, Sexuality: Lovers, Strength, the Horned Lord (Devil), 2 Cups, 4 Wands, Cups Court cards; Queen of Disks, Wands Court cards

Family, Friendships: Empress, Emperor, 9 Cups

Career and Home: Chariot, Fortune, Temperance, Sun, Ace Disks, 3 Disks, 4 Disks, 6 Disks, 9 Disks, 10 Disks, Disks Court cards; 2 Wands, 6 Wands

Art and Creativity: the Magus, the Star, Ace Wands, Wands Court cards, 8 Disks, Princess Disks, Knight Disks, 4 Swords, Ace Cups,

Spirituality: The High Priestess, the Empress, the Hierophant, Death, the Star, the Moon, the World, 3 Wands, 9 Wands, Ace Cups,

Despair and Depression: the Hanged Man, the Tower, 5 Swords, 7 Swords, 5 Cups, 5 Disks, 7 Disks,

Addictive Problems: the Hanged Man, Judgment, 7 Cups, 8 Cups

Violence and Anger: the Tower, 10 Wands, 9 Swords, 10 Swords

Appendix

Suggested Decks

Remember, your best bet is to buy a deck that appeals to you visually. If you don't enjoy looking at it, then you probably aren't going to be interested in learning to read the cards.

Having said that, here are some of my favorite decks, in order of preference.

1. The Aleister Crowley Thoth Deck
2. The Röhrig Tarot
3. The Elemental Tarot
4. The Robin Wood Tarot
5. The Dragon Tarot
6. The Art Nouveau Deck
7. The Haindl Deck

Other decks that I like, but which are more specific in terms of path and references, are:

1. The Arthurian Tarot
2. The Greenwood Tarot
3. The Kalevala Tarot
4. The Norse Tarot

I know I've left out many decks that I've seen over the years—some have been oracles rather than tarot, and so they don't quite fit this category. Other decks I just found little interest in. I'm also equally certain that, in the future, there will be other decks in which I delight. There are hundreds of decks, each with their personal slant on the subject. Remember, the truth is relevant. Each deck is correct for the person who created it and for those who find it easy to read with.

Resource Guide

Most, if not all of the shops listed here offer mail-order service and catalogs. Be aware, however, that retail shops go in and out of business with alarming frequency, so some of those listed may not be in service when you write to them. Others will spring up after the writing of this book.

As far as local supplies go: look for tarot decks in bookstores and gift shops; candles in drug stores, stationery stores, grocery stores, and gift shops. Grocery stores and florists carry flowers, as do your friends' gardens. You can sometimes find essential oils in gift shops or perfume shops, and crystals can be located in gift shops and rock shops. Gather your herbs wild or purchase them through grocery stores or food co-ops, herb shops—or buy the whole plant at a local plant nurseries.

Unusual altar pieces can often be found at local import supply stores and second-hand stores. Altar cloths are easy—go to your favorite fabric shop and buy a piece of cloth large enough to cover your altar table.

Lastly, don't overlook the Yellow Pages. Look under the headings Metaphysical, Herbs, Books (bookstores often carry far more than books), Lapidary Supplies, and Jewelry.

Magickal Supplies

1. **Abyss**
   48-NWL Chester Road
   Chester, MA 01011-9735
2. **White Light Pentacles**
   P.O. Box 8163
   Salem, MA 01971-8163
3. **Eden Within**
   P.O. Box 667
   Jamestown, NY 14702

4. **Gypsy Heaven**
   115 S. Main St.
   New Hope, PA 18938
   (catalog $3; they say it's refundable
   through purchase/Money Orders only)
5. **MoonScents and Magickal Blends**
   P.O. Box 3811588-LL
   Cambridge, MA 02238

Pagan/Magickal Journals and Magazines

1. **New Moon Rising**
   12345 SE Fuller Rd. #119
   Milwaukee, OR 97222
2. **Green Egg**
   P.O. Box 488
   Laytonville, CA 95454
3. **SageWoman**
   P.O. Box 641LL
   Point Arena, CA 95648
4. **Shaman's Drum**
   P.O. Box 430
   Willits, CA 95490-0430

5. **Open Ways**
   P.O. Box 14415
   Portland, OR 97293-0415
6. **The Beltane Papers**
   P.O. Box 29694
   Bellingham, WA 98228-1694
7. **The Sacred Horn**
   Unickorn Press
   P.O. Box 143262
   Anchorage, AK 99514-3262

Other Resources

American Tarot Association
P.O. Box 17164
Boulder, CO 80308-0164
(303) 938-1408
email: tarot101@juno.com

Crossroads Learning Center
P.O. Box 12184
Seattle, WA 98102

Aquarian Tabernacle Church (ATC)
P.O. Box 409
Index, WA 98256

Glossary

Altar: the ritual layout of magickal/ritual tools and symbols.

Aura: the energy field existing around all living things.

Balefire: a fire lit for magickal purposes, usually outdoors. Traditional fires were lit on hills during Beltane and Samhain.

Beltane: May 1 sabbat, celebration of life and sexuality.

Bower: an outdoor boudoir specifically set aside where couples may retreat to make love.

Caer Arianrhod: the castle of Arianrhod, Goddess of the Silver Wheel.

Censer: an incense burner.

Centering, to Center: to find an internal point of balance.

Chalice: a ritual goblet.

Chariot, the: the eighth card of the major arcana, representing direct action, focused will, and setting boundaries.

Circle: a sphere constructed of energy, created by a Witch. Sacred space.

Cleansing, to Cleanse: to remove negative energy, to purify.

Craft, the: Witchcraft, natural magick.

Crone: the aged aspect of the Goddess representing wisdom, experience, and the Underworld.

Death: the fourteenth card of the major arcana, representing transformation and change—voluntary or involuntary.

Deosil: clockwise (sun-wise).

Deva: a powerful Faerie land or mineral spirit; a collective oversoul.

Devil, the: the sixteenth card of the major arcana, (in this book) representing the Horned God, the wild and chaotic energy of the Hunt, spontaneity, creation.

Divination: magickal arts of discovering the unknown through use of cards, runes, stones, crystals balls, etc.

Elements: the four building blocks of the universe. Earth, air, fire, and water. Major forces used in natural magick.

Emperor, the: the fifth card of the major arcana, representing the Divine male, authority, the taking of responsibility.

Empress, the: the fourth card of the major arcana, representing the Divine female, the Goddess, mother-energy in all forms.

Equinox, Autumnal: The point during autumn when the Sun crosses the celestial equator; day and night are of equal length (see Mabon).

Equinox, Spring: (see Vernal Equinox) (see Ostara).

Equinox, Vernal: The point during spring when the Sun crosses the celestial equator; day and night are of equal length, (see Ostara).

Faerie: one of many nature spirits that inhabit a realm or dimension next to our own.

Faerie Kingdom: the realm of Faerie.

Fey: to be like or of the Faerie.

The Fool: the first card of the major arcana, representing new beginnings; new cycles.

Green Man: a male aspect of divinity, symbolized by the vegetation and forests.

Grounding, to Ground: to root self firmly in the physical world in preparation for magickal/meta-physical work.

Hanged Man, the: the thirteenth card of the major arcana, representing sacrifice, loss so that growth may take place.

Hermit, the: the tenth card of the major arcana, representing solitude, inner searching, wisdom.

Hierophant, the: the sixth card of the major arcana, representing teachers, education and knowledge.

High Priestess: See Priestess

Hunt: the Wild Hunt led by (various) Gods and/or Goddesses.

Hunter: the Horned God of the Witches.

Imbolc: festival of the Goddess Brid; sabbat celebrated on February 2 each year.

Initiation: a process of formally introducing and/or admitting the self or someone else into a Coven, group, religion, etc.

Invoke, Invocation: an appeal or petition to a God/dess, element or energy.

Judgment: the twenty-first card of the major arcana, representing karma, introspection, self-observation.

Justice: the twelfth card of the major arcana, representing truth, actions matching words, a balance of energies.

Litha: (see Solstice, Summer) sabbat festival honoring the Oak King and the Goddess in Their prime.

Lovers, the: the seventh card of the major arcana, representing unity of polarities, harmony of male and female.

Lughnasadh: festival of the God Lugh; sabbat celebrated on August 1 each year.

Mabon: (see Equinox, Autumnal) sabbat festival honoring the harvest. A Pagan Thanksgiving.

Magic/Magick: the manipulation of natural forces and psychic energy to bring about desired changes.

Magician, the: the second card of the major arcana, representing clarity and communications.

Maiden: the youthful aspect of the Goddess, representing freedom, adventure and playfulness.

major arcana: the first twenty-two cards of the tarot. The major arcana uses universal symbolism in order to spur the subconscious into understanding and revealing various concepts and beliefs.

Maypole: a tree or long pole used for dances during Beltane, representing the phallus of the God (see Beltane).

Mead: an alcoholic drink made of honey, yeast, and water.

Meditation: a state of reflection, contemplation.

Metheglin: mead with spices added (see Mead).

Midsummer's Eve: the night preceding the Summer Solstice. Often celebrated for its connections with the Faerie Kingdom.

Minor Arcana: the last fifty-six cards of the Tarot. The minor arcana uses events and emotions from daily life to predict and/or mirror what is happening in the querist's life during a tarot Reading.

Moon, the: the nineteenth card of the major arcana, representing initiation, the Dream Time, the hidden depths of the psyche.

Mother: the fertile, full-grown aspect of the Goddess, representing the prime of life, creativity and adult sexuality.

Ogham: the Celtic runic system, using either twenty or twenty-five symbols, depending on whether you accept the last quintet (added some time after the first four quintets) as valid.

Old Religion: Paganism, in all its myriad forms. A religion predating the Judeo-Christian religions.

Oracle deck: a deck used for divination, different from the tarot by the number and meaning of its cards.

Ostara: (see Equinox, Vernal) sabbat festival celebrating the Goddess Eostre and the advent of Spring.

Pagan, Paganism: (a follower of) one of many ancient (and/or modern revivals) Earth-centric/eco-centric religions.

Pentacle: a ritual object or piece of jewelry with a pentagram inscribed or woven into it.

Pentagram: five-pointed star.

Perseids: an annual meteor shower through which the Earth passes every August.

Polarity: the concept of equal, opposite energies.

The Priestess: (also the High Priestess) the third card of the major arcana, representing psychic growth and intuition.

Reincarnation: the doctrine of rebirth. Most Pagans and Witches accept this as a fact and see it as a part of the Wheel of Life.

Ritual: ceremony.

Ritualist: one who takes part in ritual.

Runes: symbols carved onto rocks, crystals, clay, etc., which embody powerful energies to be used during magic. Also, symbols used in early alphabets.

Sabbat: one of the eight Pagan holidays comprising the Wheel of the Year.

Samhain: sabbat festival celebrated every November 1, to honor and remember our ancestors and the dead.

Scry: to gaze into or at an object while in trance, to open oneself to visions from the future; to discern hidden motives and energies behind an event or situation.

Shaman: a man or woman who has attained a high degree of knowledge concerning altered states of consciousness. Usually an honored title associated with a structured form of study in what are generally regarded as primitive or aboriginal religions.

Shamanism: the practice of shamans.

Sidhe (Daoine Sidhe): children of the goddess Danu. The Celtic Faerie-Folk.

Smudge, Smudging: to purify or cleanse the air through the use of smoke (see Smudge stick).

Smudge stick: a bundle of herbs used for smudging (see Smudging).

Solstice, Summer: when the sun is at its zenith over the Tropic of Cancer, during the month of June. The longest day of the year (see Litha).

Solstice, Winter: when the Sun is at its zenith over the Tropic of Capricorn, during the month of December. The shortest day of the year (see Yule).

The Star: the eighteenth card of the major arcana, representing cosmic awareness, intuition, hope.

Strength: the ninth card of the major arcana, representing inner will, self-esteem, a holistic persona.

The Sun: the twentieth card of the major arcana, representing growth, expansion, the world conscience.

Tarot: a system of divination using a deck of seventy-eight cards, divided into the major arcana (twenty-two cards) and the minor arcana (fifty-six cards).

Tarot deck: a deck of tarot cards.

Temperance: the fifteenth card of the major arcana, representing enlightenment, integration.

Totem: an animal spirit to which a human soul is linked.

Tower, the: the seventeenth card of the major arcana, representing destruction of insecure foundations, liberation through trauma.

Tradition: a specific subgroup of Pagans, Witches, Wiccans or magick-workers.

Turning of the Wheel: movement from one sabbat/season to another—the cycle of life.

Underworld: the realm of the spirit; realm of the dead.

Visualization: the process of forming mental images.

The Wheel: the eleventh card of the major arcana, representing fate, fortune, better times ahead.

Wheel of the Year: the cyclic turn of the seasons.

Wicca, Wiccan: (a participant of) a modern revival of ancient Earth-centric religions focusing on the god and Goddess of Nature.

Widdershins: counterclockwise.

Will-o'-the-Wisp: Faerie lights/energy beings that can and will lead humans astray in swamps, marshes, moors and the forest.

Witch, Witchcraft: (a practitioner of) the craft of magic, (usually also a member of a Pagan religion).

The World: the twenty-second card of the major arcana, representing the end of a journey or cycle; rest and regeneration.

Yggdrasil: the World Tree. Taken from Norse mythology, Yggdrasil symbolizes the tree on which Odin hung to discover the nature of the runes. The World Tree links various realms together along its branches and trunk.

Yule: (see Solstice, Winter) midwinter sabbat festival celebrating the rebirth of the Oak/Sun King.

Bibliography

Arrien, Angeles. *The Tarot Handbook.* Sonoma, CA: Arcus Publishing Company, 1987.

Conway, D. J. *The Ancient and Shining Ones.* St. Paul: Llewellyn Worldwide, 1993.

Crowley, Aleister. *Aleister Crowley's Thoth Tarot.* Stamford, CT: U.S. Games Systems, 1978.

Culp, Stephanie. *How To Get Organized When You Don't Have The Time.* Cincinnati: Writer's Digest Books, 1986.

Cunningham, Scott. *The Complete Book of Incenses, Oils and Brews.* St. Paul: Llewellyn Publishing, 1989.

———. *Encyclopedia of Magical Herbs.* St. Paul: Llewellyn Publishing, 1985.

———. *Magical Herbalism.* St. Paul: Llewellyn Publishing, 1982.

Donaldson, Terry. *The Dragon Tarot.* Stamford, CT: U.S. Games Systems, Inc., 1996.

Egyptian Book of the Dead

Farrar, Janet and Stewart. *The Witches' Goddess.* Custer, WA: Phoenix Publishing, 1987.

———. *The Witches' God.* Custer, WA: Phoenix Publishing, 1989.

Galenorn, Yasmine. *Trancing The Witch's Wheel.* St. Paul: Llewellyn Worldwide, 1997.

———. *Embracing The Moon.* St. Paul: Llewellyn Worldwide, 1998.

———. *Dancing with the Sun.* St. Paul: Llewellyn Worldwide, 1999.

Haindl, Hermann. *The Haindl Tarot Deck.* Stamford, CT: US Games Systems, 1990.

Hope, Murray. *The Way of the Cartouche.* New York: St. Martin's Press, 1985.

Matthews, Caitlin and John. *The Arthurian Tarot.* Wellingborough, Northamptonshire, England: The Aquarian Press, 1990.

Murray, Liz and Colin. *The Celtic Tree Oracle.* New York: St. Martin's Press Press, 1988.

Rodway, Howard. *Tarot of the Old Path.* Germany: Urania Verlags AG, 1990.

Röhrig, Carl W. *The Rohrig-Tarot.* Woodside, CA: Bluestar Communications, 1995.

Ryan, Mark and Chesca Potter. *The Greenwood Tarot.* San Francisco: HarperCollins, 1996.

Schueler, Gerald and Betty. *Coming Into The Light.* St. Paul: Llewellyn Publishing, 1989.

Shaw, Ian and Paul Nicholson. *The Dictionary of Ancient Egypt.* London: British Museum Press, 1995.

Smith, Caroline and John Astrop. *Elemental Tarot.* New York: Bantam Doubleday Dell Publishing Group, 1988.

Index

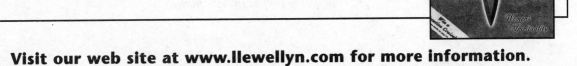

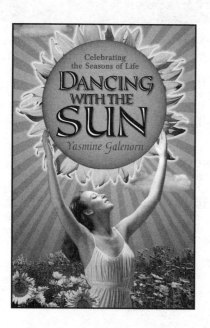

Dancing with the Sun

Celebrating the
Seasons of Life

Yasmine Galenorn

This year, in addition to celebrating the Sabbats, why not celebrate Einherjar? How about Kalevala Day? With *Dancing with the Sun* you'll find in-depth information and complete rituals for each of the Sabbats, which you can use "as is" or as a foundation on which to build your own rites. You'll also discover ceremonies for such Pagan-oriented days as the Feast of the Fallen Warriors, Lupercalia and Kamehameha Day.

Are you getting married soon? Perhaps you are separating from your partner? Is your child graduating and leaving home? Maybe you're ready to dedicate yourself to the Gods? This book provides the directions and texts for thirty complete rituals, ready for use. In addition, you'll discover recipes designed for each holiday and spellwork for different seasons of the year. You'll learn how to knot up the wind during the season of Ostara, what woods to use to kindle the Midsummer's Fires, and how to create Brighid's Bed for Imbolc.

1-56718-300-X, 6 x 9, 336 pp. $14.95

To order, call 1–800–THE MOON
prices subject to change without notice

Embracing the Moon

*A Witch's Guide to Rituals,
Spellcraft and Shadow Work*

Yasmine Galenorn

Do you feel like toasting the Gods with a glass of mead as you revel in the joys of life? Ever wish you could creep through the mists at night, hunting the Wild Lord? *Embracing the Moon* takes you into the core of Witchcraft, helping you weave magic into your daily routine. The spells and rituals are designed to give you the flexibility to experiment so that you are not locked into dogmatic, rigid degree-systems. Written to encompass both beginning and advanced practitioners, *Embracing the Moon* explores the mystical side of natural magic while keeping a common-sense attitude.

Packed not only with spells and rituals, but recipes for oils, spell powders and charms, this book is based on personal experience; the author dots the pages with her own stories and anecdotes to give you fascinating, and sometimes humorous, examples of what you might expect out of working with her system of magick.

1-56718-304-2, 6 x 9, 312 pp. $14.95

Trancing the Witch's Wheel

A Guide to
Magickal Meditation

Yasmine Galenorn

Meet the Wind and the Queen of Air; stand watch as the Sun King is reborn on Yuletide day; cross the barren lava fields with Pele; and learn to shapeshift like Gwion in his flight from Cerridwen.

In *Trancing the Witch's Wheel,* you will find twenty intricate and beautiful guided meditations, written to lead you into the very heart of the seasons, the elements, and the nature of the Divine. This book offers beginning and advanced students a guide as they journey through the cycles of the Pagan year.

Discover how to hone your sense of focus and clearly envision what you want to create in your life. The meditations in *Trancing the Witch's Wheel* are designed for both solitary and group work, and each chapter includes an overview of the subject and suggested exercises to help you in your explorations.

1-56718-303-4, 6 x 9, 224 pp.   **$12.95**

To order, call 1–800–THE MOON
prices subject to change without notice

The Sacred Circle Tarot

A Celtic Pagan Journey

Anna Franklin

Illustrated by Paul Mason

The Sacred Circle Tarot is a new concept in tarot design, combining photographs, computer imaging and traditional drawing techniques to create stunning images. It draws on the Pagan heritage of Britain and Ireland, its sacred sites and landscapes. Key symbols unlock the deepest levels of Pagan teaching.

The imagery of the cards is designed to work on a number of levels, serving as a tool not only for divination but to facilitate meditation, personal growth and spiritual development. The "sacred circle" refers to the progress of the initiate from undirected energy, through dawning consciousness, to the death of the old self and the emergence of the new.

The major arcana is modified somewhat to fit the pagan theme of the deck. For example, "The Fool" becomes "The Green Man," "The Heirophant" becomes "The Druid," and "The World" becomes "The World Tree." The accompanying book gives a full explanation of the symbolism in the cards and their divinatory meanings.

1-56718-457-X, Boxed Kit: 78 full-color cards; 6 x 9, 288 pp. book   **$29.95**

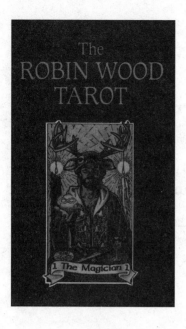

The Robin Wood Tarot Deck

Created and Illustrated b
Robin Wood

Instructions by Robin Wood
and Michael Short

Tap into the wisdom of your subconscious with one of the most beautiful Tarot decks on the market today! Reminiscent of the Rider-Waite deck, the *Robin Wood Tarot* is flavored with nature imagery and luminous energies that will enchant you and the querant. Even the novice reader will find these cards easy and enjoyable to interpret.

Radiant and rich, these cards were illustrated with a unique technique that brings out the resplendent color of the prismacolor pencils. The shining strength of this Tarot deck lies in its depiction of the Minor Arcana. Unlike other Minor Arcana decks, this one springs to pulsating life. The cards are printed in quality card stock and boxed complete with instruction booklet, which provides the upright and reversed meanings of each card, as well as three basic card layouts. Beautiful and brilliant, the *Robin Wood Tarot* is a must-have deck!

0-87542-894-0, boxed set: 78-cards with booklet   **$19.95**

To order, call 1–800–THE MOON
prices subject to change without notice